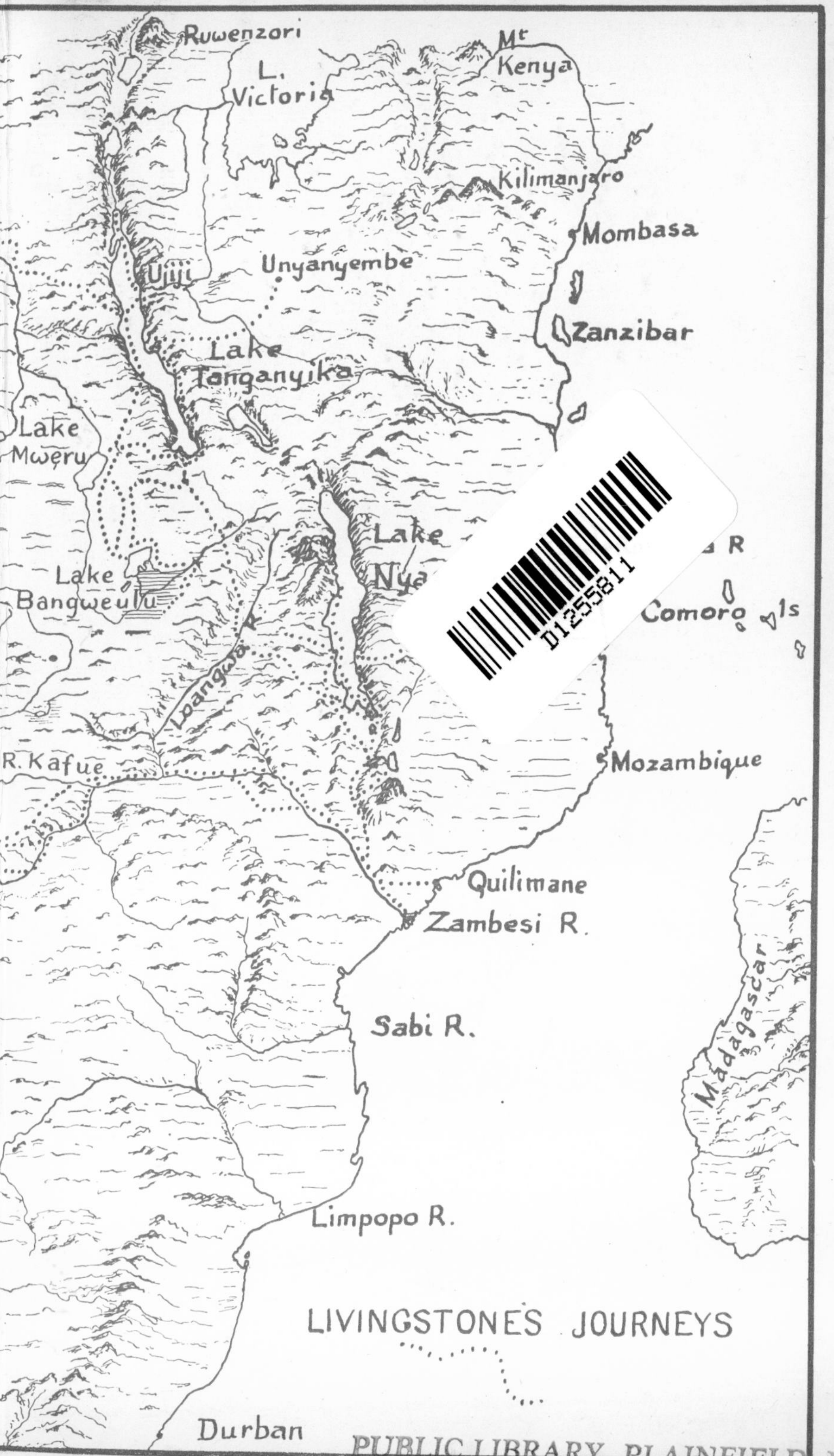

D1255811
PUBLIC LIBRARY, PLAINFIELD

THE WAY TO ILALA

David Livingstone in middle age

from *The Last Journals of Livingstone*, ed. H. Waller (John Murray, 1874)

THE WAY TO ILALA

David Livingstone's Pilgrimage

by

FRANK DEBENHAM, O.B.E.

Emeritus Professor of Geography
Cambridge University

LONGMANS, GREEN AND CO
LONDON ♦ NEW YORK ♦ TORONTO

PUBLIC LIBRARY, PLAINFIELD, N. J.

B
L763D

LONGMANS, GREEN AND CO LTD
6 & 7 CLIFFORD STREET LONDON W I
BOSTON HOUSE STRAND STREET CAPE TOWN
531 LITTLE COLLINS STREET MELBOURNE

LONGMANS, GREEN AND CO INC
55 FIFTH AVENUE NEW YORK 3

LONGMANS, GREEN AND CO
20 CRANFIELD ROAD TORONTO 16

ORIENT LONGMANS LTD
CALCUTTA BOMBAY MADRAS
DELHI VIJAYAWADA DACCA

OCT 10 1956
142298

First Published 1955
New Impression 1955

PRINTED IN GREAT BRITAIN BY
ROBERT MACLEHOSE AND COMPANY LIMITED
THE UNIVERSITY PRESS GLASGOW

FOREWORD

This is a fine book: my honour to be asked to put a foreword to it. My honour to have known 'Deb', who has written it, for many years. My honour and joy to have served years ago as one of a succession of District Commissioners in the Bangweulu region, and to have travelled constantly on foot and by canoe and by boat in the steps of Livingstone. With this difference: that thanks to Livingstone, and to those many who followed him fired with his spirit and motives, I knew when I started my day's journey that I would meet friendship by the way; I knew that on the other side lay warmth and comfort and health; and always I knew, above all, that if need be I could be back amongst my own people in a matter of days.

Not so the first geographer in that trackless swamp, whose instruments failed him; not so that same first administrator who, long before Lugard, wrote: 'One or two pious agents are equal if not superior to Europeans in the beginning of the work. The natives look so much upon the Gospel as just ways and customs of white men that little progress is made, but from their fellow natives the truth comes directly.' Not so that first Christian, whose pilgrimage decided that most of the first white men to enter this part of Africa would come as friends and helpers of the people. Not so that first Great-heart who never knew whether he would survive the day, nor how many months or years lay between him and one of his own kind. Still in this modern age when our men are chosen for work in Her Majesty's Overseas Service in Africa one of the essential qualities looked for is the ability to support loneliness—that affliction which, above all others, may destroy judgement, upset moral values, and send a man mad.

Who better to know these things than the author, who went with Scott on his last journey? How easy to have glossed over the weaknesses, the indecision, the vanity, the human desire to be more successful than others, which, when all is said, is a main spur to achievement by man. These are faithfully recounted, and it is well: for it is the fashion in these days, for motives other than truth, to foul our own nest. There seems today to be a temptation for a biographer to be 'a man that could look no way but downwards, with a muckrake in his hand'. Any so tempted will find his poison already frustrated.

We who work in Northern Rhodesia strive to work in the spirit and with the motives of Livingstone, and because of Livingstone our work is easier than the same work elsewhere. For him in this country all the trumpets will always sound.

ARTHUR BENSON

GOVERNMENT HOUSE
LUSAKA
NORTHERN RHODESIA

CONTENTS

Published for the Trustees of
the Rhodes-Livingstone Museum with the
aid of a Grant from the Government
of Northern Rhodesia

PLATES

MAPS

Maps

INTRODUCTION

by DR HUBERT F. WILSON

One of the amazing things about the great Victoria Falls discovered by my grandfather is how very close it is to London. At dinner in the Falls Hotel there you may meet people who lunched in London the day before. Such is the measure of progress in transport in the hundred years since David Livingstone took months, even years, to reach it by ox-waggon and canoe from Cape Town.

The contrast is bewildering. How can our generation realise that the interior of Africa in those days was completely unknown, a blank on the maps of the geographers, which had to be filled in with elephants and potentates, and other savage pictures instead of rivers and towns?

Professor Frank Debenham has made us his debtors by giving us a picture of David Livingstone as a geographer, placing on the map rivers and lakes whose very existence had not been suspected before. Here we can read of the solitary pioneer turning to good use the simplest of instrumental equipment and with a singularly alert eye observing hills, rocks, animals, birds and fishes as if trained for that work. A Pilgrim indeed—ever on the move and always with a high moral purpose driving him on. Sir Reginald Coupland has well pointed out that through all his exploratory work, his ultimate object was still the spread of Christianity. We must not lose sight of that. This picture is not of an ordinary missionary—what Livingstone himself dryly styles 'a dumpy sort of man with a Bible under his arm'—but rather of one to whom the mapping of a river, the quiet teasing of an obstructive headman, or even the shooting of game for his companions, was the prosecution of a definite missionary venture.

Some forty years after the death of my grandfather I found myself at Ilala, working amongst the people with whom he spent the last few days of his life. The older men still remembered him and one worker at the mission station, who had no ears or hands, recalled Casembe's methods of ruling his people—although it was actually a Bemba chief who had thus mutilated him. When my mother came out to visit her father's African grave we gathered several of the older men to meet her there, so that she might hear what they remembered of his death. Chifono was amongst them, the successor to Chitambo, the chief of the village where he died, who always referred to Livingstone's arrival as 'when God came to our country'. Chitambo's son was there and a toothless old blacksmith who was ready of speech and alert of mind. Their story corresponded so closely to Susi's account in the *Last Journals* that we could detect no discrepancy.

'The white man's people', they said, 'tried to hide from us that their master had died. They were afraid of what we might do, but there was no need. We knew what had happened and we knew that men can die anywhere. When they confessed their trouble to us we did what we could to help them, as they wanted to take their master's body away with them. They buried his heart in an iron box under the big Mpundu tree. Did we not see it ourselves? A man read out of a book and then they wrapped up the body in bark and went away.'

There was one headman there, the successor to Kalunganjovu, the chief who had directed from an anthill the crossing of the flooded Lulimala 'sponge'. This man remained silent. Pressed to speak, he shook his head, and not because he remembered nothing. I was surprised. But the old blacksmith broke the silence, 'Chitianka has nothing to say,' he said with a chuckle, 'because he and the other boys ran away to hide in the gardens, they were frightened by the white man's black boxes.' There was a general snigger and Chitianka's growl betrayed the truth of the imputation.

The anthill was still there; the Lulimala was just as it had been forty years ago, and the villages to which Livingstone's men had been sent, in vain, to buy 'Milch goats', but Chitianka's youthful timidity deprived us of a picture which might have been memorable.

The talk then turned to the island of Nsumbu, seventy miles to the north across the swamps and to the old chief Matipa. We turned up the picture in the *Last Journals* of Matipa's head—taken from a sketch by Livingstone, the last he had done—and showed it to them. It was passed round and not only recognised at once but pronounced to be a good likeness, so that if my grandfather was no artist at least his work was realistic and easily understood by those who remembered the original.

I have always felt, personally, that my grandfather possessed a genius for understanding how to treat pagan Africans. He knew equally when to be patient and when to be blunt. Through all his dealings with Africans he showed a respect for his companions and the local villagers which evoked their loyalty and their unwavering confidence. A pattern this might well be today for those who, under conditions so vastly different, live with and administer, or who work with the same African people. And as the white race moves forwards into a new age in that country, progressing from benevolent fatherhood to a new companionship, Livingstone's methods and Livingstone's principle can still be an example for those who are trying to link the two races with the bonds of mutual service and mutual respect.

Professor Debenham is fortunate in having served his apprenticeship in the Antarctic under Scott and Wilson; and in having in later years struggled among the Bangweulu Marshes and toiled over the arid plains of Bechuanaland. He has first-hand knowledge of much of the country first visited by his hero. But more than that here is an author who has fallen in love with his Scottish pioneer. With a kindred sympathy he can understand his problems and enter into his difficulties. He can make allowances for his shortcomings. He can appreciate his unavoidable mistakes—and place a true value on the patience and thoroughness without which such sound work could not have been done. He is ready, too, to teach us a little of his own craft and can make technical points comprehensible—if not actually simple.

David Livingstone has always been fortunate in his biographers—and they are many. But Professor Debenham, in the present volume, shows himself to resemble, in many ways, 'his pilgrim'. He has the same friendliness, the same thoroughness, and something of the same sense of humour, above all the same avoidance of overstatement, and in it he has placed the wanderings of Livingstone onto the modern map. With this help we can now follow where exactly he went, what his route, and generally why that route was chosen.

It makes a fascinating volume, and for many of this Pilgrim's admirers it will rouse dreams of spending a retirement tracing out those tracks of long ago and following him, book in hand, but understanding what was obscure and hidden before.

CHAPTER ONE

Then said Evangelist, keep that light in your eye, and go up directly thereto, so shalt thou see the Gate; at which, when thou knockest, it shall be told thee what thou shalt do.

JOHN BUNYAN

In the spring of 1841, when the young Queen Victoria had been but four years on the throne, there stepped ashore at Algoa Bay a spare young man of twenty-eight who was to become the greatest geographer that Africa has ever seen.

At least twenty of his twenty-eight years had been spent in such labour of body and mind as only a young Scot could survive. As a boy at work all day in a cotton factory he yet had energy to attend evening school and learn his rudiments of Latin, and this habit of industry stayed with him throughout his youth. He had devoured every book he could come by, on medicine, on Greek, on divinity; and had taught himself to abstract his mind from noise and rack of machinery. Even more he learnt to go his own way, to be independent in spirit, even while he was what we would now call a wage-slave, tied to a spinning-jenny all day.

He, who was to become the loneliest man in all Africa, had learned to be alone even in the busy factory at Blantyre, alone in his thoughts and schemes for the future. And when he took the decision that landed him in Africa he looked back with some regret to those days of study when, mentally, he called no man his master.

When he had offered himself to the London Missionary Society for the mission field to become as he said 'in a measure dependent on others', he could write that delightful comment on his own action: 'and I would not have been much put about, though my offer had been rejected'. Truly 'nature hath framed strange fellows in her time'; to shape a boy from a cotton mill into a medical student, and then into a minister, and finally to turn him loose in the wildest continent of that day to use his gifts of industry and concentration to an end which must have been far from his youthful philosophy.

Books alone could not have made him the geographer he became; it was his intense love of nature that bent him in that direction. If you go to the Livingstone Memorial Museum at Blantyre to-day you will see the bare, almost sordid, atmosphere of industry that the boy grew up in, but you will also see the countryside he roamed over in his few spare hours. There was the river below his parents' tenement, teaching him to become an expert on rivers; the flowers of spring that he longed to study; and the quarries that made him more aware of the structure of his Africa than almost any other traveller of his time. Even while a slave to his ambition he was laying all nature under tribute, finding everything he saw of absorbing interest.

We must account this absorbing interest, this divine curiosity, as the greatest spur to his travels, for it endured when all else failed. A week before he died, he was scribbling notes on the fish and the plants of that vast swamp of Bangweulu, in the middle of Africa. Even when exhaustion had robbed him of common sense he was fain to observe and record the little facts of nature. Even at death's door he remained 'the interpreter of nature, dipping his pen into his mind'.

We are accustomed to say that David Livingstone was turned by chance from being a missionary into an explorer and geographer. I think that is the wrong way to put it; he was a geographer from the first and by nature, and became a missionary as a sort of aside, or *en route*.

It was perfectly natural for him, on the voyage out, to take lessons in navigation from Captain Donaldson, a first step towards his becoming the best navigator and surveyor of all African travellers; and he saw nothing unusual in his description of it, as he wrote: 'The captain of our vessel was very obliging to me and gave me all the information respecting the use of the quadrant, frequently sitting up till 12 at night for the purpose of taking lunar observations with me. The captain is of a most agreeable nature, a well-informed shrewd Scotchman but no Christian.'

We may presume, perhaps, that the skipper's lunars were interlarded with many strange oaths, and that young David Livingstone was beginning the discipline of pursuing the object of his desire despite attendant shocks, just as in later years he, the liberator of slavery, was to journey for months on end with slavers, the end justifying the means.

For, in spite of what we have said, there is no doubt that his prime object was to become a missionary, a far travelled one, and an unsectarian one; free and untrammelled by the doctrinal controversies which so horrified him in his first few months in the mission atmosphere of Cape Colony.

We could wish for a pen picture of this product of the anatomy school and the divinity college as he walked into the strange world of that beautiful bay of the Port Elizabeth-to-be, beautiful even then in spite of the rough pioneer atmosphere that man had imported. It was the taking-off place for the hinterland, for the bleak Karroo and the High Veld beyond, with that mixture of British and Boer and native Bantu that is still striving to achieve some degree of harmony and still failing to do so.

A farming fraternity was not new to him, since his own Lanarkshire was full of careful farmers, but farmers who carried rifles and sjamboks, who travelled by ox waggon driven by Hottentots or 'coloureds', who carried little with them but salt and gunpowder, must have been very new indeed.

Each pioneer country, according to its climate and resources, has worked out its own peculiar mode of transport, and in South Africa this had long before taken the form of the 'Cape Waggon' drawn by oxen, able to carry up to a ton and more, and to act as a house on wheels for months at a time.

The Cape Waggon was usually about eighteen feet long with a wheel-tread of from four to five feet. The body of the waggon would have sides between two and three feet high, the bottom of which would be well clear of the water when crossing drifts and fords across rivers, or wherever the oxen could walk. A semi-circular tent on bent rods surmounted half or even all of its length, the front seat being 'the fore-chest' for stowing things. There were also side-chests, long boxes overhanging the wheels for other goods, particularly tools. Canvas bags tied to the tent-supports held clothing and provisions for immediate use, while pots and pans travelled in a 'trap' or net slung under the body. A full span of oxen was a dozen to fourteen, the favoured type of ox coming from the sour-veldt country, a tougher breed than those from the sweet-veldt. Since they gathered their own food they were cheap, from £3 each in those days, so that a team or a span of twelve cost about £40, much the same as the waggon itself, or 1200 Rix-dollars in the then currency of the 'Colony'.

The front wheels were swivelled under the waggon and attached to the disselboom, a long and strong pole to which were yoked the wheelers, the rear pair of oxen. Beyond this the pairs were fastened to the 'trek-tow', or trace of thick hide, by rough wooden frames or 'skeys', by which the pull was taken just in front of the beasts' withers. They were fastened by 'reims', thongs of raw-hide about eight feet long, the universal binding material of South Africa. The span was led by a reim held by a native 'forerunner', or 'voorlooper', whose chief duty was to prevent the leaders from taking short cuts round corners of rocks or trees.

Like the bullock-waggons of Australia at the same period the oxen were driven by a man who walked alongside the team with a whip some twenty-five feet long fixed to a slender pole up to twenty feet long. The heavy thongs on those whips could make mincemeat of the flanks of an ox—I have seen Australian 'bullockies' cut a triangle of metal out of corrugated iron with three slashes—but the good driver rarely used them on the oxen, relying more on the sharp crack given by the cord, or even fine leather, at the end of the whip.

The best drivers were usually Hottentots, perhaps because, as someone unkindly said, their intelligence was on a level with that of the oxen, and they certainly did much of their driving by talking to the oxen, who all have their individual names and know when they are being addressed. In driving a span of oxen you can use bad language if you like, but the worst thing to do is to lose your temper.

A very useful attachment to a waggon was a revolution counter, or trocheameter as it was then called, for registering the distance travelled, and Livingstone in particular always had one. The standard practice in waggon travel was to give the oxen eight hours of work, eight hours of grazing, and eight hours for rest and rumination.

Somehow the young missionary managed to adapt himself quickly to the strange mode of life which he was henceforth to follow, and began to show that handicraft and inventiveness with which he was to build three houses in as many years almost entirely by himself. He learned without effort how to choose his oxen, order his stores, arrange his waggon; to mend a broken wheel, or ship a new disselboom.

All his early journeys were done, in the Boer fashion, with a Cape waggon, an ideal way of transporting all that was needful in a country so widespread, so full of game and grass. It was only when he reached country infested with the tsetse fly and the fatal disease, *nagana*, that it transmitted to oxen, that he had to go on foot. Livingstone himself describes this method of travelling as 'a prolonged system of picnicking, excellent for the health, and agreeable to those who are not over-fastidious about trifles, and who delight in being in the open air.' In fact, immediately after his first long journey of nine hundred miles to Kuruman, taking ten weeks, he wrote of it as 'so pleasant I never got tired of it. My waggons are very comfortable affairs indeed, little houses in fact . . .'

He went by the standard route at that period, passing through Graaf Reinet and Colesberg. He must have passed close to a farm near Colesberg whence five years earlier a small boy of nine, named Paul Kruger, had started off with his father and mother, of Prussian descent, on what is known somewhat grandiloquently as The Great Trek. It was indeed a very important episode in the history of South Africa, but the story has become somewhat embroidered in the telling until the number of families taking part in it rivals the number of beds scattered all over England in which Queen Elizabeth I is reputed to have slept.

While Livingstone was making this first journey Paul Kruger was on commando with his leader Potgieter against the Matabele and other tribes in the area towards which Livingstone was heading. They probably never met, but Kruger was second-in-command of the raiding party which sacked Livingstone's house in 1852. In the battle which preceded the burning, Kruger was hit by two bullets from the five muskets which the Bakwena tribe had to oppose to the long rifles, or 'roers', of the attacking Boers.

This raid was the last straw as far as Livingstone's opinion of the Boers was concerned, though at an earlier date he gave them full credit for the way in which they endured hardship and adapted themselves to the country of their choice. His first letter from Cape Town showed his attitude: 'The Boors are again shooting the Caffirs—levying their cattle and making their prisoners slaves.' There was in fact never any chance of Dr Livingstone's living in amity with the Trek Boers; their aims were diametrically opposed. In Cape Town also he had met Dr John Philip, the Superintendent of the London Missionary Society's activities in South Africa, who was so hated by the Boers for the major part he took in securing the freedom of their slaves.

On this journey to the hinterland he preceded several famous big-game hunters, including Gordon Cumming, whom he helped in an emergency but called 'a mad sort of Scotchman', Oswell, Vardon, Webb, Murray and others, with most of whom he became firm friends for life. Gordon Cumming found him very kind and helpful with advice as to places in which he might find elephants to shoot, but Livingstone's pithy remark about Cumming may have been due to the latter's habit of hunting in a kilt, or else because he found out that he had sold twenty muskets to Sekomi, the chief of the Bamangwato, at a profit of 3000 per cent.

I can find no details of this first journey of Livingstone, but we can imagine that he was drinking in all the experience and trek-lore that he could, and was enjoying the free life of the open sky and the broad plateaux. He must have seen the countless herds of game so soon to be decimated by the sportsmen who followed him, but in his first book the whole journey is dismissed in one impatient sentence, saying that his oxen were pretty well tired by the long journey, so that he had to rest them for a few days at Kuruman before pushing on again for another two hundred miles to Shokuane, where the chief of the 'Bakwains' (Bakwena tribe), Sechele, lived.

Dr Moffat, the pioneer missionary of that region, was at home in England at the time so we have no means of knowing what the people there thought of their new recruit. We therefore have had only a glimpse of how he plunged into the troubled waters of South Africa as to the manner born, and can but guess how his varied training, and his wide interests, fitted him so well for the career he was about to carve for himself.

It would be unfair to Livingstone to gloss over certain defects which were later to hamper him, and to invite criticism from those with narrower vision than his. He was, at this time, very trenchant and critical in what he wrote and, no doubt, said about his fellow missionaries in South Africa, and even when his censure was just it was rarely couched in diplomatic language. He was ever one to prefer calling a spade a spade. It was not surprising therefore, that some of his colleagues took umbrage at this new and gifted broom which was apt to sweep aside hesitation and confusion in so brusque a manner. This is perhaps saying no more than that he had the defects of his qualities, and that it was often these defects which carried him to resounding success when a smoother manner and a more forgiving spirit might have halted him half-way. To amplify this statement we may quote from a letter, written many years later to his brother-in-law, John Moffat, in which he says: 'When I was a piecer (in the cotton mill) the fellows used to try to turn me off from the path I had chosen, and always began with "I think you ought, etc." till I snapped them up with "You *think*! I don't need anyone to think for me, I assure you." I never followed another's views in preference to my own judgment.'

Livingstone soon became acquainted with the dissensions amongst the missionaries, and in particular the quarrels between the Griqua Town group of Messrs Hughes and Wright and the Kuruman group of Messrs Moffat and Edwards. The former used native teachers as soon as they could be trained, while Moffat did not approve of that principle; but there were other reasons as well for a sort of armed neutrality between the two stations.

Livingston's opinion of the matters in dispute exhibits his fairness and balanced judgment so well that we quote from a letter to his friend T. L. Prentice which is in the Rhodes-Livingstone Museum at Livingstone. It was written in December 1841, that is, only six months after he had reached his destination and it is an appreciation of the situation, meant to prepare his friend for what he should find when he joined them, as was the original intention. 'I mentioned that the tribes near us to the North and North East are all hostile to Christianity. The different villages in the other directions are not so but these are all taken possession of by the Griqua Town missionaries. In fact they have nearly encompassed us. Don't imagine I am sorry at it. I love to see their arms encircling for it will force us towards the dark Interior, if no other motive impels us this will. . . . Quarrels somehow or other arose between the Griqua missionaries and the Kuruman ones, and at different times there have been squabbles and bickerings. You must not think I speak disrespectfully or censoriously of anyone. They are all excellent men. I have a great regard for them all and their wives too are excellent characters.'

He then goes on to declare himself, very humbly, in favour of native teachers: 'I have no hesitation in saying one or two pious native agents are equal if not superior to Europeans in the beginning of the work. The natives look so much upon the Gospel as just ways and customs of white men that little progress is made, but from their fellow natives the truth comes directly.'

An amusing summing up of his first impressions of chiefs follows: 'In general the chiefs of the Bechuanas are hereditary asses, born idiots or little better, good at nothing but begging.'

The rest of the letter is full of geography too long to quote, including a full description of how the natives make iron: 'The

Iron trade is not a whit improved in their hands I should think, but just in the *statu quo* that it was left by old Tubal Cain of glorious memory. Using no limestone it is no wonder they repeatedly fail, but then they satisfy themselves it has been bewitched.'

This letter was written immediately after his journey to Mabotsa to select that site for his future station.

Even at this early stage it was clear that he preferred to travel without white companions, perfectly happy with his black helpers, with nobody to question his authority. In years to come he was to plumb the very depths of loneliness, but we must realise that it was his own choice and that never, till his very last days, did he complain of that choice. There can be no doubt that he did his best work when alone and single-handed, but there is also no doubt that it spoiled him as a leader of a white man's party; he simply could not delegate jobs, but had to have at least a hand in everything that was doing.

In his early letters we remark a restlessness, a desire to push on to the far north, a reluctance to stay very long at Kuruman, a fretting at control by the Directors of his Mission and a longing to go off alone. Judged by the standards of to-day we are apt to assess these as grave defects, as intolerant and reactionary, whereas in the standards of the period, especially in South Africa, they were signs of tolerance, and a spirit of reform. For the young Scotsman now found himself in the strangest world of contrasts, surrounded by villains enough and saints too, yet the saints could be villainous at times in their very righteousness and could swear at each other in the most genteel Billingsgate.

Neither the great Dr John Philip nor the even greater Robert Moffat knew the word 'compromise'; neither could budge an inch from their own standpoint. Truly, tolerance and charity seem to have been rare virtues amongst the missionaries there, and one can hardly wonder that Livingstone wished to get away from such an atmosphere of bickering, and take refuge with the heathen tribes to the north. He recognised well enough, like Cassius, that the fault was not in their stars but in themselves, and he saw no remedy but to avoid the forum, and betake himself to what he regarded as the real battle-front for Christianity, that looming territory which he always called 'The Interior'.

There are signs that, even on his first journey to the scene of his labours, he felt some impatience with the rigid, unrelenting attitude of his fellow missionaries towards such things as keeping the Sabbath; with their indignation at native nudity, their conviction that all were damned who did not exactly follow their own rules of conduct. For instance, it is noteworthy that even at the beginning of his missionary career he felt a certain degree of revolt against the ultra-rigid observance of the Sabbath as taught by the first missionaries. When, nearing the end of the journey, they were forced by lack of water to travel on Sunday, he was severely reproved by a Bushman whom he passed. Then the local chief came along and 'requested on explanation of our conduct'. He himself was always careful, within reason, to observe the Sabbath, but he must have been greatly tickled at being taken to task by a Bushman for an apparent defection from his duty.

Whether we ascribe his wanderings of the next few years to an urge to explore, or to a desire to avoid too close an association with 'the brethren', as he usually called his colleagues, the fact is that he at once began to turn himself into the most accomplished traveller of them all. By the time that Moffat had returned from a long stay in England to his oasis in a cultural desert at Kuruman Livingstone was just as courageous and expert as that past master of African travel.

If we are bent upon finding still further reasons for Livingstone becoming an explorer we can find one in the beckoning quality of Africa itself, especially the southern half of it. Whether you call it a challenge or a welcome does not matter; Africa beckons. Whether you travel at the pace of the patient ox or at that of the noisy lorry, you feel the urge. Whether you merely seek the time-honoured 'new thing out of Africa', or have some more particular reason, travel in Africa is always interesting and may be exciting.

It was not only the dissatisfied Boer who was always trekking on; it affected the hordes of Bantu, centuries before, and the Englishmen of to-day. Each will have an apt reason, conquest or room to live, gold or fame, missionary fervour or philanthropy; but behind all these is a strong element of what one can only call plain curiosity, and we may as well confess to it. To 'go and find out and be damned' was not the sole prerogative of Kipling's Lost Legion; and whether you chivy the slaver or cherish the black, you will even to-day have that inclination to pretend to be a gentleman rover abroad.

Livingstone had a busy mind. It was always at work, inquiring, theorising, seeking relationships between phenomena, the very foundation of science and philosophy. He wanted to carry the Word of God to the minds of the heathen but, nearly as much, he wanted also to know their circumstances; to study their conditions and environment; to know why, under Providence, droughts happened, rivers failed, disease came, and so on.

He found himself in what we now call 'marginal country', where scattered villages could just support themselves by cattle and occasional crops. But it was also marginal country in a far more risky sense, in that it was seething as a result of wars and raidings from the east.

He was on the edge of the great eddy of disturbance caused by the clash of forces at the south-east corner of Africa. The well-nigh irresistible force of the Bantu pushing down the eastern side had met the nearly immovable object of the White Man spreading eastwards from Cape Colony. The Bantu recoiled as each surge broke against the firearms of the settlers, helped at times by British troops, and threw off wisps of their people, swarming across to the north of the whites, The Matabele under the leadership of Mosilikatse formed the major swarm, but there were others before and after, one of which very nearly succeeded in driving Dr Moffat from his Kuruman settlement.

The Whites, too, threw off swarms, discontented swarms like those which left the Zulus, and one of them broke through the Bantu ring, as the Great Trek of the Boers. This caused further eddies in the movements of peoples whose choice was plainly whether to raid or be raided. The Matabele were pushed northward and westward by the Boers; others and lighter insurgent parties of Bantu were thrown back by the Griquas, that odd collection of coloured peoples able to use the guns and the horses of the white man.

Under the strain of all this commotion, both sides, if they can be called sides, threw up leaders of considerable stature who did their best, according to their lights, to lead their people to some sort of victory.

On the Bantu side there were Moshesh, the wise leader of the tribes now collectively called the Basuto, and Sebituane, who led an offshoot to the west and north to found the brief empire of the Makololo on the Zambezi. The Matabele leader, Mosilikatse, fought successfully and fled at the proper moment, yet dominated the scene for the middle part of the century. On the more civilized side, a word to be read with the utmost elasticity of meaning, there was Potgieter, followed by Pretorius, and later by Paul Kruger. Their reasons for fighting were not really very different from those of the Bantu, but they had better weapons and superior tactics.

The only 'invaders' to have a moral purpose were the great Robert Moffat of Kuruman, the pioneer missionary, and his son-in-law Dr Livingstone. Close to them they had those most surprising Griquas, 'Africaner' and his successor Andries Waterboer, without whom the mission field would have been swept away like chaff. Yet to each and all of these leaders no doubt his cause was just, and he hoped the path of duty, as he saw it, would become the way to glory.

It was through the confusion of these troubled waters that the young Livingstone had to steer his way, and he began his self-training by ceaseless journeying. Within the compass of his first year he travelled some two thousand miles, and his annual average was little less than that for years to come. We cannot follow these preliminary journeys in detail, but we can illustrate his gains in experience of flood and drought, of dangers run from men or beast, with a few examples.

He had been less than a year in Africa when he undertook his first journey alone, for three hundred and fifty miles to the north, to the tribe of Sekomi, the chief of the Bamangwato, the father of Khama, then about twenty years old. He wore out his oxen before he reached his destination and did the last fifty miles on foot.

It was on this journey that he overheard his Bechuana boys telling each other; 'He is not strong, he is quite slim and only appears stout because he puts himself into those bags (trousers). He will soon knock up'. Whereupon the slight but wiry Scotsman 'kept them at the top of their speed for days together', until he overheard a changed opinion of his walking powers.

Before this he had dug his first irrigation channel for Bubi, a chief of the 'Bakwains', with whom he stayed for a month. It was dug with the sharpened sticks and the bare hands of his people and was five hundred feet long and three feet wide. He was learning his hydraulics the hard way, since the dam diverting the stream for his channel was twice swept away by the floods of that rainy season, till presumably he designed a large enough spillway to prevent such catastrophes.

It was just a year later, on the same route, that fear of the Matabele halted his waggon party two hundred miles short of Sekomi. Little daunted he showed the persistence in spite of all obstacles that was to be his outstanding characteristic, and did the two hundred miles forward, and back again, on ox-back. This was a mode of travel which carried him later on for many times that distance, but he writes of it: 'It is rough travelling, as you can conceive. The skin is so loose there is no getting one's great coat, which has to serve for both saddle and blanket, to stick on. And then the long horns in front with which he can give one a punch in the abdomen if he likes, make us sit as "bolt upright" as dragoons.'

It was on this trip, too, that he learned to accommodate his digestion, with difficulty, to the dangers and chances of the native foods that were to be his portion for more than half of his future wandering. They included some of 'the 40 different kinds of roots and 30 different kinds of fruits which they use as food, some of them by no means unsavoury'. The writer has tried one or two of these only, and is inclined to echo that cautious phrase 'by no means unsavoury', the double negative meaning that they are better than nothing.

Having broken a finger against a rock on this journey, he broke it again by firing his pistol with his disabled hand at a lion, which had chased his ox into their camp. This second fracture prevented him from using his gun for shooting game, so the party had to take to locusts and wild honey. Their resort to the food of St John the Baptist in the wilderness turns him whimsical, as reverses often did, and he writes of it to a doctor friend: 'The locusts are the most constipating food I ever ate; they taste just like the vegetables on which they subsist, generally like the soft juicy parts of a stalk of wheat, and far better than shrimps at home. The wild honey has the very opposite tendency, the two combined form one of the best kinds of food the Bakalahari have.'

Perhaps Shakespeare's blunt Iago was not so far wrong when he described Othello's surfeit of love for Desdemona to be as 'luscious as locusts', but inclined to turn bitter later on.

Livingstone then goes on to describe the honey bird, which enabled them to find the honey by means of 'a peculiar kind of chirping, and following it we are very seldom disappointed'. The honey-guide is a rather insignificant little brown bird, about the size of a sparrow, which seems to carry a map in its head of all the nearby bee-hives in hollow trees. You rarely see one without its perching near on a bare branch and calling your attention by a persistent 'chk-churr! chk churr', until you go towards it. It will then fly off to another bare twig about one hundred yards away, and so on in short swoops from tree to tree till you reach the bees-nest. It now becomes your duty to smoke out the bees, prize off the wax and clay over the opening, and leave a thank offering for your guide.

It is on this journey, too, that Livingstone first mentions the rumour of a lake to the north-west of Sekomi's territory. He was given to understand that it was only a short distance beyond his farthest point, and that it was 'a fresh water lake called Mokhoro, or the lake of the boat, on account of the canoes which are found upon it'. This, of course, was the Lake Ngami, the object of his first definitely geographical journey some six years later, and it rings particularly true because of the name his informers gave it.

The Bechuana themselves have no canoes since they have no water to put them on, but Makora is the native name for the dugouts which the Batawana use in Ngamiland.

The next rainy season, that is, the first three months of 1843, saw him again in the north, on which journey, in his own words: 'The greater portion of my time I employed in itineracy to the agacent tribes'. He was, in fact, selecting a place for the mission which he hoped to establish. When he returned to Kuruman he showed his pleasure at such a prospect, writing to the London Secretary of the Society of 'the feelings of inexpressible delight with which I hail the decision of the Directors that we go forward to the dark Interior'.

Later that year he rode on horseback one hundred and fifty miles south to meet Dr Moffat, just beyond the Vaal River, who was returning from a long visit to England. We must presume that it was these constant journeyings that were bringing out the latent geographer in him. Chapter II of his *Missionary Travels* will always stand as a model of what a succint geography should be, a potted yet comprehensive study of the Kalahari, its structure, its natural resources, its people, politics and panoramas.

He seems to have acquired very quickly an eye for country, to use that quaint phrase which expresses so well that combination of wisdom and understanding which enables a huntsman to choose his fences, a soldier to plan his attack, and a scout to lead his party by the best and surest route. It implies also a more or less subconscious feel of the country, just as a good sailor gets the feel of his boat. Every sight and sound and scent is learned and understood, each giving the traveller its message, be it of warning or of welcome. It is the faculty that makes a man perfectly at home in the wilds; a competent, self-contained, assured explorer. But Livingstone was far more than a mere explorer, which need not mean more than the ability to travel into the unknown. He was a geographer, able to observe accurately, to appreciate the pattern of what he saw, and the myriad relationships between the physical environment and the living things that had accommodated their habits to those conditions.

In those years, when Darwin was working out his theory of

evolution based on the laws of survival of the fittest, his unconscious disciple, David Livingstone, was feeling his way to similar conclusions. The difference was, perhaps, that Livingstone would call it a dispensation of a Divine Providence which enabled an eland, for instance, to live without any surface water, whereas Darwin would ascribe it to a process of natural selection. Livingstone would say that God looked after the eland while Darwin

'The showy gambols of the white-tailed wildebeeste'

would say that God had fashioned a plan whereby the eland could evolve so as to look after itself, a more remote control so to speak.

Livingstone was a great keeper of notebooks of observations on every topic, and these are the stand-by of his biographers of to-day. Unfortunately nearly all the journals of the earlier years were destroyed by the Boers when they sacked his house at Kolobeng in 1852. From his letters we get the impression that his attitude to all the strange things he saw was mainly objective: only rarely does a flash of feeling come into his descriptions, as when he calls the baobab tree 'that upturned carrot', or names the ostrich as 'the most wary and the most stupid of all birds'. Yet it is just such momentary injections of humour and fancy that show us the real Livingstone who, once he had satisfied himself as to the utility or otherwise of a tree or an animal, could sit back and admire its beauty or smile at its oddity. I feel sure that the lost notebooks would have been full of evidence of intimate and personal appreciations of this kind. He was, for instance, the most humane of hunters and was the despair of his native followers as a provider of meat from 'those lovely creatures, the antelopes. If we had been starving, I could have slaughtered them with as little hesitation as I should cut off a patient's leg: but I felt a doubt, and the antelopes got the benefit of it'.

'The outraged air of the grey lourie and the swooping antics of the lesser bustard'

We can be fairly sure that Livingstone enjoyed, just as much as we should, the showy gambols of the white-tailed wildebeeste, or the hurtling gallop of the hartebeeste. He knew well enough the malevolent stare of the black rhinoceros, and he could see the lion in true perspective, as when he wrote: 'One is in much more danger of being run over when walking in the streets of London than he is of being devoured by lions in Africa.' He also must have revelled in the cheeky cavortings of the herds of springbok, those *gamins* of the dusty veldt, and have stared with amazement at the rocking-horse canter of giraffes, those enormous toys-come-to-life, swishing disdainful tails as they wheel so cleverly round the tall thorn trees that are their chief source of food.

He was, perhaps, more interested in birds than in animals, and we can imagine him smiling at the outraged air of the grey lourie, shouting its hoarse 'Go'way' from the top of a tree at the sight of the gentle missionary. In the Kalahari, particularly, he had every variety of bird behaviour at his elbow, from the soaring and swooping antics of the lesser bustard (koorhaan) to the sedate but purposeful stalking gait of the secretary bird, that giant hawk which forsook the skies for the broad plains and grew long legs for its new mode of life.

With his own animals, too, he probably put use before beauty, and his attachment to his horses and his oxen, though evident, was not a sentimental one as was the case with some hunters of his time. He was a dog-lover but not a besotted one. Like Oswell, he found dogs very useful in camp to give warning of visitors of all kinds at night, but he scorned to use them for bringing big game to bay merely to save the hunter's legs.

He would have agreed with Oswell's own words, written some years later: 'I don't think it would have been possible, save with a large number of armed watchers and fires, to keep your oxen in anything like safety without dogs. You went to sleep in peace as soon as the dogwatch was set and the fires made up for the night.'

Yet Livingstone never took a dog with him until his third and last visit to Africa when his 'poodle dog Chitane' served him well as watch dog, more against thieves perhaps than wild animals.

It is obvious that he found a deep satisfaction in this gipsy life or, as he would call it, this picnic life of travel with a waggon; the sense of independence that it gave; the close companionship with the wild things, and the interest of coping with whatever of risk or pleasure the day might bring forth. No one who has ever travelled in this way will underrate the risks or overstate the pleasures, nor will he easily forget the scenes it recalls.

Dawn is the best hour of the day in Africa, and it is heralded by the murmur of the 'boys' as they rise to make up the fires, and the contented lowing of the oxen standing close to the fires, watching with mild eyes these black humans who will lead them to water and grass, and who have shared with them the minor alarums of the night. As the sun rises, kindly rather than fierce for the first hour, the pattern of the flat-topped thorn trees begins to show against the eastern sky, and the birds are giving their dawn chorus before they start on their search for seeds or insects or honey. The routine of breaking camp goes steadily; the morning cup of tea—it would have been coffee in Livingstone's day,—the stowing of the bedding under the tilt of the waggon while the boys lead up the oxen to where the trek-tow and skeys have been laid out for the inspanning. It is not always so, of course; some of the oxen may have strayed; water may be a long distance off; repairs to the waggon may be required; checks and hindrances and delays of all kinds. The real point is that the camp unit can meet them all, its motto is self-help. It is a small kingdom in the wilderness and you can observe with judicious eye all that happens therein.

To a man like Livingstone, for whom every single thing had an interest of its own and usually a meaning, such a life had an intense appeal. The more expert he became at coping with its ups and downs the more wrapped up he became in the places he visited, the people that he found there, and the life they led; the whole content of geography, in fact. Africa to him was becoming one vast intriguing enigma, one which he felt he could play a part in solving, to the glory of God and the benefit of man, and he was full of impatience, as usual, to begin the task in earnest.

Early in 1845 he and Mr Edwards, a very senior 'brother', went off to their chosen site, Mabotsa, to start the new mission, and it must have been soon after their arrival that the lion incident occurred, which for every afterwards hampered his shooting. Livingstone was not in the least interested in hunting as a sport, but he seems to have been a competent shot and quite fearless. Not long afterwards he wrote explaining his fractured arm to a doctor friend, and related that the worst damage was done 'when only partially recovered a jerk received in lifting a stone (for building his house) has led to a false joint in my left humerus'. He ends by saying that he could use the adze and hammer and lift heavy weights notwithstanding the injury, but had difficulty in holding that arm out straight, and that affected his shooting; in fact he had to learn to shoot from the left shoulder.

There were compensations, because it was during his convalescence at Kuruman that he abandoned his former opposition to matrimony and became engaged to Mary Moffat. He could hardly have been an ardent suitor, judging from the way in which he announced it to the London Secretary of the Mission: 'Various considerations connected with the new sphere of labour having led me to the conclusion that it was my duty to enter into the marriage relation, I have made the necessary arrangements for union with Mary.' In spite of such language we know that it was a love-match and it was not the last time that he ensured that inclination should run in harness with duty.

In March Livingstone took his bride to Mabotsa which, aptly enough, means 'a marriage feast', and it was there in June that William Cotton Oswell called on him and 'stayed two days with the Rev. Mr Livingstone, the best, most intelligent and most modest of the missionaries'.

It was but three days earlier that Gordon Cumming, the other great hunter, passed through and wrote merely that he was 'kindly received by Dr Livingstone'. These and other hunters were all going to the parts towards the north where he himself had been some years before, and it was his advice that was sought. His geography and exploration now had to be carried out by proxy, as he was very fully engaged in his true missionary work. Between 1843 and 1848 he moved twice, from Mabotsa to Chouane and then to Kolobeng. That meant three separate houses and schools to be built, and the Bakwains moving with him each time.

At each place a promising water supply gradually failed in a long spell of drought, and troubles piled up around him. There was trouble from the brethren at Kuruman who criticised his frequent moves; there was trouble in the tribe who accused him of keeping the rain away; there was trouble from his having persuaded Chief Sechele to dismiss his surplus wives. There was more than a hint of trouble, too, from the Boers across the Limpopo, whom he twice visited as a sort of ambassador on behalf of his Bechuana people. He got little satisfaction from their commandants, one of whom was a brother of Paul Kruger.

From his letters one has the impression that the only bright spots were the visits of those he called the 'Indian gentlemen', because most of them were on leave from military service in India; Oswell, Steele, Frank Vardon and Murray. He does not envy them their sport, nor their finances, but he does revel in their conversation and their travel talk. Yet with all these worries and frustrations he wrote in 1848 to a friend: 'Never yet has a wish crossed my mind to return homewards. All my desires tend forwards, towards the North. Why, we have a world before us.'

The period of his apprenticeship was over; he was now the most competent and knowledgeable traveller in Bechuanaland, and chafing against his pleasant harness. As a missionary, 'passing rich' on £100 a year, all spent in advance, there was no chance of great journeys for him; he was bound by lack of funds. But if his hoard was little his heart was great, and that fact was recognized by his friend William Cotton Oswell, in whose generous hands his future lay.

CHAPTER TWO

Yet so it was, that, thorow the incouraging Words of he that led in Front, and of him that brought them up behind, they made a pretty good shift to wag along.

JOHN BUNYAN

The three journeys made by Livingstone in association with Oswell, the partnership period in fact, were all made to the north-west of the Bamangwato country, which up to that time represented the farthest known reached by white men.

The region is so curiously contrasted in character, part being almost desert and part having an embarrassment of water, that it is convenient to have recourse to a crude simile in order to convey the contrast in a simple way. Think of an old-fashioned German tobacco pipe with a curved stem, the whole representing country which is fairly well watered and therefore possessing many tall trees, as well as the kind of game which goes with a good water supply, elephant, buffalo, rhino, together with the two antelope most closely identified with marshy country, the lechwe and the situtunga (nakong).

Outside the pipe is typical Kalahari country, covered with sand and barren of rivers or any surface water except for a few weeks

The headpiece represents an incident mentioned long afterwards by Oswell, when, on the banks of the Zouga, the five-year old Agnes Livingstone entertained him to a pretend tea party.

in the rainy season. It is very sparsely wooded but fairly well grassed, and shelters the typical animals of the sandveld, gemsbok, eland and springbok, with ostrich, bustards and the ubiquitous doves as bird-life.

On each journey Livingstone and his partner struck north-westward from the Bamangwato, zigzagging across the dry area from one well to the next, till they approached the mouthpiece of the pipe-stem, represented by Lake Kumadau (the modern Lake Dow), with the perennial water of Chokotsa a few miles to the eastward.

The curved stem itself represents the zone of country on either side of the Botletle river, the river always called the Zouga by Livingstone, a name which has disappeared since it was merely that of a local chief living at that time.

Along the pipe-stem the population is dense by Kalahari standards, the people being Makalaka, Bahurutse and Batawana in succession as one passes along, until the bowl of the pipe is

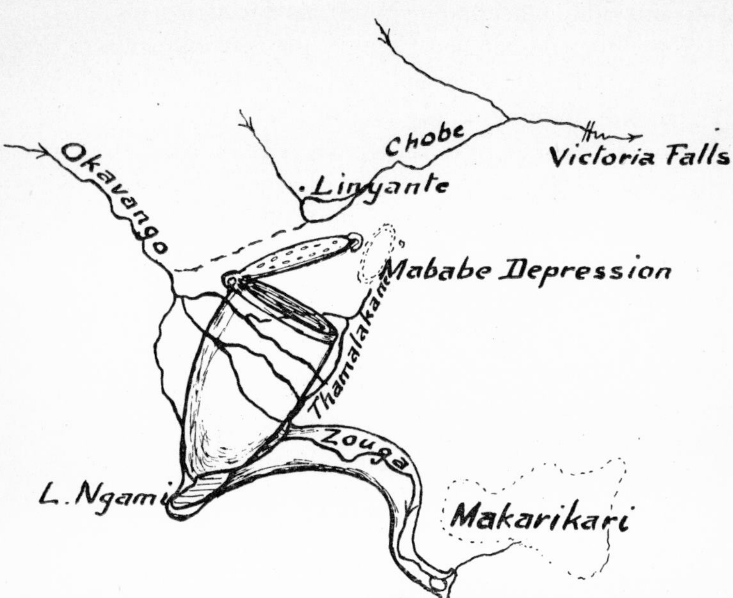

Map to illustrate Livingstone's three journeys with Oswell—German pipe as an 'aide memoire'

reached. This is the vast expanse of swamps best described as the delta of the Okavango River. Here dwells the original tribe of the Bakoba, serfs to the more recent and warlike Batawana, and entirely different in appearance and character, being canoe-men, fish eaters and swamp dwellers.

At the base of the pipe-bowl lies Lake Ngami, looking like the hand-hold of the old-fashioned pipes and, like that device, being a temporary convenience only, not essential for the pipe, just as Ngami has long since dried up. Much of the pipe-bowl is tsetse-fly country, and that is the reason why Livingstone always travelled outside it with his ox waggons. Yet he had an extraordinary understanding of the whole river system, which he achieved by constant questioning of the inhabitants, added to a real sense of hydrology. There can be little doubt that it was these early journeys in a thirsty land that made him so 'river-wise' and 'water-conscious' for the rest of his life. So ingrained was this feeling for water that in his future journeys he hardly ever crossed a stream without mentioning its size and direction in his notes.

Continuing this simile of a pipe, the first journey was along the lower side of the stem and down to the heel of the pipe bowl. The second, with his whole family, was along the upper side of the stem till he reached the bowl, where he met tsetse fly and had to recross the river to the former route and reach Lake Ngami that way. On coming back to the Zouga (Botletle) they met Oswell who, as usual, treated them with the greatest generosity. On his third journey, with his whole family and Oswell, he went due north from the mouthpiece, taking a short cut to the lip of the bowl, in order to avoid the fly belt.

The only critical part of the first journey, therefore, was the thirsty stretch from the border of Chief Sekomi's territory to the lake at the end of the Botletle, the mouthpiece. Once the whereabouts of the watering places was established this part of the journey should have lost its terrors. That it did not, but was a cause of anxiety at each crossing, was due to the unpleasant habit of Sekomi in sending men to fill in the wells already dug, so as to hinder the white men's passage.

Livingstone himself never regarded that first journey as

deserving the stir it caused, since he looked upon it as simply a case for keeping on, a faculty at which he was pre-eminent himself and Oswell equally so. The only hint of disagreement was given later by Livingstone himself, when he wrote that Oswell and Murray were 'not pleased' at his giving Wilson, the trader, permission to accompany them. Wilson was the only one to make money out of the expedition, and contributed least towards its success, yet it was he who later claimed that he had taken a major part. Evidently Oswell was a better judge of Wilson's character than Livingstone in this case.

The reason for Wilson begging to accompany them must have been the tales brought by some coloured travellers from the lake who arrived at Kolobeng shortly before the white men started. Livingstone's remark on it was that 'they brought flaming accounts of the quantities of ivory to be found there, and talked of cattle pens made of elephants' tusks of enormous size'.

Having crossed the dry zone of about two hundred miles, in which there was one stretch of seventy miles without certainty of water, they came to a type of country new to them all, a region of scattered palms, of salt pans and mirages, the mouthpiece of the pipe-stem. So vague had been the accounts of the lake they were seeking that they all thought they had arrived there, whereas they had still three hundred miles to go. It was not exactly a highway along the zone of the river, as it was the first time waggons had been there, so there was much tree cutting to be done, not to mention avoidance of the many game pits dug by the inhabitants.

It was, to say the least of it, a great puzzle to Livingstone to find a considerable river coming out of the lake he sought, and he set himself to solve it. His success in doing so is at once a tribute to his ability as a geographer and an example of the value of his method of supplementing what he actually saw with what he heard in conversation with local people. This required a faculty of discrimination between what the Africans said truthfully and what they said to please him, a faculty which he studiously cultivated all his life. He soon had a picture of the region, which, in all respects but one, is correct, in spite of the fact that he was never able to penetrate the swamps themselves, the actual bowl of the pipe.

It is, perhaps, a dispensation of Providence that while pioneer countries attract Nature's refuse, the dregs of men, they also hold a lure for those who may be adjudged the salt of the earth. Of such a band was William Oswell, and of almost equal savour were Steele, Vardon and Webb, all of whom became Livingstone's friends and helpers in the bright future immediately ahead of him. If anyone encouraged him in his geography it was Oswell, who not only aided him in things material, but was as curious as he to cross the desert and find the mysterious lake. More remarkable still, he was that rare type of selfless explorer who, when all was done, stood aside and let others have the fame of the exploit.

There are, in the history of exploration, so many examples of quarrels and jealousies between partners in travel, that the association of Livingstone and Oswell stands out in high relief as an instance to the contrary. The way in which the partnership worked is put very well by Oswell himself many years later: 'We were the firmest of friends, both a trifle obstinate, but we generally agreed to differ, and in all matters concerning the natives I, of course, waived my crude opinions to his matured judgment. I had the management of trekking and the cattle, after he, with his great knowledge of the people and their language, had obtained all the information he could about the waters and the distances between them. This worked well.'

Livingstone was about to begin no less than three successive journeys to the north, two of them with his whole family, and we must understand his persistence in doing so. Some of the brethren at Kuruman were apt to murmur that he wanted to be an explorer rather than a missionary, and there has been a good deal of misunderstanding on this point. He had already moved his mission station three times, from Mabotsa to Chouane and then to Kolobeng, and had firmly cemented his friendship with Sechele, the chief of the Bakwena tribe.

Meanwhile the Boers over the Limpopo were steadily moving westward towards him, and threatening to take action against

Sechele for allowing Englishmen in his country. Unfortunately they had a shadow of legal support as one result of a recent treaty made between Sir George Cathcart, Her Majesty's Commissioner in the Cape Colony, and the Boers north of the Orange River. This gave independence to the Boers but included certain articles which, through ignorance on the part of the English negotiators, put the missionaries and the Bechuana tribes at the mercy of the Boers. There was to be free passage to Englishmen wanting to pass through Bechuanaland, but no mention of the white men who resided there at the three missions.

The Bechuana tribes were to be prevented from securing guns or ammunition, and any one supplying such things to them was guilty of breaking the treaty.

Livingstone was not the man to keep silent about such a one-sided treaty, and he made two trips into the northern Transvaal in order to reason with the Boers themselves under Pretorius, who were not slow to realise that he was the real hindrance to their penetration to the west. He was forestalling them in precisely the same way as Cecil Rhodes did a generation later.

It was in March 1849, just before Livingstone was joined by Oswell for the journey to the Lake, that his mother-in-law, Mary Moffat, wrote to a friend: 'The Boers in the interior have written to the Committee of our mission here insisting on Mr Livingstone's being immediately removed to the Colony (Cape Colony) and that for ever. They add that if the Committee does not comply with this demand, they will carry it into force themselves.'

Livingstone understood the situation far better than his colleagues at Kuruman, and knew that he and his family were in danger at Kolobeng. He must either go back tamely to Cape Colony where he would have been most unhappy, or go north out of the reach of the Boers. Mary Moffat wrote again in June 1851: 'Livingstone is again away to the Lake, intending to seek a field there, or rather beyond it. He seems determined to get out of the reach of the Boers.'

If we are to seek any major reason for his subsequent career as explorer-missionary it is in this avowed intention of the Boers to make the Bakwain country too hot to hold him. It was the declared enmity of Pretorius and Kruger which thrust upon him the choice of whether to go forward or to retreat. That too was the reason why he took his whole family with him on those two journeys; he dared not leave them behind at Kolobeng. The hardships and danger that his patient wife endured have been laid at times at Livingstone's door as an instance of disregard for his family, whereas it was exactly the reverse. Even his father-in-law was a little slow to understand Livingstone's motive when he wrote in October 1851: 'Livingstone and Oswell were in Sebitoane's country by last accounts. Think only what a journey for a wife and children.' The plain fact of the matter is that on his £100 a year Livingstone could not afford to send his family south to Kuruman or the Cape, and he dared not leave them at Kolobeng, where they could live cheaply, so he took them with him.

On the threats of the Boers Livingstone was very forthright in his letters home at this time. In one written in January 1851, from Kuruman, after he had returned from his second visit to Lake Ngami, he says: 'We hear our station (Kolobeng) is again menaced by the Boers and I feel anxious to be back again. They are great plagues to the progress of missions, these same Boers. They are of Dutch extraction. Each has his big bible which he never reads. Each has his horse and gun with which he can kill the blacks. They look upon themselves as the peculiar favourites of Heaven—that they resemble the children of Israel when led by Moses. And the blacks are the descendants of Cain and may be shot as so many baboons.'

At the same time, he was always careful to distinguish between the Dutch in Cape Colony itself and their cousins who had trekked northwards in protest against the various Government regulations, and particularly the emancipation of slaves.

There is little to show how and when the plan was made between Oswell and Livingstone to find the lake so often rumoured. Both were rather quiet about it in their letters and for a very good reason. The Boers in what is now western Transvaal were jealous enough of the English hunters, including Oswell, who were so successful along the Limpopo, but if they had heard of an attempt to open up the country by the lake they would have gone to almost any lengths to prevent it.

The plan must have been complete when Oswell arrived at the Cape from England at the end of 1848, for his friends Vardon and Steele wrote to him then wishing him success. His arrangement with Livingstone must have been made long before that, for he wrote saying that he would bring 'all books, instruments, etc. thought requisite', and was clearly anxious lest Livingstone should be prevented from coming with him.

It is, I believe, fairly clear that the idea was first mooted by Livingstone, who mentioned it to Steele, and it was taken up eagerly by Oswell, who thereupon made himself responsible for all preparations and expenses. Their common interest in geographical discovery had already occasioned correspondence between them as to the course of the Limpopo, along which Oswell and Vardon had hunted in 1847, and had attempted to map the river.

It is probable that the friends themselves were perfectly clear as to their respective rôles; it was only their friends in England who were inclined to wrangle later as to which was to have the greater glory for the exploit. Oswell was provider and organizer; Livingstone acted as guide, interpreter and surveyor. The latter had in addition the well-defined purpose of finding a suitable centre for a mission, and that aim claimed priority as soon as the lake was reached.

A vital preliminary, nothing less than that of conciliating Sekomi, the chief of the Bamangwato tribe, fell to Livingstone's share in the preparations. This was outwardly successful, but in fact that wily chief sent men ahead to create as much opposition as they could to the travellers' progress, even to the extent of telling the local people that the white men would rob and enslave them. It was one of the early instances, to be repeated often in days to come, where Livingstone met a blank wall of opposition but overcame it by his manner of handling the people.

Livingstone never boasted of his influence over native chiefs, but in some of his anecdotes its powerful effect is very obvious. In a letter to his friend Mr James MacLehose of Glasgow he says of Sekomi: 'When sitting one day in the hut with Sekomi he was silent for some time and at length, looking steadfastly at me, he said, addressing me by the pompous title by which I was usually addressed, "I wish you could give me your eyes." I asked why. "Because," he said, "I like them." He remained quiet and thoughtful again, and then abruptly said, "You must give me medicine to change my heart, I want a heart like yours. Mine is always proud and angry, angry with people. It is very proud and very angry, always, always."'

Their first and immediate difficulty was to get across the dry zone of almost waterless country between the Bamangwato tribe and their vassal tribes to the westward. The critical part of the journey was that between the perennial water of Mashue, where they left the usual road leading to the Bamangwato stronghold of Shoshong, and the end of the Botletle river near the Chokotsa wells. This is a distance of about one hundred and eighty miles by the route taken, which followed a course dictated by such wells as were likely to be holding water.

On this, the first passage made by a white man, dependent upon eighty oxen and twenty horses, they were fortunate in finding water, but in later years there were many tragedies due to its absence, the most notable being those of a party of Boers in 1876. It was really a case of the capacity of the waterholes, most of them being ample for a small party of men on foot, sorely taxed when the travellers had oxen with them, and hopelessly inadequate for a trek such as the Boers attempted with their families and stock.

The local people understood that these occasional wells or soak-holes depended upon a stratum of impervious material which must not be pierced, but it was Livingstone who first perceived the origin of the stratum when he called it 'incipient sandstone'. All this part of the Kalahari is covered with a fine sand from ten to one hundred feet in depth, the remains of the desert that it once was. The few inches of rain which fall each year upon it sink in, carrying down some lime and silica in solution, some of which cements the grains in favourable circumstances into precisely what Livingstone calls it.

He went much farther than that in his understanding of the

water resources of this so-called 'desert', and was not far off the modern conception of what we might call the 'regimen' of water. He was one of the first to recognize that the low rainfall was due to the south-east winds bringing the rain from January to March, and that they lost most of their moisture when surmounting the Drakensberg Mountains. He saw, too, that there must be a moderate amount of water in the sand, since grass grew high in the rainy season; while shrubs and trees must reach more permanent supplies to enable them to survive the eight or nine months of the dry season. The character of the rainfall being capricious, mainly in the form of localised heavy thunderstorms, it was obvious that any area which was lucky in its storms one year would have a surplus of water. This surplus, after germinating the annuals, giving the grass a good start, and refreshing the trees' roots, would accumulate somewhere underground as it sank into the sand, and seep very slowly to the lower parts of the region.

What was often mistaken, even by Livingstone himself, as a sign of progressive desiccation, was usually the result of this capricious, almost haphazard, choice of locality for the heaviest storms. The dependence of all nature in the Kalahari on such bounty as it may receive in one area is so extreme that it affects all living things, from plants up to man. The plants cannot migrate but must have a mechanism by which they can survive a bad rainy season, yet be quick to take advantage of a good one. The animals and man can move to the lucky district, and it is interesting to note the working in this connection of that phrase in the parable of the unjust servant, 'Unto every one which hath shall be given; and from him that hath not, even that he hath shall be taken away from him.'

For in the district which has less than an average fall of rain, the annuals fail to germinate, or germinate and die before maturing; the shrubs put forth fewer leaves and the grass fewer stems; the damp layer of the sand falls lower still, until it is beyond the reach of the smaller trees, which therefore die; there is more sand bare to the pitiless sun, and greater surface desiccation in consequence.

In the lucky district, on the other hand, the grass puts forth early stems from its tussocks, the ground is covered with the trailing stems of the melon family shading the damp soil from too rapid evaporation, and surplus water seeps beyond the reach of roots and replenishes the water-bearing strata. To balance that, animals flock to the feast and help to reduce the plant cover, yet at the same time provide a certain amount of manure and assist in distributing seed. In fact we may indulge in the fanciful idea that, as the rains begin, all the mobile population of the Kalahari

Tsama melon

is doing its best to find out where the greatest rains are happening, and girding up their loins to make their way there as soon as certain news is received. What we cannot imagine is just how the news is carried, if at all. The only possible couriers are the vultures, who are not in themselves very directly interested in a surplus of plant growth.

We will not follow the journey in detail, since it could never be told better than in Livingstone's own words in his *Missionary Travels*, but we may present a picture of what the country looks like even to-day. It is conveniently but inaptly called 'desert' because it is waterless, but it looks little like a desert for the first few months after the rains because there is plenty of grass. There can in fact be no death from starvation here, only from thirst.

Nature has provided some palliatives, however, and it is on these that the Bushmen, the real denizens of the Kalahari, exist in a land where for two-thirds of the year there is practically no surface water whatever. The chief of these is a small melon, about the size of an ostrich egg, which grows wild in the sandy country. It is an annual and therefore depends on showers coming at the right time for it to germinate and get its roots down into the damp sand well below the surface.

There are several kinds of melon, including a small yellow one with prickles on it which tastes exactly like a cucumber. The real standby is a melon called *tsama*; this has two varieties which are

The Kalahari grapple plant

exactly alike in appearance, but one is tasteless and the other extremely bitter, like quinine in fact. Animals will eat either kind of *tsama*, and even get a modicum of nourishment from it as well as quenching their thirst, but for horses it must be sliced otherwise they may try to swallow it whole and will be choked. The value of these melons lies in the fact that, once mature, the skin becomes tough, and the flesh inside remains sweet and turgid with water till the next rains come, when it rots and releases its seeds. The standard method of getting a drink from a *tsama* is to cut off a segment at one end, cut up the flesh inside, and then pound it with a blunt stick to reduce it to a juicy pulp. The bitter kind can be used if roasted, but even then one has to be thirsty to try it without nausea. The leaves of this variety have a bitter smell when crushed. Allied to the melons is the Devil's Claw or grapple plant, lying in wait for an animal's nose to cling on to and looking more like a wizened ogre than any plant should.

In the western part of the Kalahari the little yellow Bushmen spend the dry season literally living on the melon, moving from patch to patch and not seeing water as such for months on end. It was a very different story for a party of twenty men with twenty horses and eighty oxen, for even if it had been a good melon season it would have been difficult to 'water' such a company from them.

They were using the standard method of travelling fast from water to water, often at night to spare the oxen; of carrying enough water in casks for the men, and of sending the horses and sometimes the oxen on ahead to reach water, and walking them back to haul the waggons on. They were relying on a guide who was rarely at fault as to direction, but he could not know whether the various wells and pans held water at that moment, and there were times when they had to risk going forward with the prospect of finding no water, and then having to decide whether to take another jump, or retreat and save some at least of the oxen.

There was the pleasant incident, at one of these critical junctures, when Oswell rode after what he took to be a lion and discovered to be a Bushman woman trying to escape from what she no doubt thought meant death. She took them the eight miles to the now famous well of Chokotsa, which has been the Mecca of many a caravan since that day. It is in the salt pan country, quite featureless and flat except for the tussocky grass which grows right up to the salt incrustation; a land of mirage and illusion as to distance, where at one season of the year one can take an ox waggon over a perfectly hard level surface for miles and at another can sink it to the axles through the dry crust to the gluey mud beneath. Many a waggon wheel has found its funeral round the outskirts of the vast Makarikari Salt Pan, which is half the size of Ireland, and is even now not fully mapped as to its boundaries.

They had scarcely passed these dreary flats, either blinding white with scum of salt, or holding waters of bitterness, when they came to one of those strange contrasts which one only meets in arid lands. Instead of dryness they found an embarrassment of water; instead of open plains a thicket of trees and shrubs, grass and reeds; instead of an occasional nomad Bushman a succession of villages of the Bahurutse, a settled community, vassals to the Bamangwato.

No wonder Oswell gave a loud huzza and threw his hat into the air, to the astonishment of the natives, and the undemonstrative Livingstone wrote 'the news gladdened all our hearts'.

They were told that the river came out of the lake they were seeking, and that therefore 'by following it we should at last reach the broad water'. They had only exchanged one difficulty for another, of course, and it needed a lot of axe work to clear a track for the waggons, the first wheels which had ever passed that way. They could rarely use the elephant paths because they were dotted with the pitfalls dug by the natives to capture game, into which no less than eleven of their own animals fell and had to be rescued. So, after one hundred miles of this arduous travelling, they decided to take a short cut with only the light waggon towards the lake of which they now knew the direction.

Livingstone called the river the Zouga, and this is one of the rare instances when he accepted a local name, that of a chief, instead of the more general native name, the Botletle, and with characteristic persistence he stuck to that name throughout his writings. As they progressed up the river they were conscious that it was growing bigger instead of smaller, and when they reached the curious junction of the Thamalakane (Tamunak'le of Livingstone) with the river coming from the Lake, the news they had of it from the local people overshadowed in Livingstone's mind all news of the lake that had been their goal: 'I inquired whence it came. "Oh, from a country full of rivers—so many that no one can tell their number—and full of large trees." The notion that there might be a highway, capable of being traversed by boats, to an unexplored and populous region, grew from that time stronger and stronger in my mind; and when we actually came to the lake this idea was so predominant that the actual discovery seemed of little importance.'

This is the first clear instance of a quality in Livingstone's character as an explorer that, whenever he reached an immediate goal, led him to cast his mind forward to what was beyond. He was never satisfied with what he discovered, but at once projected himself into more distant aims. He was in fact a living exponent of Browning's lines

> '*Ah, but a man's reach should exceed his grasp,*
> *Or what's heaven for?*'

He was, of course, pleased to reach the mysterious lake which had been his objective for several years, but he instantly assessed it at its proper value; 'It is shallow and can never be of much value as a commercial highway.' He would not have been greatly surprised, one imagines, had he heard a prophecy that his lake's real value was to be as a pasture, a grazing ground of sheep and cattle.

It was only twelve years later, when Livingstone was travelling up a very different kind of lake in Nyasaland, that Thomas Baines visited Lake Ngami and wrote of it: 'We descended to the shores of "the Dam" as it is generally called among our people. The bit of water in sight was a mere strip and the horizon was bounded by reedy islands less than three quarters of a mile distant.'

Forty years later Arnold Hodson has his say of what he saw: 'The once famous Lake Ngami now presents the appearance of a vast and reedy marsh, intersected by streams, no large expanse of water being visible from its shores. The surface of the "lake" is covered with a crust which gives way at every step precipitating the unwary into unknown depths of mud. It gradually dried up till it reached its present depressing condition, being a mere parody of a lake.'

These were the melancholy stages in the death of a lake, yet we know now that lakes, like men, can rise on stepping stones of their dead selves to higher things. It was exactly a century after Livingstone and Oswell had stared across the fifteen miles of water that the writer, in a convoy of four lorries, drove right across the 'lake' through grassy plains, the home of some thousands of Damara people, possessing some score of thousands of their long-horned cattle as well as sheep and goats. It is true that half way across we met a full-sized thunderstorm and had to race our lorries at their utmost speed, lest we too should be stuck in 'unknown depths of mud', overtaking ostriches and gemsbok on the way. 'Lake Ngami' is now, in fact, the richest part of that district, known as Ngamiland.

The region into which Livingstone had now penetrated was the first large-sized geographical problem he had met, and he rose so magnificently to meet it that, even now, we can find only one thing wrong in his explanation of the queer situation he had encountered. For queer it was, and still is, to pass across a semi-desert and reach a river flowing towards him which grew larger instead of smaller as he passed up it; which divided into a two-way river, flowing either way according to the season; and to reach a region where there was, after the rains, more water than dry land.

The dwindling river was his first puzzle and he seems to have recognised at once the true reason for its behaviour, namely, that it was lost by evaporation from the brackish waters of Lake Kumudau, or in wetter seasons, from the vast salt pans of the Makarikari.

'There is', he writes, 'I am convinced, no such thing in the country as a river becoming lost in the sand. This fancied phenomena, so convenient for geographers, haunted me for years, but I have failed in discovering anything beyond a most insignificant realisation of it.' Then he rightly concludes that the Zouga (Botletle) is a 'prolongation' of the Thamalakane, and that 'a narrow arm of the lake reaches up to the point where one ends and the other begins'. This channel, now known as the Ngabhe river, a name sometimes applied to the lake, he regarded as just 'as stagnant as the lake itself'. It is, however, the outlet to the lake and therefore does flow into the Thamalakane when the lake level is high. On the other hand, when the latter river is first in flood the water will run along the Ngabhe into the lake depression, even at times showing rapids capable of upsetting a canoe.

The Ngabhe is in fact a two-way river, and Livingstone rightly judges that it could be so, as he says that under certain circumstances 'we should then have the phenomenon of a river flowing two ways'.

As to the origin of the lake, the value of his ceaseless questionings and skilful analysis of the answers he got is very apparent. He was never able to penetrate the flooded area we now know as the Okavango swamps, because they were tsetse-ridden, yet he

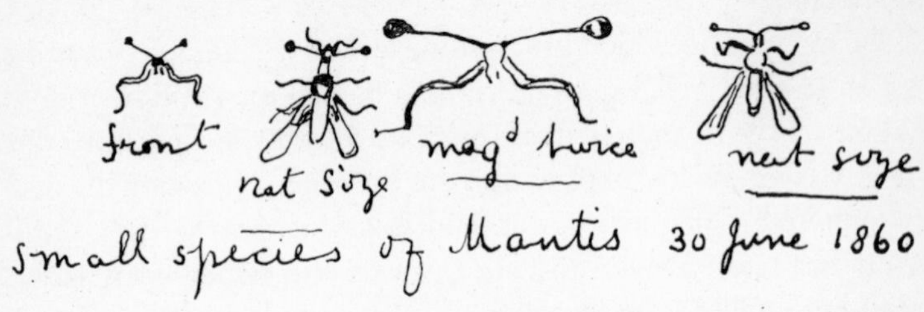

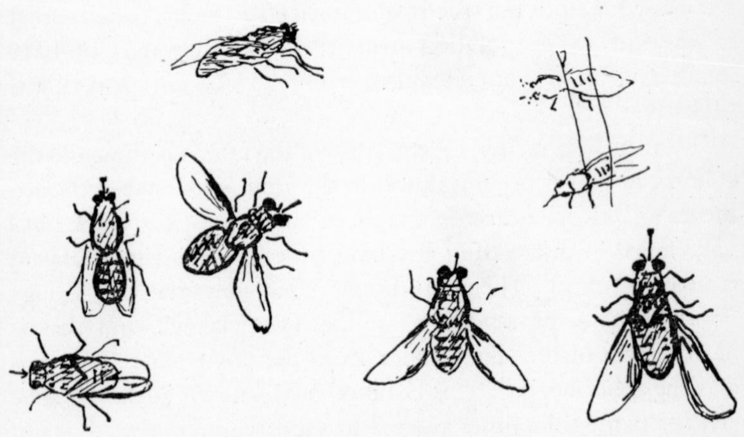

Above: A stalk-eyed Diopsid. Below: Tsetse flies
Tracings of Livingstone's insect sketches

not only mentions rivers he had never seen but deduces correctly their junction. He describes how the water of the Embarrah (a local name for the Okavango) divides into the Tzo and Teoughe, the former feeding the Thamalakane and the latter 'falling into the lake as into a reservoir'. This, in simple terms, describes accurately what happens, and is the basis of all the plans now being suggested for making the Okavango swamps the most productive region in the whole of the Bechuanaland Protectorate.

The only mistake he makes is in ascribing the progressive diminution in size of the lake, which he noted, to a general desiccation and decrease of rainfall, whereas it is really due to a blocking of the channel of the Teoughe and diversion of the supply to other parts of the swamps. In fact, at his very first encounter with a puzzling river system he shows his mastery of the principles of hydrology.

Livingstone tried hard to persuade Chief Lechulatebe to sell him canoes in which he and Oswell could journey up these countless rivers towards Chief Sebituane, and when this was rudely refused Oswell 'settled the matter by nobly offering to bring up a boat next year, at his own expense, from the Cape'.

The next year, 1850, he comes back again to the lake, but this time with his wife and three children, and, for much of the way, with Sechele, intending to go up the Thamalakane to visit Sebituane, the paramount chief of the Makololo tribe, only to find that that route was blocked by tsetse fly on the east bank of the river. It is interesting to note that the fly is no longer on that bank except for a belt about ten miles wide near the Mababe depression, across which the Ngamiland cattle for the Northern Rhodesian market are driven at night, when the fly is inactive. He must have turned back from his second attempt to reach the Makololo, very sorrowfully, at some point opposite the present chief centre of the whole district, the thriving little township of Maun. Here there are plenty of cattle though the fly zone begins about ten miles to the west.

So the family and their small retinue recrossed the Thamalakane and made their way to Lake Ngami. There they found a party of traders, struck down by fever, too late to save an artist who was with them, Alfred Rider, but in time for Mary Livingstone to nurse the other sufferers back to health again. The well-known picture of the family viewing the lake was based on an unfinished drawing by Rider lent by his mother.

Livingstone then made a bold plan, none other than that of leaving his wife and children under the care of that most untrustworthy chief, Lechulatebe, while he went alone and on ox-back to Sebituane. Sechele had persuaded Lechulatebe to help Livingstone, and the whole trip was planned and paid for with a very superior gun. By what we must consider a stroke of good fortune he delayed his start by one day, to find next morning that the two elder children were down with fever, to be followed by the collapse of some of their servants.

From this incident we may judge both the persistence of Livingstone himself and the noble support in it that always came from his wife. Such was her capacity that we may be confident that she would have coped with the fever well enough, but we now know enough of the chief's character to be very doubtful whether he would have kept her party supplied with food as he promised.

This was the second time Livingstone was foiled in pressing northward, and though he would probably have reached Sebituane on ox-back, travelling quickly and avoiding the fly belts, he might well have come back to find tragedy had overtaken his family.

Oswell was to have been with him on this 1850 trip, but for some reason there was misunderstanding between them as to their rendezvous. The mistake apparently was made by Livingstone, for when Oswell reached Kolobeng he found that his former partner had gone north a month earlier than he had expected. Although Oswell had purchased the boat as promised and brought it on his waggons all the way he, with characteristic generosity, makes very little of the upset to the plans, and journeyed on to the Zouga, where he met the returning Livingstone party. The relationship between these two men is underlined by a remark in a letter from Livingstone to a friend in London: 'We met Oswell on our return—brought supplies for us from the Colony and returned a bill of £40 [that is, he paid for them himself]—seemed very anxious to get me to promise to allow him to accompany me next trip.'

For even then, returning with an ailing family, he had made plans for the next year, nor were they affected by what happened when he got to Kolobeng; Mary Livingstone was delivered of a daughter a week later, was seized wth a paralytic attack after her confinement, and the children all caught a prevailing sickness from which the baby died. As a result they all went to Kuruman, where Mary Moffat was rather aghast at their appearance.

Livingstone's natural resilience to misfortune shows itself in the same letter when he records the receipt of an award of twenty-five guineas from the Royal Geographical Society. His occasional playfulness in letters comes out when he writes of this sum, 'I think they must have left out a cypher (250) by mistake, but unfortunately it was written in words.'

The Makololo chief, Sebituane, in his turn, was equally desirous of meeting this redoubtable and kindly missionary, and sent messengers down to him at Kolobeng, bearing delightful bribes for the three chiefs whom Livingstone would have to pass on his way. These were 'thirteen brown cows for Lechulatebe, thirteen white cows for Sekomi, and thirteen black cows for Sechele'.

Oswell, back in England, was busy getting an outfit, including instruments for navigation for Livingstone, who might well have quoted to him: 'A judicious friend is better than a zealous; you are both.' Yet when he reached Kolobeng he found difficulties. Livingstone dared not leave his family within reach of the Boers, and he had no waggon fit for the prolonged journey it was bound to be. Oswell surmounted these hindrances by giving the family a waggon, and went ahead of them on the first thirsty three hundred miles, opening up the wells so that the children should not again undergo the trials of thirst.

The two sections joined again before they had reached the Chokotsa wells, near the mouthpiece of the pipe in our simile, from which point they were to strike north into new country, known only to a few of the tall Masarwa Bushmen of that district, who are a foot taller than the little yellow Bushmen of the southern and western Kalahari, and very black.

A curious situation presented itself to the party when they were crossing the Zouga. They heard that a party of traders, which included the Wilson who had been with Livingstone and Oswell when they discovered Lake Ngami two years before, was a few days ahead of them, purposing to visit Sebituane. It was in fact a race between them as to who should get there first, and Livingstone was most anxious that the first impressions of white men should come from the missionary party. He therefore procured guides who were reputed to know the direct way north, instead of following the traders along the Zouga and Thamalakane.

We can only guess at the relations between the two parties. They can hardly have been cordial, for it was Wilson who had claimed that neither Oswell nor Livingstone but he himself was the real discoverer of Lake Ngami. On the other hand Livingstone was coming to see that trade could work in well with missionary effort, and help to undercut the commerce in slaves of which he had already heard. Perhaps because the journey had become a race the crossing of this unknown quarter of the Kalahari receives rather scant notice in his *Missionary Travels*. It was a feat at least as great as their Lake Ngami journey, and became doubly so, as they had only two white men instead of four, and the encumbrance of a wife and young family.

After crossing the then dry bed of the Zouga and several salt pans, which were only just hard enough to let them pass over safely, they came upon a type of country quite new to the travellers. It is aptly described in one sentence in Livingstone's notes: 'The whole of the adjacent country is hard, and covered over with Mopane and Baobab trees; the underlying rock is white tufa and springs abound in it.'

The belt of country immediately to the north of the Makarikari Salt Pan is now well known, as the main lorry track from the railway at Francistown to Maun runs along it. What Livingstone calls 'the madrepore limestone' or 'the tufa' is now called 'calcrete', and it is the result of prolonged seepage of water, some of which no doubt comes very slowly underground from the higher ground up in the north. Water can therefore be found underneath the calcrete by digging, and the large number of natural springs and grass makes this good country for cattle, provided it is not too heavily stocked.

It is difficult to follow Livingstone's track across it since few of the names he uses for the springs seem to have endured, and later travellers have failed to recognise most of them. Possibly they were Bushmen names as given by his guide, and some have been replaced in usage by Sechuana names. The route seems to have been more to the westward than that usually followed by later travellers, but the pace was hot, about thirteen miles each day, till they met the heavily wooded country some sixty miles south-east of the Mababe depression.

This is the Kalahari at its best; monotonous perhaps but full of game and particularly of birds. After leaving the glare and arid sameness of the salt pans one meets palms and an occasional baobab, which break the skyline with fine effect, and the going, though sandy, is only slightly hindered by trees and shrubs. Of these, two types were to be the constant companions of Livingstone in many of his future journeys, the *mopane* and the *mohonunu*.

The mopane is one of the *Bauhinia* group of plants, which includes climbers, shrubs and large trees, all with leaves which are more or less split into two lobes, rather like butterfly wings. In the case of the mopane these leaves have the faculty of closing their wings, exactly as does a butterfly, in strong sunlight, presumably to reduce the rate of transpiration. Consequently just when shade would be most appreciated you can find very little under a mopane tree. On the other hand you can find a most pestiferous little insect known as the mopane fly, which by its numbers and persistence is a menace even though it does not sting.

The presence of the fly may be connected with a sweetish secretion on mopane leaves which interested Livingstone, as it furnished a food for the Bushmen. It appears as countless white patches on the leaves which can easily be scraped off and have a sickly sweet taste. It is precisely similar to the scaly excrescences to be found on certain types of eucalyptus bushes in Australia which, in the writer's youth, were called 'manna', and were gathered by him and his companions when pretending to be living in the wilderness.

The mopane favours harder ground than most trees and seems to inhibit the growth of grass, for which reason 'mopane country' has come to be considered poor country in the minds of stock owners. Nevertheless it is a fine hard wood for repairing waggons and so resinous that it makes an excellent camp fire. The elephants are fond of the foliage and break down the trees to get it, so that nothing but its ubiquity saves it from extinction. Its light green foliage, which falls in the winter, is an emergency fodder for stock, especially when dry.

The mohonunu is also to be met with over much of central Africa, growing to tree size in Nyasaland, and only shrub size in the dryer parts of the Kalahari. Its botanical name of *Terminalia sericea* describes it well enough as having its silvery, silky leaves in tufts at the ends of twiggy branches. It too furnishes food for the browsing antelopes, and its sweet bark is much favoured by elephants. In the part Livingstone was now traversing, it grows in dense thickets, needing much axe work when one is clearing a passage for the waggons, but the alternative is equally dense thickets of thorn-bush. In the modern method of travel by lorry furnished with a strong steel bumper, neither type is an obstacle, but the choice is usually for the thorn scrub since one can see rather better through it than through the leafy mohonunu. Its curious winged fruit turns pink and even red when mature, and worthily matches its musical native name.

Half way across to the Mababe Depression, of which they knew the existence, they got beyond the region of springs and into thorn bush country where 'not a bird nor an insect could be seen for three dreary days', a sure sign of absence of surface water. Things were becoming critical, and their Bushman guide had deserted them; when they came across the spoor of a rhinoceros, which never strays far from water, they took to the rather desperate expedient of setting the oxen free to find their own way to the water ahead, followed by the drivers. Oswell and Livingstone stayed with the family at the waggons, till the men returned with water from the Mababe river.

The Mababe is an occasional river, an overflow from the Okavango swamps which runs into the famous Mababe Flats, or Depression as it is now called, the favoured haunt of many hunters from Chapman up to F. C. Selous. The tsetse belt projects eastwards from its real centre in the marshes just to the south of the Depression, and some of their oxen had entered it when seeking water and were therefore doomed. At that date the Mababe was a place of refuge for the people driven from their true homes to the eastward by raids of the Matabele, and it was very unhealthy from the large number of mosquitoes which find it a more or less permanent home.

The Mababe is in fact an exact parallel to Lake Ngami itself, but at a later stage in its evolution. Perhaps a century before Livingstone's visit it, too, had been a lake of much the same size as Ngami, and it almost certainly had two sources of supply; one via the Mababe river from the south-east, which is another of those baffling rivers of this region which can run either way according to where the greater floods are; the other from an overflow channel from the Chobe River, known as the Savuti channel. This is still a well-defined but dry river bed, and in fact it now has very large trees growing in it.

As a result of its past history the Mababe Depression has a number of requirements for migratory game which has made it a happy hunting ground for the big game hunters. There is grass there long after it has become sere and sour on the sandy belt beyond; there are salty patches in the lower parts; and there are water holes in and around it which are either permanent or nearly so.

One such is the Tsotsoroga Pan, which is worthy of description since it is so typical. It is on the eastern flank of the depression proper. Before you get to it through rather dense mopane forest you are conscious of the spoor of numerous animals heading in the same direction; that of the buck and buffalo running along the rough track for waggons or trucks; that of the wiser elephant always crossing it, since he knows it to be the track of man. Quite suddenly the trees get larger, the spoor more concentrated, and one comes to a delightful pond some fifty yards across in a barely noticeable depression.

There is a twittering of all the small birds, which cannot live far from water; there are often small flights of duck adventuring far from their real home in the swamps; and the mud at the edge holds the story of months in the countless footprints of animals;

a real palimpsest for the sportsman. The veritable pits made by the feet of elephant tend to obliterate all others though the enormous cloven hoof of the giraffe is usually clear enough, especially where it has straddled its forefeet so as to lower its body and enable it to reach the water; a most awkward and defenceless posture for an animal whose only weapons are its mighty kick and its speed in the open.

The Livingstone family went up the centre line of the depression on this journey, but on his next one he himself passed that pan and came to the other unique feature of the district, the hill N'Gwa as he calls it, now rendered as Goha. 'This being the only hill we had seen since leaving the Bamangwato, we felt inclined to take off our hats to it.'

He could not resist climbing it, of course, and he saw before him a new and fascinating type of country of big trees, a sufficiency of water, the end of the Kalahari in fact, but also the beginning of malarial Africa. It was indeed the Africa of his future, where rain and swamps and dense forest were to be his portion rather than sand and salt pans and rare water holes.

He soon made contact with Sebituane, who had come a long way to meet him, and they immediately took to one another. Oswell's account of the meeting is less matter of fact than Livingstone's: 'Presently this really great Chief and man came to meet us, shy and ill at ease. I felt troubled at the evident nervousness of this famous warrior (for he had been and still was a mighty fighter with very remarkable force of character). Surrounded by his tribesmen he stood irresolute and quite overcome in the presence of two ordinary-looking Europeans. He was far and away the finest Kaffir I ever saw.'

Sebituane was destined to die within a fortnight, yet it was the impression he left on the two white men that brought Livingstone back next year and determined a great deal of his future career. To emphasize that statement we must quote further from Oswell: 'In the dead of the night he paid us a visit alone, and sat down very quietly and mournfully at our fire. Livingstone and I woke up and greeted him, and then he dreamily recounted the history of his life, his wars, escapes, successes and conquests, and the far distant wanderings in his raids. By the fire's glow and flicker among the reeds, with that tall dark earnest speaker and his keenly-attentive listeners, it has always appeared to me one of the most weird scenes I ever saw.'

Sebituane died from inflammation of the lungs, possibly as a result of a fall off Livingstone's horse and Livingstone's comment was: 'I never felt so much grieved by the loss of a black man before; and it was impossible not to follow him in thought into the world of which he had just heard before he was called away. The deep dark question of what is to become of such as he, must, however, be left where we find it, believing that, assuredly, the "Judge of all the earth will do right".'

In spite of the sudden death of Sebituane the two white men were fascinated by the prospect of seeing more of this strange watery country they had discovered, and they made plans to that effect. Oswell was to try to go down the Zambezi to the Portuguese settlements on the east coast, while Livingstone would remain in the country and establish a mission station when he could find a suitable place.

The geographer in both of the men was all agog to hear of as well as to see what they had found. Livingstone records of one of the chief's head people: 'He was of much use in drawing maps and Mr O. and I drew or had drawn for us, upwards of sixty. The tablet was frequently only the ground, but the agreement of different individuals in their delineations of rivers etc., shows that what we furnish on their authority is worthy of credit.'

The map facing page 64 is obviously made up from the memory of these consultations, and we reproduce it here in facsimile because it was made by Oswell, and in fact drawn by him six months later on the back of a letter to his brother. On the reverse side of the map there is a note which is so characteristic of these two explorers that it is quoted in full: 'It is not pretended that the accompanying sketch is correct, or even near correctness. The dotted line shows our course, and this we have laid down as well as we were able; let others prove us wrong. The greater part of the whole is on hearsay evidence, but this was as good as such can be and tested to the best of our ability; it must of course be looked upon merely as an approximation to the truth. Livingstone and I rode out to Seshetse on horse back, swimming our horses through the little rivers. We considered the distance about ninety-five or a hundred miles, we were eight days absent.'

In this journey they discovered the Zambezi, which the Portuguese had never suspected to be there, though they had lived on its lower course for two centuries. They heard also of the 'Mosi-oa-tunya', 'the smoke that thunders', and Oswell writes it on the map. This was the Victoria Falls, and they were told by the Makololo that it was a feature beyond belief. It was characteristic of Livingstone that he did not bother to go and look at these Falls till he found himself near them four years later when journeying to the Eastern side of Africa. What could be more laconic than his first sentence concerning this visit? 'As this was the point from which we intended to strike off to the north-east I resolved on the following day to visit the falls. Of these we had often heard since we came into the country: indeed one of the questions asked by Sebituane was, "Have you smoke that sounds in your country?" '

The 'hearsay evidence' referred to by Oswell was of course interpreted by Livingstone, whose own maps were more polished than this one, and were used by the Royal Geographical Society to compile the one accompanying Livingstone's paper published by the Society. It will be realised that it is an immense area to be mapped by hearsay from the dotted line representing their 'course'. Yet a comparison with a modern map will show how very sound was most of that hearsay. The note in the corner about the Sabi river shows Oswell's continued interest in the course of the Limpopo river below the point which he and Vardon had reached. The Sabi is in fact quite separate, but it was a reasonable guess.

Their plans were doomed to disappointment. Livingstone recognised that the swamps of the Chobe and even the rather higher banks of the Zambezi were no place in which to settle his family of young children, of whom a fifth was on the way, and tsetse fly would have made Oswell's journey down the Zambezi impossible except on foot. So after talking it over Livingstone took the enormous decision that he could do no other than send his family home to England and return himself to Central Africa alone.

They therefore made their way back southwards, with oxen given them by the Makololo, and in Livingstone's diary there is an entry when they reached the Zouga: 'A son, William Oswell Livingstone, born.' It was during the halt required by this domestic event, so curtly noticed, that he wrote of his new plan to his Missionary Society authorities: 'I feel that two years alone in that country are required for the successful commencement of a mission.' We may note that word 'alone', for that is what Livingstone meant and he later had some difficulty in avoiding a companion being given to him.

Later in the letter his additional purpose in going back is disclosed, and it is the one that ruled the remainder of his life: 'If we can enter in and form a settlement we shall be able to put a stop to the slave trade in that quarter. It is probable that the mere supply of English manufactures in Sebitoane's part [of the country] will effect this for they did not like it [selling slaves] and promised to abstain.

To orphanise my children will be like tearing out my bowels but you will perceive it is the only way except giving up the region altogether.'

Oswell, as always, came nobly to the rescue and in a characteristic way. Instead of staying a few days with them at Kolobeng he pushed on to Cape Town alone. When the Livingstones arrived there some time later, they found that he had made arrangements to outfit the family and help with their passages. Without that help it is doubtful whether the plan could have been carried out. But it was a sad father who wended his way back to Kuruman, bereft both of family and friend, and one of the most poignant sentences in all his letters is one in which he dramatises the sacrifice to his mission, not of himself but of his children. To their questions at this time: 'When shall we return to Kolobeng? When to Kuruman?' the father has to reply; 'Never! The mark of Cain is on your foreheads; your father is a missionary.'

Unavoidable delay on his journey back may well have saved his life, for only a few days before he reached Kuruman there occurred the attack by four hundred Boers on the Bakwain tribe at Kolobeng, and the spoiling of Livingstone's house and library, already mentioned. As usual Livingstone takes the loss with more philosophy than the average man, though he used, rather delightfully, that figure of speech known as meiosis, or deliberate understatement, when he writes to a friend: 'I cannot say I take joyfully the spoiling of my goods. If they had made any use of my books and medicines I could have forgiven them—but tearing, smashing and burning them was beyond measure galling.'

The worst effect of this raid on his plans was that he could not get any servants to go north with him, knowing, as they did, that he would have to run the gauntlet past the Boers and would get short shrift if they caught him. 'They intend, it is reported, as soon as they hear of my passing, to send a party on horseback after me, and if I will not come back they must kill me. I intend to lighten the waggons as much as possible and then we shall have a run for it.'

The start of his final journey to the north was therefore scarcely an auspicious one: '. . . our servants were the worst possible specimens of those who imbibe the vices without the virtues of Europeans, but we had no choice, and were glad to get away on any terms.'

The expedition of only eight men, including a coloured man, George Fleming, who was formerly with Oswell and now intended to become a trader, reached the town of Sechele on the last day of the year, where they were safe enough since the Boers, had lost thirty men in their raid and were not likely to attack again.

An incident, with an interesting sequel, took place here. Not far from the town there is a cave which was viewed with awe and even abhorrence by the natives, who said that everyone who went in remained there for ever. Livingstone wanted to know if there was some precipice inside to account for these rumours and he paid it a visit; he found it to be rather ordinary, dividing into two branches, and in the upper branch he left a leaden medal he had with him. The sequel is that in 1953 his grandson, Dr Hubert F. Wilson, also paid a visit to this cave, precisely one hundred years later. Naturally he tried to climb up and find this leaden medal. He had to give up the attempt, coming away, as he confessed to me, with a profound admiration of the clambering powers of his grandfather, and declining to accept my proffered excuse on his behalf that Dr Livingstone was twenty years younger when he accomplished the feat.

By keeping to a western route, on the fringe of the desert, the party kept out of reach of the Boers, and as the season of 1852 had been a rainy one they had less difficulty than before with water supply. Livingstone remarks that such a rainy season was the completion of a cycle of eleven or twelve years, now known as the sun-spot frequency cycle, a rather remarkable observation from a man who had been living far from scientific men for just that period of years. In fact it was one of the rare years when a party could, with the aid of *tsama* melons, travel right across the 'desert' from Kolobeng to Lake Ngami. He met one such party, and their oxen had subsisted on melons alone for a period of three weeks, 'and when at last they reached a supply of water they did not seem to care much about it.'

It is very noticeable in his account of this, his first journey far to the north unaccompanied by white men, that his notes and observations on what he sees are far wider in scope and in detail than before. He would have said, perhaps, that he had more time to ponder on what he saw when untrammelled by company, however pleasant. It was a state he was to enjoy or endure for almost the whole of the next four years. Nothing escaped his notice; the age and character of the baobab trees, for instance, of which he says 'though it possesses amazing vitality it is difficult to believe that this great baby-looking bulb or tree is as old as the pyramids'.

His reflections on hunting, especially hunting at night when it is impossible to be certain of a killing shot, are enlightening if a little scathing to some hunters he had met, as he calls it a form of insanity. He had kept records of the numbers of elephant reported killed, and makes the interesting calculation that the average for native hunters was one elephant per man, for the Boers two and 'for the English officers twenty each', the difference being entirely due to the fact that the Englishmen rarely fired till they were within thirty yards of their target while the others blazed away at a hundred yards.

The route was now well-known to him, nevertheless he had plenty of privations as soon as he broke off from the old Ngami route to cross the northern triangle of the Kalahari; this time it was due to fever seizing upon all but one of his small party. He promptly put this adversity to geographical uses by calculating several longitudes by the method of lunar distances, a method which had been refreshed in his mind by the instructions from his friend Maclear of the Royal Observatory at Cape Town, and one which needs some considerable practice both in observing and in working out, and at which he became an expert.

Meanwhile his forty oxen had been stampeded by a hyena, and were lost for two days although followed faithfully by a Bakwain youngster. The labour of clearing a new route to the Mababe, to avoid the tsetse belt, was severe on such a small and ailing party but fortunately he himself remained fit. And so, by slow degrees, they came to the Sanshureh, a southerly branch of the Chobe and only had to make contact with his Makololo friends.

In his *Missionary Travels* the text on this journey spreads over some fifty pages full of anecdotes of the country, the people, the animals, and incidents of travel formerly passed over in silence or with the barest allusion. One is inclined to say that Livingstone had now found his true bent, to journey alone over Africa with the minimum of paraphernalia, amongst which his real treasures were his sextant and compass, his nautical almanac and his Bible. In fact the many statues of him reflect these characteristics; in most of them he has a walking stick to show his favourite method of travel, and the artist then has to decide between a Bible or a sextant for his other hand; not a few designs include both.

As we are about to leave the Bechuanaland Protectorate finally, we might glance at it as it is now, just over a century since Livingstone first 'put it on the map'. It remained a no-man's-land for many years and was ultimately saved by Chief Khama from being either annexed by the Transvaal republic or attached to

Cecil Rhodes's South Africa Company. Khama avoided the emissaries of both aspirants and went to see Queen Victoria, after which it became a Protectorate of Her Majesty's Government in 1885.

With a population of about one per square mile, scattered over a vast area, with no permanent surface water except in the Okavango triangle, and with few minerals of economic value, it is not surprising that it has lagged behind the rest of Southern Africa in development. In the eastern margin the railway has given at least an air of modernity to the tribes who helped or hindered Livingstone. West of the railway belt there is not a great deal of difference; it is still dependent on the few water-holes and on the seasonal profusion of melons; there are still the little yellow Bushmen on the western fringe, living their life of freedom.

In the part crossed by Livingstone to reach Sebituane, now known as the Chobe Crown Lands, there are very few inhabitants. In a journey of two weeks there the writer only encountered one man, a tall Masarwa Bushman looking for honey.

To the west of those arid areas, however, in the Okavango swamplands and Ngamiland, there is promise of a change. Here is water and to spare and a reasonable population, and here too is a possible outlet to the Atlantic for the Rhodesias.

There is always a chance for development of the cattle industry in the Bechuana Protectorate, but it depends upon underground water and that is a question of pumping and maintenance.

Few travellers now use the route of Livingstone's choice, since there is a road, of a kind, between railhead at Francistown and the centre of administration for the north-west, at Maun, where there is also an airstrip for quicker travel still.

History has repeated itself in the tribal lands of the Bamangwato, where in Livingstone's day the chief Sekomi was at loggerheads with his great son Khama. Yet Khama was also at odds with his senior son Segkhoma the Second and banished him for twenty years. Segkhoma was succeeded by his infant son Seretse, under the Regency of his uncle, Khama's youngest son Tshekedi, as wise a ruler as his father. Recent years have disclosed a new type of family disharmony through Seretse marrying a white wife, the outcome of which at present is exile for him and the loss to the tribe of Tshekedi's leadership. These are minor matters, however, compared to the uncertainty of the Protectorate's political future.

It would not be hard to imagine what would be Livingstone's comments on the present situation, with the Union of South Africa claiming the Protectorate, yet he would be pleased to know that ever since protection was confirmed in 1885 there has been no war inside its borders and comparatively few tribal upsets.

'That heraldic beast, the sable antelope'

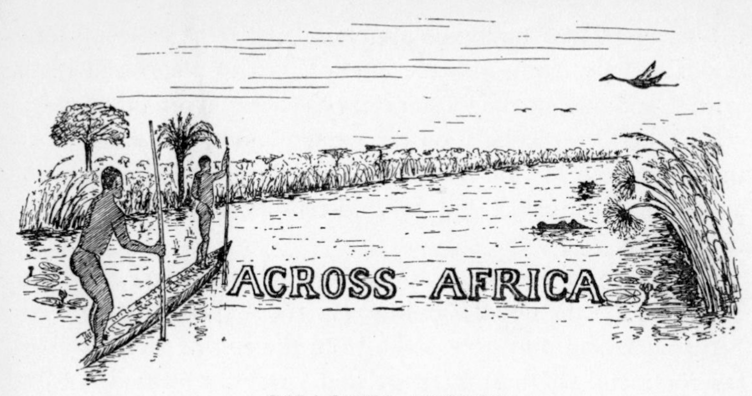

CHAPTER THREE

Then I thought with myself, who that goeth a pilgrimage but would have one of these Maps about him, that he may look where he is at a stand, which is the way he must take.

JOHN BUNYAN

When Livingstone met Sekeletu, the young man who had stepped into the shoes of the great chief Sebituane, he was more or less 'at a stand'; he did not quite clearly see the way he must take. His first purpose was to find a suitable place for a mission station, for which he wanted higher and healthier land than he had so far seen in the country of the Makololo. But behind that straightforward task another one was shaping which was shortly to engulf the first one, and become his ruling motive; the task of wrestling with the curse of slavery.

Slavery as an institution he had already met, thinly veiled as serfdom, but now he had come upon slavery as a trade, one in which men, women and children were sold as chattels, transported as slave gangs to the coast and lost for ever to their own people. Even at this early stage he saw it as a problem in economics. It was a trade of a kind, and it must be combated by devising a trade which could undersell it and make it a poor proposition.

And, after a fashion, it was maps which held the solution, for only by finding a way of getting goods cheaply from the coast to the centre of Africa could he hope to undercut the profits of the slavers. Their trade was simple; a matter of carrying light goods, mainly cloth, into the interior, buying slaves and ivory with it, and making the former carry the heavy ivory down to the coast where, particularly on the western coast, it was the ivory that accounted for the real profit. The slaves had already eaten a part of their value, and by mid-century were not so easily disposed of.

The lesson of the map was plain enough. The slave trade just beginning on the upper Zambezi was 1600 miles from the Cape Settlements and only 1000 miles from the east or west coasts of the continent. He must therefore find a way for his traders from the nearest coast.

The first rebuff to his plan for what would essentially be cheaper transport was the most lasting one, the presence of the tsetse fly. The white man's waggons would soon have undercut the slave gangs could they have been used, but the fly put an absolute stop to that. Therefore he must find navigable or semi-navigable rivers for means of transport. He had already seen one, the Zambezi, and had seen canoes that had come down it for several hundred miles—there was a good starting point at all events. If not that way, then he must go down the Zambezi to the east coast. In the end he did both, and quite single-handed.

A great change was about to take place in the circumstances of his travel, and he was not slow to see it coming, else why did he bring his clumsy pontoon, a present from his friend Murray? For ten years his travel had been largely a search for water holes in a dry country; now and henceforth it was to be for rivers and lakes; it was the problem of where they were and where they went that was to be the centrepiece of the rest of his life.

Here we may find a 'ghost' map of Central Africa useful in finding a measure for his travel, a map which shows what was known of African rivers in the year 1850 and, in thinner lines, what is known now.

There was a complete blank in the geographical centre of the continent, although Mounts Kilimanjaro and Kenya had just been discovered—and discredited. The known Congo was but two hundred miles long, apparently coming from the north-east, somewhere in the direction of where the ancients reputed the Nile to rise, but that river was still not on our maps. The only other river whose course was known for any great distance was

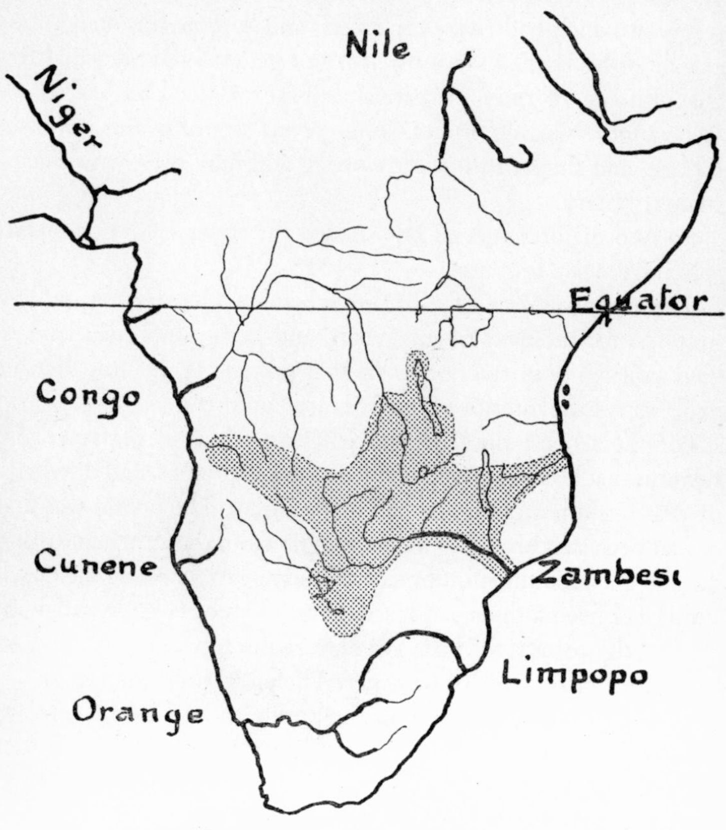

African rivers as known in 1850

five hundred miles of the lower Zambezi, and that had been known for over a century.

Who could have guessed from the 1850 map that the ultimate source of the Congo was within five hundred miles of the *east* coast of Africa, while that of the Zambezi, together with the Okavango, was within two hundred miles of the *west* coast? The only guess nearly correct was that of Herodotus, that the Nile was the longest river in the world and came from south of the Equator.

In 1852 Livingstone himself had added five hundred miles to the known Zambezi, which he called the Liambye, but he was in a region which had two-way rivers, and he therefore had a local puzzle of his own. Even now it is not generally appreciated that the ultimate, if only occasional, source of the Zambezi is the Okavango, which empties some of its flood waters into the Chobe, and thence into the Zambezi, and may once have been a main tributary.

So two major rivers all but crossed the continent, and another split it from top to centre.

The river systems of Africa were to be the despair of geographers for the next twenty years, and Livingstone was later to have colleagues in the north. At that date, 1853, he was the sole explorer for the interior of nearly half a continent.

For the second time he was entering the land of rivers and swamps that he and Oswell had seen the year before, and of which, by ceaseless questioning, he had made a map. The puzzle was that he had been steadily rising as he came up from the Zouga, crossing the gap between the mouthpiece of the pipe to the lip of the bowl, and it had been a thirst-land, a weary stretch of sandy forest with never a sign of a river bed; yet here at the top of the long slope he stepped into a wealth of water. The enormous inundations of the Chobe alone were a part of the puzzle and no wonder, for in a region of strange rivers it is perhaps the strangest of all. Though quite respectable in size its watershed is only one-third of the area of that of the Okavango to the west, and one-fifth of the Zambezi to the east; yet it seemed to supply a lake and attendant swamps far beyond the warrant of its size. One peculiar phenomenon discovered many years after Livingstone had used it was that it sometimes flowed *backwards* from its junction with the Zambezi. This was because the Zambezi near that junction, with its earlier flooding, can be some feet higher than the Chobe and, by swamp channels, flow into it. At such times the lower Chobe is full, and either stagnant or flowing slightly backwards; yet it may be dry between its own swamps and its lower reaches.

The even stranger phenomenon of its lake and swamps rising long after its own flood had subsided was not explained until 1900 when Major Gibbons, who was, if possible, an even more stalwart walker than Livingstone, was making his way westward to the Okavango from Linyanti. To his profound surprise he was taken to a wide but dry river bed, called the Makwegana, coming from the west. Could it be the original bed of the Okavango itself? To solve the mystery he journeyed westward along it, and it was solved most dramatically for him after five days of long waterless marches. Half a mile in front of them they saw myriads of water

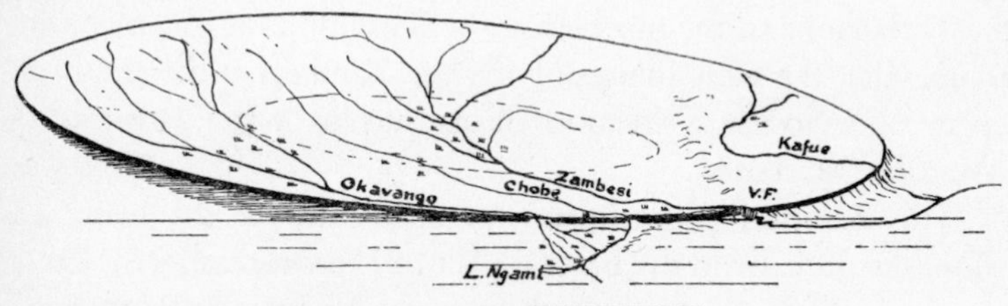

Upper Zambezi watershed in perspective to show structural similarity to a tilted plate

fowl circling in the air, and his Barotse companions 'grunted their disapproval and informed me that the water was coming'. Ten minutes later they were ankle deep in the annual overflow of the Okavango, which sends its surplus water along the Makwegama Spillway, as it is now called, to join the Chobe and thence the Zambezi, finally reaching the Indian Ocean on the far side of the continent. The overflow lasts for about two months, after which the bed dries up again.

It is indeed a strange regimen of rivers here, and one that has not even yet caught the public eye. Partly because it is difficult country to travel in, but even more because it is hopelessly partitioned by the ridiculous Caprivi Strip, that enormity of political geography, its possibilities have been recognised by only a few men as yet.

When politicians become more broad minded, and when engineers are let loose upon that curious intermingling of three great rivers, that area should become the granary of all the surrounding territories.

In order to understand this queer geography of the Upper Zambezi we may adopt a simile which was later used by Livingstone himself, and liken the region to a vast saucer or dinner plate.

As illustrated in the diagram on p. 73 we have this plate slightly tilted to the south and east. The Okavango and its large tributary, the Kwito, gather their water on the western rim of the plate, and flow in the direction of its tilt, lipping over the edge into the great Okavango Swamp, and Lake Ngami, but sending some of its surplus along to the Chobe.

The Chobe to the north-west, or Kwando as it is named, does somewhat the same thing, joining the Zambezi at the rim of the plate, but losing a fraction of its surplus water towards the Mababe Depression.

The Zambezi proper occupies the centre of the plate, and floods it annually in the Barotse plain. Where it reaches the rim of the plate it has worn its way to form the Victoria Falls, whence it zigzags its way down its gorge towards the East.

The Kafue rises in the north-east rim of the plate and swings round as though to join the Zambezi in the Barotse plain. It then makes its great hook bend to the east, forms a flood plain only second to that of the Barotse, and slips over the edge of the plate down the 2000 foot drop of the Kafue gorge.

The lowest part of the plate is 3000 feet above sea-level, while the far rim is from 5000 to 7000 feet high, and beyond it is the Congo system. On the hither side of the plate is the great sandy plain of the Kalahari, which receives water from the Okavango, but it never gets farther than the great salt pan of the Makarikari.

In coming back to the Makololo alone Livingstone was risking a great deal, since he had left them the year before soon after the death of Sebituane, and he did not know what might have happened to the succession. His immediate success with young Sekeletu is perhaps the best proof we have of the way in which he could form lasting friendships with chiefs, however tyrannical. He was not alone in that sort of personal magnetism, for his father-in-law Robert Moffat had done the same thing with

Mosilikatse, a much more violent character than Sebituane or Sekeletu.

What was it in these two men that could appeal to dictators with absolute power? Their utter fearlessness must have impressed these rulers, but mere admiration would not be enough. Their transparent honesty was another attribute which no doubt was so rare that it imbued an image of trust on their part.

It seems that we must seek other qualities than these to account for these strange friendships. Their forthright declaration of right and wrong, their immediate criticism of these rulers for cruelty and war-mindedness were something so new to such men that they may well have been taken aback, yet again it could hardly breed affection.

I believe myself that it was their trust in God. Every dictator is a lonely man, a watchful man, able to give his uttermost trust to no one. Yet here were two white men risking death and destruction, who obviously had a heavenly ally, an unseen friend who was with them in spirit always, and who therefore were the most trustworthy men the chiefs had ever met.

It is true to say that both these potentates opened their hearts to the two missionaries in a way they could not possibly do to their own people and had no fear in doing so. The feat was greater on the part of Moffat perhaps, for his rigid unbending attitude to what in his view was wrong had less of the element of Christian love in it, and the affection,—it was nothing less,—of the cruel Matabele leader for this stern man of God seems almost miraculous.

Livingstone was more resilient, more able to turn a blind eye to sins till the time came, more interested in the man himself as well as his soul. Neither of them had what we would call a sense of humour, but Livingstone had more of it than his father-in-law, and could use a quip or a joke or a laugh at the minor accidents of travel like falling off an ox. Whatever the reasons, there seems no doubt that the eighteen year-old Sekeletu came at once under the spell of the missionary, and a lucky accident confirmed it.

He was still uneasy on the throne with at least one pretender aiming at his assassination. Livingstone himself, present at the meeting of his chief rival, Mpepe, and Sekeletu, seems to have stepped between them at the precise moment when Mpepe had plotted to strike his enemy down with his axe. Livingstone's curt but graphic account of the affair of Mpepe, this would-be murderer, reads so like *Macbeth* that one can picture Sekeletu, when he says, 'That man wishes to kill me,' and ordering him to be speared away from the camp, echoing Macbeth with

'If it were done when 'tis done, then twere well it were done quickly.'

The incident took place when Sekeletu and Livingstone were going from Linyanti to the Zambezi to carry out the latter's plan to ascend that great river to look for a healthy locality for a mission station.

He remarks in a matter-of-fact way that 'the commotion which followed up Mpepe's death' made it 'unadvisable' to proceed with the plan for the moment. In fact Sekeletu had but scotched the snake, not killed it, and though he had no Lady Macbeth behind to spur him on, he found sufficient murderers, like her, to do his bidding in ridding him of Banquos, innocent or otherwise. In that Makololo empire, where an odd thousand or two of that breed were ruling some hundred thousand of the Barotse the leaders were most certainly

'cabined, cribbed, confined, bound in
to saucy doubts and fears'

and their methods of relieving those fears were those of medieval Europe.

If a closer analogy still be sought it lies in the blanket of superstition that overhangs all the Bantu tribes, even to this day. The witches' cauldron was no new thing to Central Africa, and if it could not summon ghosts of murdered Banquos it could, by throwing of the bones, impress policies on the leaders of the greatest moment. It was one such soothsayer, as related by Livingstone, who turned Sebituane back from his dreams of conquest down the Zambezi, where he would meet fire (the fire arms of the Portuguese) to seek a land of water and black men (the Barotse plain with its jet black inhabitants).

In the meantime Livingstone had to stay at Sekeletu's headquarters, Linyanti, for a month, during which he must have been acquiring still more influence over the youthful chief. When they began their postponed journey they travelled with a long caravan in the greatest amity, each with a small 'gipsy-tent' to sleep in, and a cavalcade of mounted men, Sekeletu on Livingstone's horse and the Makololo trying to ride on ox-back and causing

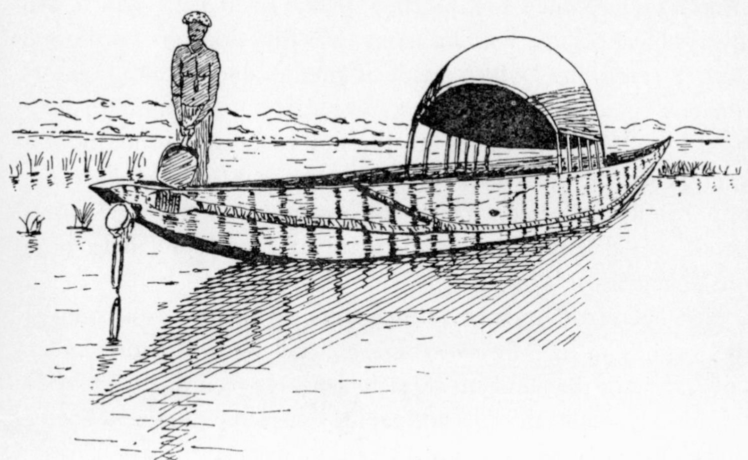

The 'Nalikwanda' or royal barge of 1895, 60 feet long, 9 feet broad

from a photograph

'much amusement' with their frequent falls. When they reached the Zambezi a few miles above Sesheke, they spent some time in collecting canoes for the more or less triumphant voyage up the river to the district which had been under Mpepe's sway till his death. Livingstone was given his choice of canoes and took one which was thirty-four feet long by twenty inches wide, with six paddlers. The one hundred and sixty men were in thirty-three canoes but many of them must have been far smaller than this, and the white man was greatly impressed with the watermanship of the Barotse men who managed them, or Makalaka as they were called by their conquerors. This skill with their canoes remains to this day, and was shown to the late King George VI on his visit to the town of Livingstone in 1947. The royal barge of the paramount chief was then manned in the original fashion, and was itself but a modern version of the one pictured on p. 77, of seventy years earlier, in the days of the famous paramount chief, Lewanika.

The Makololo themselves were not watermen, in fact few could swim, and on the very first day a canoe was filled by waves in a strong wind and a Makololo was drowned while the Barotse swam. Livingstone's first journey on the great river which will always be associated with his name, was thus done on a scale, and with a ceremony, which made it memorable to him. Unfortunately his detailed notes and journal about it appear to have been lost. When he left on his journey to Loanda some months later, he left the book with Sekeletu, to be sent to Dr Moffat if the opportunity occurred. 'This book,' writes Livingstone, 'with a letter, was delivered by Sekeletu to a trader, and I have been unable to trace it.'

However, from memory, Livingstone writes a lively account of the journey in his *Missionary Travels*, and we will comment on only a few of the incidents there related. He records the tsetse fly on the west bank, the falls and rapids where the canoes had to be carried or rolled past the obstacles till he reached the true Barotse plain above the most serious of them, the Gonye or Sioma falls of about twenty feet. His first view of this plain excited in him all the emotions of a geographer to whom discovery was but the prelude to development for the betterment of man. 'It bears a close resemblance to the valley of the Nile and is inundated annually, not by rains but by the Liambye exactly as Lower Egypt is flooded by the Nile.' 'The soil is extremely fertile, and the people are never in want of grain.' 'The Barotse are strongly attached to this fertile valley; they say, "Here hunger is not known".'

Nevertheless, he was cautious in his enthusiasm, citing the floods as unhealthy for humans and causing the cattle to be driven to the higher bush country where they fall off in condition. When they came to Mpepe's village, his father and another of the conspirators were thrown to the crocodiles in the river, and near the same place they came upon the stockade of the 'Mambari', the slave dealers from near the Atlantic coast, whom Mpepe had encouraged.

It was proposed to attack them at once, and, if Livingstone had not been there, they would have had such a lesson that they would have sought other parts for their future traffic. By the irony of fate it was the great Foe of slavery who saved their lives, and in a way which may almost have encouraged them to come again. 'As the chief sufferers in case of such an attack would have been the poor slaves chained in gangs, I interceded for them, and the result of an intercession of which they were ignorant was that they were allowed to depart in peace.'

The Mambari were accompanied or led by half-caste Portuguese who could all read and write, and they had come to Barotse land for the first time only a year or so earlier. The Scourge of the slavers had arrived just in time to teach them a wholesome lesson, but his humanity prevailed over wisdom.

The curious economy of the flood plain was taken in by the first white man to see it, perhaps even more quickly than by those gallant missionaries, Arnot, the Coillards and others who were to follow him, and by the able administrators from Coryndon onwards who were to follow the missionaries. To convey a picture of that economy I cannot do better than to quote from the reminiscences of one such administrator. Thirty years ago Mr R. S. Hudson was in charge of the Nalolo Boma, right in the middle of the plain and he wrote of it in the journal of the Northern Rhodesia Society in the 1953 issue:

'Nalolo Boma was built on a slight rise in the middle of the plain, by a canal which cut off a bend of the Zambezi. It was put there because that was the piece of land allocated for a Government station by the Murena Mokwae who lived at the Barotse capital across the river. She wanted her Native Commissioner near enough for convenient business and social intercourse, but she wisely liked to have the river between us.

'On the low rise on which the Boma was built there was just room for a house, an office, a gaol and African staff quarters. Only the heights of the rise could be built on because the hollows were flooded each year. One had to wade to the office for a week or so and the garden was always flooded.

'There were always solitary fishermen working their way along the reed beds in their narrow dug-out canoes. Up these lagoons came the barges for Mongu or Lealui from Katombora three weeks away, and one often heard the songs of the paddlers before catching the gleam of the tops of their long paddles above the reeds.

'The sunsets over the Barotse plain are very lovely and one used to watch quantities of ducks, geese and other wild fowl flighting as the sun disappeared. It was this peaceful beauty of the plain with its constantly changing moods and its life and movement which constituted the main charm of Nalolo.'

It more than compensated for the other features for which it was notorious, the snakes, the *serui* (soldier ants), the mosquitoes, and the floods:

'One encountered snakes continually, but nobody was bitten while I was there. I inherited a "snake boy" from my predecessor. He was of the "uncle" class and he used to wander about with a forked stick, and he was paid 1/- a snake. One snake which haunted the office at night he had failed to catch when I handed over. I entered him under the heading "livestock" in the handing-over form.

'The *serui* ants were harder to pin down and we had to be content with a night guard patrolling the Boma with a lamp when the flood was up.

'But the flood was fun and the great expanse of water was a grand sight until the vegetation covered it. On the rise of the flood the Murena Mokwae would migrate from her capital at Nalolo to her flood-time capital on the sand belt. She travelled in state heading a great procession of canoes, loaded to the limit with wives, children and household effects.'

The Paramount Chief would have migrated in his *Nalikwanda* from Lealui earlier. The Murena Mokwae of those days was Matauka, sister of Lewanika. 'She was of great size and great age, but had all her senses and wits very much about her. I believe she was aged about ninety then. She had great personality, and ruled her people with a rod of iron, but she was greatly respected, and had a grand sense of humour. She belonged to the old glories of

The Murena Mokwae of Barotseland

from a photograph taken about 1925

the Barotseland of Lewanika.' A very redoubtable old lady indeed who must have been the belle of her village when Livingstone was passing through, but, her tribe being in the position of the conquered, we do not hear of her then, nor of her distinguished brother Lewanika. In 1894, and again in 1899, Major Gibbons met her, and speaks of her in terms similar to those of Mr

Hudson: 'I found this capricious but hospitable old lady as kindly disposed as of yore, but very much stouter. She is the king's eldest sister, who, in accordance with the terms of the unwritten constitution, shares with her brother the prerogatives of the Marotse chieftainship. She claims the same honours as her brother and a precedence second only to his.'

Livingstone stopped with Sekeletu at Naliele, the then capital of the Barotse, which, like Nalolo and the later capital of Lealui, was built on a largely artificial mound, raised high enough above the floods to preserve the buildings but deserted at that season for a temporary capital some miles to the eastward on the low sand ridges, at Katongo, which Livingstone walked over to see. He is constrained, like Mr Hudson, to say that 'the scene from the ridge, looking back, was beautiful. We could not see the western side of the valley on that cloudy day but we could see the great river glancing out at various points'. But, beautiful or not, he recognised that these flats were no place for a mission station, especially one with children, and he went on up the great river for another hundred miles leaving Sekeletu at his capital.

Even at the junction of the two main source-rivers of the Zambezi, the Leeba and the Kabompo, it was clear to him that there was little prospect of a healthy station; his first aim was foiled. He realised that he had ample excuse to come home and say that the 'door was shut', but instead he resolved to follow out the second part of his plan, that is, to find a route to the coast along which legitimate trade could come to undercut the slave trading. The reconnaissance journey had in fact settled his future in favour of more exploration and less missionary work.

Back at Linyanti the plan had to be put not only to Sekeletu but to his counsellors as well and there was some opposition from a 'noted croaker'.

Rarely could a major expedition, for it was nothing less than that, have been planned in odder circumstances, the one man who knew what he was in for, being at the mercy, albeit the tender mercy, of a chief only recently secured in his seat of power. The easier route to the coast would have been westward by the way the Mambari used but 'there the slave trade had defiled the path' and he decides on the much longer, and quite unknown, north-west direction to Loanda. His desire for a certain amount of companionship declares itself for a moment, when, having heard that there were some English there, he said, 'the prospect of meeting with countrymen seemed to over-balance the toils of the longer march.'

There was little that he himself could do in preparation except to send back his retainers from Kuruman who remained true to their character. The incident was an important one though it is not in his book, only in his journal. After the actual start he writes: 'I now became aware of a theft inflicted on me by the people I brought from Kuruman. I was compelled to order them home with full wages. They would not go nor would they take their wages, they would remain, eating up my stores. When they did go the package containing my stock of ammunition and prepared medicines was stolen by one of them, Thebe. This has crippled me badly and I feel the loss of the medicines severely.'

Sekeletu allotted twenty-seven men to accompany him, of whom only two were true Makololo, and Livingstone reduced his impedimenta to the minimum so that they should not be discouraged by heavy loads. They only had five firearms for the whole party, not including his own pistol, and took very little food. His stock of books reveals his character—the Bible, a Nautical Almanac and Thomson's Logarithms. His navigation instruments were 'the best of their kind' a Troughton and Sims' sextant and a chronometer watch by Dent, with a seconds hand that could be stopped independently. There were also two compasses, a thermometer and a small telescope. Perhaps the most useful item of the instrument kind was a magic lantern with a set of slides on biblical incidents, for it did more to calm the savage breast than all the others. This had been given to him by his friend, Murray.

For camp comfort he took his small gipsy tent and a horse rug as a bed, scant comfort indeed for a thousand-mile journey. 'The outfit was rather spare, and intended to be still more so when we should come to leave the canoes,' but, as he added, he 'did not forget to carry his wits about him'.

The journey to Loanda and back occupies one-third of his *Missionary Travels* and, as before, we leave it to speak for itself, selecting only certain incidents, mainly from his original journal, kindly lent to the present author by his grandson Dr Hubert F. Wilson. This journal is a heavy leather-bound book of nearly one thousand pages with a brass clasp which could be locked. It was his custom to jot down notes of the day in very small note-books, and write up his journal from them whenever opportunity offered. The original note-books would have been more valuable still, but they appear to have been dispersed or lost, and were not available. These small note-books would certainly contain little sketch maps and observations with his instruments, from which he would compile his final manuscript maps. Of these we reproduce two in facsimile. One of them is the map he sent to his friend Mr Maclear at Cape Town, when he had reached Loanda, with a request that he should send a copy to Sir Roderick Murchison at the Royal Geographical Society. The other is probably of the same date as it shows the route on the early part of the same journey. For permission to use these I am indebted to Dr Livingstone's great grand-daughter, Miss Diana Livingstone-Bruce. They contain an immense amount of geographical information, and are monuments to his navigational ability and accuracy.

His habit was to find his latitude by observing suitable stars as they crossed the meridian. This involved using an artificial horizon of mercury in a special iron dish together with his sextant. Longitudes were more difficult, and less frequent. He used his pet method of 'lunar distances', which meant observing with his sextant the angular distance between the moon and a star, or occasionally, the sun, and noting the time by his chronometer watch. There must also have been frequent observations of the altitudes of stars in order to find out the behaviour of his watch.

Readers who are not versed in such matters must accept the statement that most of this work had to be skilled, both in the observations and the computations, and some of it exceptionally so, as he did not hesitate to observe occultations of stars by the

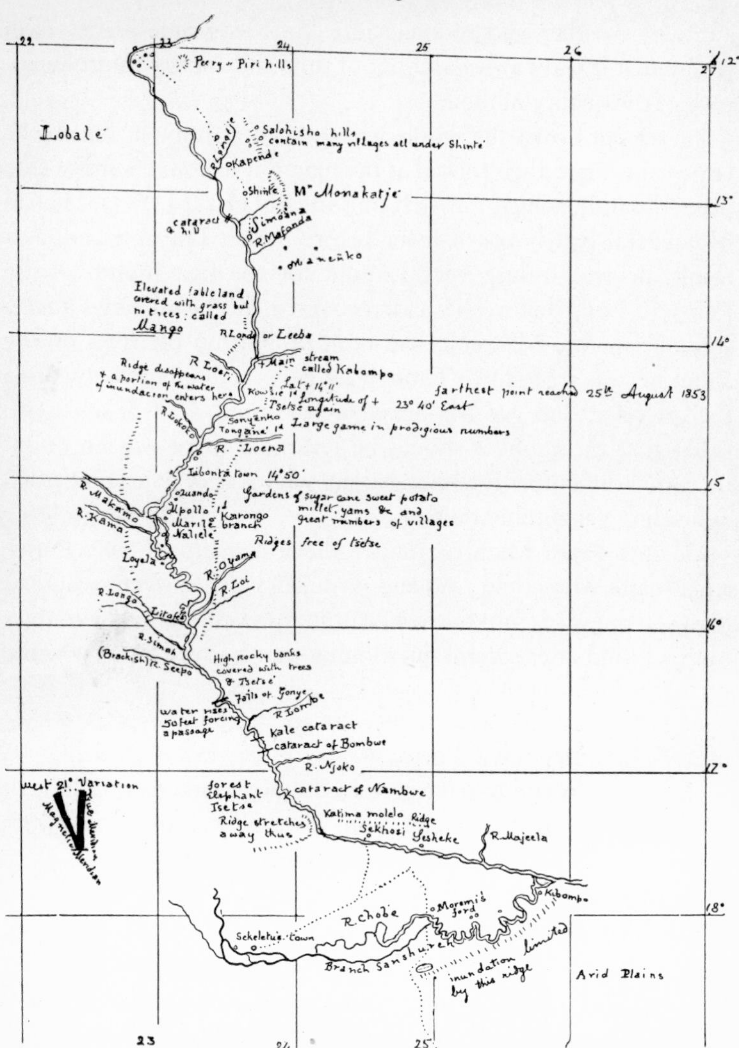

Reduced facsimile of Livingstone's map of Barotseland

moon and Jupiter's moons behind its disc, both of which would be done by using his telescope and his chronometer watch, with protracted computations to follow, and also to precede. They must also do their best to imagine the minor difficulties of night observations in the tropics, insects, lack of a suitable light, animals, weather and so on. More knowledgeable readers will realise that it takes a vast amount of time and energy to produce a map of the quality of these.

He set out down the whole length of the Chobe in the chief's large canoe, and then turned at the junction to reach Sesheke (the place of sand), which they left on November 23rd, 1853. He had had several bad bouts of fever before he left Linyanti and, as a result, he was feeling very languid for the first month of the journey. Long before he had recovered, he heard news that a sub-chief of the Makololo had been raiding up the river on the route he was to follow. Though he gave verbal chastisement to the offender, and got Ma-Sekeletu (the mother of Sekeletu) to order that the captives should be returned, there was no doubt it created difficulties for Livingstone, who was of course regarded as heading yet another raiding party.

He met more Mambari under the leadership of one, Porto, a half-caste who could read and write, and also an Arab who had come all the way from the east coast in his search for ivory to buy, but he found after careful questioning that he was the first white man they had ever seen.

Nevertheless these two men were to affect Livingstone's later life not a little. Silva Porto was a trader, who according to Livingstone, 'is said to have preferred ivory to slaves. It is difficult to ascertain his real character from his acts here and it is always necessary to be slow in forming a judgement'.

Yet his Mambari followers carried off between three and four hundred slaves, and he became a slave trader on a very large scale in days to come.

Livingstone got on good terms with the Arab, as usual, and, having got him to write his name in Arabic in the Journal, Rya Syde ben Habib ben Salem, he says 'Met this Arab from Zingebar. He has been across the continent to Loanda'. We shall meet him again in this book as he was of some assistance to Livingstone nearly twenty years later, but more often a hindrance. The modern spelling of his name would be 'Said'.

The part of the journey by canoe was restful for him and in spite of his languor, his notes are full of descriptions, especially of birds. He was not a specialist on birds, but an enlightened observer nevertheless and his journal is full of entries such as 'an ibis had perched her home on the end of a stump. Her loud, harsh scream of "Wa-wa-wa" and the piping of the fish hawk are sounds which can never be forgotten.' He was more interested in their songs and their general behaviour than in their generic names, and the following description is typical of his attitude: 'The fish hawk sometimes plunders the purse of the pelican. Soaring overhead and seeing this large stupid bird fishing beneath, it watches till a fine fish is safe in the pelican's pouch; then descending, not very quickly, but with considerable noise of wing, the pelican looks up to see what is the matter, and, as the hawk comes near, he supposes that he is about to be killed, and roars out "Murder!" The opening of his mouth enables the hawk to whisk the fish out of the pouch, upon which the pelican does not fly away, but commences fishing again.'

The charm of travelling on Central African rivers like this is one that has not yet been fully advertised, but the day will come no doubt when peaceful river journeys will become as fashionable as are big-game safaris now, and the idea is to be commended to the tourist agencies. All that is needed is a launch big enough to be made proof against mosquitoes, and against hippos, when even elderly people would be able to revel in the same scenes as did Dr Livingstone. When the engineers have had their say, and made their locks round the rapids, when the river has been made to 'roll obedient through the land', a trip to Barotseland by water will be the natural sequence to visiting the Victoria Falls.

Livingstone's progress had to be slow, as he had a land party marching along the banks with the oxen, and their passage was an arduous one, with so many tributaries to cross. Meat supply was difficult, not for any lack of animals to shoot, but because his men were new to guns, and shot so badly that he had to do all the shooting himself. 'Having but little of the hunting furore in my composition, I always preferred eating the game to killing it.' He is modest about his own shooting, which, if poor, was due to his injured arm with its false joint; he had to shoot from the left shoulder and in his own words, 'I wanted steadiness of aim and it generally happened that the more hungry the party became, the more frequently I missed the animals.'

The party took seven weeks to reach the head of navigation, which was on the Leeba about seventy miles beyond its junction with the Kabompo, which is a major stream but came from the wrong direction for him. He had come into the district of the chief paramount of the Balonda tribe here, Shinte, and he had at first some difficulty with him and even more with a niece of his, Manenko, a chieftainess in her own right, who would not abate one jot of her rights. She was 'a tall strapping woman about twenty in a state of frightful nudity' and obviously a person of great strength both of mind and of body.

The trial of will powers between Manenko and Livingstone makes excellent reading, especially when, after saying that he was not going to give in to 'her sable highness' he has to admit that he 'was not inclined to encounter her tongue any longer. As the next best shift I went off to try and shoot a zebra'. In the book, as contrasted with the original journal, this incident concludes with 'with her hand on my shoulder she put on a motherly look, saying, "Now, my little man, just do as the rest have done".'

She marched with them for several days in her own style. 'Rain came on soon after we left, but this amazon went on in her ball dress at such a rate that few of the men could keep up with her. "The woman is a soldier," said our people in reference to her pedestrian powers.' He was able to keep up with her as he was on his ox, Sinbad, of whom he spoke in the same tone of rueful raillery as he used towards Manenko, for Sinbad too had a will of his own. 'He had a softer back than the others but a much more intractable temper.' He showed his independence by choosing his own path, and Livingstone was often scraped off his back by a branch, 'and he never allowed an opportunity of this kind to pass without trying to inflict a kick, as if I neither had nor deserved his love.'

Sinbad carried him all the way to a settlement near the coast, and all the way back again, so that he earned the respect of his rider, and what must have been something approaching the affection of the men. When they were nearly back again Sinbad was bitten by tsetse, and his death was only a matter of a week or two in consequence: 'Poor Sinbad had carried me all the way and back again (which would be a matter of some 1500 miles), without losing any of his peculiarities or ever becoming reconciled to our perversity in forcing him away every morning from his pasturage. I wished to give the climax to his usefulness, and allay our craving for animal food at the same time, but, my men having some compunction, we carried him to end his days in peace at Naliele.'

There is an interesting entry in the journal while he is at the village of the old Chief Shinte, who was very friendly. The Chief had tried to make a gift of a little girl to Livingstone, and when the gift was declined, sent an older one instead. Livingstone then tried to explain that if it had been possible he would have taken rather the younger one 'for it was for service when Mrs Livingstone came, when she could be properly instructed'. That reads as though he had not wholly given up the idea of a mission station in the higher land he was now crossing.

It is even arguable that, if he had been crossing this watershed, five thousand feet in altitude, in the winter instead of in the wet season, he would have been sufficiently impressed with its climate to send for his family and found a station with Shinte. As it was, the frequent showers and bouts of fever gave him a quite contrary impression.

In spite of his constant fever, in spite of the hostile reception the party so often had, the geographer in him was uppermost all the time. The pattern of drainage of the country interested him most as usual, and he felt very conscience-stricken when his illness prevented his astronomical work. When he reached Lake Dilolo, which marks the divide between the Congo and Zambezi basins, he was too ill to examine this new discovery and writes, 'if it is thought strange I should pass so near the broad end without looking at it, or taking observations to determine more accurately its geographical position, it must be remembered that I had eaten nothing for two whole days and, instead of sleep, employed the night in incessant drinking of water.' He satisfied his conscience on his return journey and mapped Lake Dilolo properly.

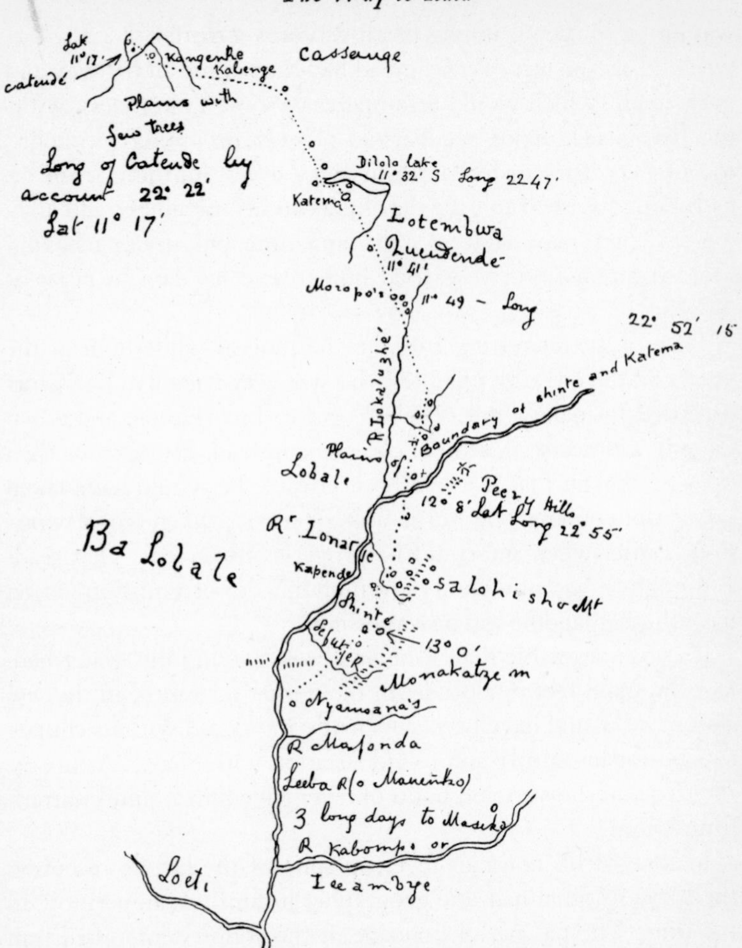

Tracing from Livingstone's journal of map made during his journey to Loanda

It is worthy of note, as showing how very remote his route was, that the next Englishman to be near the lake was the missionary, F. S. Arnot, in 1885, thirty-one years later. Though also a great traveller, Arnot had not the same interests as Livingstone and says, 'I passed Lake Dilolo far to the right, only seeing the water glistening between the hills. I would have gone by the lake but because of my ox I was compelled to avoid it, the way being marshy in places.'

The same chief, Katema, who had been friendly to Livingstone, met Arnot, and 'was sorry to hear of his death'. It is a sad commentary on the neglect of Livingstone's pioneer route that, in Arnot's words, 'Katema sent me a present of a woman slave with infant in arms—a pitiful sight' and he had some difficulty in refusing the gift. Lake Dilolo is now quite well known, as the Benguela-Katanga railway passes close to it.

As the party began to descend into the basin of the Kasai the way grew harder, because they were now entering the true African jungle, which is, in fact, rarely found outside the basin of the Congo, and which was entirely new to Livingstone, the very antithesis to the Kalahari. He delighted in the tree growth, but, on the whole, he found it a depressing atmosphere, and certainly an unhealthy one. The nearer he got to the Portuguese sphere of influence the more difficulty he had with the local chiefs. The Mambari traders had quite spoiled the route by giving in to their demands for passage-toll, the 'hongo' as it was called in East Africa. Livingstone had always strongly opposed the principle of buying the right to pass through a district, but now he was unable to pay even if persuaded of its necessity, as he had little left but his own shirts, a few beads and an ox or two. His men had become faint-hearted, and ready to give in to outrageous demands. At one stage he had to threaten with his revolver in order to maintain discipline, and at another he told them plainly he would go on alone if they deserted him, a threat which elicited more support than he had expected.

We quote one critical incident from his journal, to show the spirit in which he met the opposition of the chiefs, and how barefaced that opposition was. They were in the country of the Chiboque people at the time, on the Upper Kasai:

'The chief collected all his people and they came armed to our encampment, their object was to plunder us. All (my men) seized their arms and stood on the defensive, while the young Bachiboque brandished their short swords with great fury.

'I called on the chief and my people to sit down. Some obeyed but others stood flourishing their weapons and pointing their guns at us.

'When I got the chief to follow my example and sit down I asked what guilt we had that he came armed in that way. He replied that one of my Makololo, Pitsane, had given one of his people a piece of meat and that while they were sitting by the fire Pitsane spat on the ground and one small spark had lighted on his servant.

'This guilt we must wipe out by paying a fine of a man, ox or gun or other valuable article.

'To the demand for one of our number we were all determined never to submit, and as Pitsane admitted to the fact of spitting I said "I would pay a small fine for it. . . . I produced a white shirt and the chief seemed satisfied with it, but his counsellors objected. . . . One young man made a charge at me from behind, stopping his sword just over my head. I pointed this out to the chief and he ordered him back. . . . I gave a bunch of beads and added a large handkerchief. Then an ox was demanded and as Pitsane besought me to accede to it I allowed one to go.'

They changed their route after that, but the same kind of thing happened several times. In fact, this part of his journey reads so like Bunyan's *Pilgrim's Progress*, that it can hardly be better described. There was many a hill Difficulty and a Slough of Despond, while at least once he walked in the Valley of the Shadow of Death.

Their last difficulty was at the crossing of the Kwango where they came within range of the Portuguese. Here the local chief fired on his party when they refused to pay the exorbitant tribute he demanded, and things might have gone very badly but for the help of a young half-caste Portuguese sergeant. Once across, all their difficulties with tribes were at an end, but now Livingstone's health degenerated rapidly, and in spite of the lavish generosity of successive commandants in clothing and feeding him, he literally staggered into Loanda on the last day of May.

There are no entries in his journal for a week before and a

fortnight after his arrival, and his life must have been saved by the kindness of Mr Edmund Gabriel, the only Englishman in the city. The accumulation of fevers and attacks of dysentery of the last three months of his journey completely prostrated him. He writes a good deal in his journal about the symptoms of his illness, the doctor in him anxious to discover ways of combating this particular scourge of Africa. He is for ever noting down the medicinal properties of the plants used by the people as febrifuges, and he often makes a guinea pig of himself to test their value. It was to be forty years later that the discovery was made that malarial fever was carried by the anopheles mosquito, but Livingstone noted no more than that mosquitoes and fever were apt to occur together, and that 'paludal miasma,' his whimsical name for marsh gases, had something to do with it.

At this time he was almost too prostrated to continue these medical notes, but as he recovered he was able 'to meditate on the weakening effects of the fever': 'The complaint itself occupied many of my thoughts. One day I supposed I had got the true theory of it, and would certainly cure the next attack of it, but some new symptoms would appear and scatter all the fine speculation.' There is a curious footnote in his journal for May 20th. 'Dream of death of Charles [his younger brother]. Never dream except when health is deranged. See if this comes true.'

As they neared the sea the excitement, and fears, of his companions—it should be noted that he always wrote of them as companions—grew in spite of the assurances of their leader. There is that dramatic passage in his book when they first see the ocean: 'My companions looked upon the boundless ocean with awe. On describing their feelings afterwards they remarked, 'we marched along with our father, believing that what the ancients had always told us was true, that the world has no end; but all at once the world said to us 'I am finished; there is no more of me'." The anticlimax to that remark came when someone said, "Then you reached Ma-Robert." They were obliged to confess that she lived a little beyond the world.'

As soon as he had recovered, his stay at Loanda was crammed with observations on the country, its resources, the people, their rulers and, particularly, what was needed to develop it. The Portuguese, almost without exception, were kind and hospitable to him. Indeed their excessive generosity rather overcame his caution and in his journal he gives, in two cases, a glowing account of the wisdom and honesty of hosts which, after longer acquaintance, he has to retract. These are hardly mentioned in *Missionary Travels* but in the journal both eulogy and later disappointment appear in characteristic style: 'Senor Arsenio Carpo, Commandant of Ambaca, possesses very enlightened views on the subject of the Slave Trade. He mentions many men of high rank in Portugal who hold as he does and the knowledge of this fact makes me less desponding.' The wily Arsenio is further praised for his plans 'for schools, good roads, good magistrates and prompt administration of justice'.

Some time later Livingstone looked again at this page and inserted the note, 'Arsenio's views and practice neutralize each other' and he puts a ? at the end of every line on the page. A few pages further on there is a footnote written six months later: 'Mr Arsenio was a convict for manslaughter of his father and is one of those who never loses an opportunity of making a friend and ruining him if he thereby can promote his own interests.'

Livingstone was so transparently honest and truthful himself, that he was not a sound judge of character, being easily taken in by smooth words and by those 'that keep the word of promise to our ear, and break it to our hope'. It was in Loanda that he first met Captain Bedingfield, in command of the sloop *Pluto*. He admired his good qualities so much, that he was blind to certain deficiencies in his temperament which, a few years later, were responsible for the partial failure of Livingstone's second expedition to Africa.

His Portuguese hosts, and, still more, the kindly naval officers, all seem to have expected him to take the offer of the latter and go to England. He admits that the offers were tempting but gave it very little consideration, for two reasons. Firstly, he knew that his 'companions' could never return alone to Sekeletu, and secondly, since he had failed to find a waggon route to the Atlantic coast he must go back and try 'to make a path to the East coast by means of the great river Zambezi'. In plain words, while people in England were thinking he had made an almost miraculous journey across half of Africa, he himself was realising that, judged by the ends he had in view, his journey had been a failure.

We have not very much in his writings about the matter, because many of the letters and maps he sent to England from Loanda were lost in the wreck of the ship on the island of Madeira. In a letter to his brother Charles, written after he had started back he says with his usual brevity, 'I return, because I feel that the work to which I set myself is only half accomplished'.

The party left Loanda on the return journey on September 20th, and, if prudence had been their only guide, they would have pressed on and done their travelling before the rainy season. But there were sick animals to look after, including the horse taken as a present to Sekeletu; sick men including one of his kind hosts, and the distinguished botanist, Dr Welweitsch; and several side journeys to be made for the interest of the geography of the country. He also wished to await mails from England.

With all these lets and hindrances they were detained for months: they did not leave the occupied and moderately civilised part of Angola until February, and arrived back at Sekeletu's in a little less than a year after leaving Loanda. Once again, therefore, Livingstone was doing the most difficult part of the journey in the rainy season, the most unhealthy and dangerous time of the year. He did the same thing so often in later years that it demands some explanation, and I think the only possible one is that he refused to admit that the rainy season was dangerous. Mere discomfort never worried him, and it seems that the only attention he paid to the rains was to inquire first whether floods were liable to stop him altogether.

It does not seem to be generally known that there was a plan that Dr Welweitsch should return to Barotseland as companion for Livingstone, and Livingstone's account of it is illuminating: 'Some of the personal friends of Dr Walweitch proposed that he should accompany me bearing a message and presents from the Government of Angola to Sekeletu. . . .' Livingstone goes on to give several reasons for his opposition to the plan, ending with the best one of all, 'pretty plain evidence of an irritable temperament in my companion would render the association unpleasant. The Bishop spoke of the plan but I communicated my views freely on the subject.'

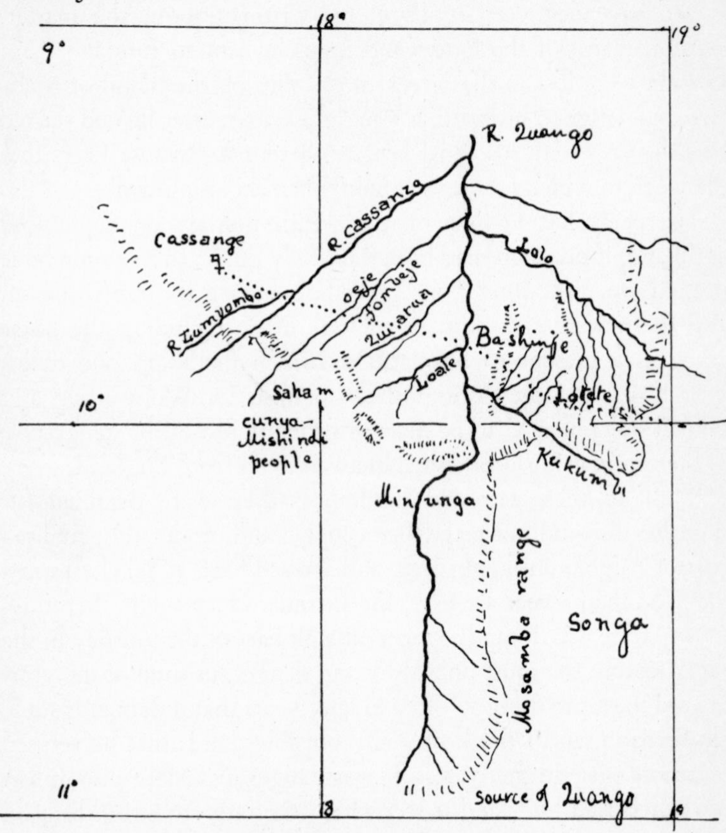

Tracing of map in Livingstone's large journal, made on his return journey from Loanda

Livingstone may also have been influenced by the fact that the learned botanist had recently been one of a commission of three to report on some affairs inland. 'The other commissioners told Dr Walweitch he had plenty of natural objects to report on, and need not say anything about slaves.'

As an example of Livingstone's practical interest in every branch of science we may note his experiments with what one hundred years later we, near Lake Bangweulu, called the rain tree. My wife, walking with a friend, discovered a tree under which there was almost a puddle, in the dry season, caused by tiny showers falling from the leaves whenever they were rustled by a breeze. I have never yet discovered any phenomenon in Africa which had not already been noted by Livingstone, and, on looking up his book, found that he had actually measured the fall of 'rain'. He was quite sure that it was not the sap of the branches passing through the bodies of the insects responsible for the fluid and he subjects them to amusing experiments by which, in spite of being robbed of the sap supposed to be the source, the little colony of insects goes merrily on with their 'distillation', yielding as much as two drops a second, or over four pints in twenty-four hours.

As soon as the party passed out of the region where the Portuguese kept small garrisons, the trouble with petty chiefs began again. There was one threatened attack in which Livingstone had to point his revolver at the chief after his men had fired at the party in a forest, but no blood was shed. He travelled for a few days with two Portuguese, who were taking slaves inland for the paramount chief Matiamvo, and he even considered whether to go there himself. It is curious to note that, if he had done so, he would have found the answer to the query which filled his horizon for the last five years of his life—whether the rivers of that region belonged to the Nile system or that of the Congo.

When he reached the divide, near Lake Dilolo, in June, he recorded his twenty-seventh attack of fever, yet he made several acute observations concerning the drainage in that district, some of the water reaching the Atlantic via the Kasai and some going to the Indian ocean by the Zambezi. A day or so later they reached the point where they had left his pontoon and found it in good order except for a hole made by mice. It was in this district, the headwaters of the Leeba River, that he thought 'a commercial and missionary station would in all probability rise to great importance as an emporium for the civilisation and evangelisation of this continent'. But he added that there is much risk of fever there.

Back in the country of the chief Shinte he began to feel he was amongst friends once more, and here he planted some young orange trees, a fig tree, besides seeds of other fruits which he had brought all the way for the purpose. They had also been carrying no less than eighty fowls of the large breed from the coast, which he was anxious to introduce to the Makololo. In the journal he discusses the value of taking the inland African to the coast to make contact with civilisation there, and bring back at least some elements of it. His argument was that 'my men learned more in one day when introduced aboard the *Pluto* and *Philomel* than I could have taught during years'.

He took more star observations on his return journey to fill up former gaps due to bad weather. His eyesight must have been extremely good, and he said on this point 'all my men can, with ease, discern the small star *Alcor* situated near *Misar* in the Bear's tail which, of old, was employed as a test of good sight. I can readily distinguish it'.

Everywhere the party was welcomed with great joy, as they had been given up for lost, and when they reached Naliele on August 2nd, they heard all the news of the region, which was chiefly concerned with murders, abductions and another visit from Silva Porto's Mambari who had carried off a large number of children. Syde ben Habib, their guide, had been well received on another visit, but Livingstone's comment was 'a more heartless expedition I have not known in Africa'. The flood that year had been excessive, the mound villages like Naliele being all but submerged.

It was at this time that he began to work out his 'trough' theory for Africa in his journal: 'The watershed (of the Leeba) forms part of the run of the continent. The interior is evidently lower than it and if I find the same everted edge on the Eastern Coast then the form may be described as a sort of trough, the rims being a little though not much higher than the hollow along the middle. This is different from the prevailing opinion and from my own when going North.' It may be that it was because of his mind running on the structure of the country at this time, that we here come across nearly thirty pages in his journal of which he makes the entry: '2/Aug.55. Yesterday and today I have written 20 pages of geology from memory.' This memorandum would be a *tour de force* on a professional geologist's part, it is quite amazing in a man who was not trained in that subject, and was very busy in other lines of activity. It is nothing less than a study of the rocks, the land forms and the water resources all the way from the Orange River to the Zambezi. The names he used for the rock varieties are a little confusing, but the only obvious mistake he made was in ascribing the holes in the calcrete or tufa of the Kalahari to the work of 'madrepores' by which we understand him to mean coral-building animals.

He adds to this geological part of the journal on November 27th and later dates, when he had seen the Victoria Falls and the country he passed over beyond that part of the river, expanding the essay to thirty pages. His attitude to waterfalls, however beautiful, comes out strongly at this point: 'I am sorry to hear that a frightful waterfall exists in the Kabompo . . . and that the Bashukulompo river (the Kafue) too is spoiled by cataracts.

'The waterfalls of Mosioatunya (Victoria Falls), Kabompo and others explain why commercial enterprise never entered the interior of the continent except by foot travellers. I am sorry for it, my dreams of establishing a commerce by means of the rivers vanish as I become better acquainted with them.' Livingstone wrote this when he was being received with acclamations of the most extravagant kind from the Barotse and Makololo, his party being almost showered with gifts of oxen, ivory, meal and milk. Truly he was a man who never for a moment lost sight of his real objective.

David Livingstone on Sinbad

CHAPTER FOUR

It happens to us, as it happeneth to Wayfaring Men: sometimes our way is clear, sometimes foul; the Wind is not always at our Backs, nor is every one a Friend that we meet with on the Way.

JOHN BUNYAN

If we need a reminder of how utterly penniless and completely alone Livingstone was when he got back to Linyanti, Sekeletu's capital, we can find it in the story of the parcels of mail and other things that his father-in-law had forwarded to him from Matabele-land. That stern and fearless minister had paid a visit to Mosilikatse a year earlier, and had prevailed upon his savage friend to send a party of warriors with these parcels up to the Makololo, their bitter enemies.

Their only means of contact was by shouting to each other across a channel of the Zambezi near the Victoria Falls, and the Makololo suspected that they were being asked to receive something in the nature of a Trojan horse, as Livingstone says in his journal. After the Matabele had shrugged their shoulders and retired, as if to say, 'Well here are the goods, if you let them perish the guilt will be yours,' the timid northerners came across and carried the parcels to an island in midstream, where a hut was built over them, and there they remained for a whole year untended.

The eatables sent by Mrs Moffat were for the most part spoiled but the letters and newspapers were all intact, though nearly eighteen months out of date. In Livingstone's book there is little mention of the contents of this delayed package, but in the journal he writes: 'A whirl of thoughts rushed through my mind as I opened my letters but, thank God, I had no cause for sorrow.' Mr Maclear says, 'I have no hesitation in asserting that no traveller on record has determined his path with the precision you have accomplished,' a typical remark of an astronomer who was also a great friend. He wrote it after he had received Livingstone's map and observations sent to him from Loanda. The mail also contained the first letters that Livingstone had received from his family for three years.

Even in the centre of Africa then, a white man had to have goods, mainly cloth, with which to pay his way, and he had expended all he had on the way back from Loanda. The presents of tusks and oxen that had been showered upon him on his return by the Barotse and Makololo might have put him in credit, but it never occurred to him to regard them as his own, and he gave them all away to his men. A very typical entry on this subject occurs the day after he reached Sesheke, where he was to await horses from Linyanti: 'Yesterday we came to a herd of elephants on an island, and having landed at 60 yards distance I shot one on the ear. The others fled but he came to a stand at a short distance, and shewed by a horizontal movement of his proboscis that he was writhing with pain. Another shot which happened to pierce the proboscis near the root made him advance again with a gruff snorting.'

That is the point at which the hunting stories of most African travellers begin to be dramatic, the charge of a wounded elephant. Not so Livingstone, for his account goes on: 'This is the first elephant I have killed. I mean the tusks for my companions should they return to Loanda.' And that is all about the matter, the next sentence being:

'A strong east wind prevails at this season of the year in these parts and will continue till the rains begin.'

For means of going anywhere, Livingstone was therefore

completely in the hands of Sekeletu, a paramount chief, whom he had just rated severely for organising raids during his absence. However, such was the ascendancy he already had gained over this young and bloodthirsty chief, that, as soon as the cost of the journey down the Zambezi was discussed by them, Sekeletu made that famous remark: 'The ivory I have is all your own; if you leave any in the country it will be your own fault.' This might have come out of the *Arabian Nights*, except that it would have ended 'and the hand of my beautiful daughter in marriage'.

Livingstone's standing with the tribe as a whole is illustrated in this context in a curious incident. The Arab, Syde ben Habib, who was to lead another party to Loanda, had asked for the twelve-year-old daughter of Sebituane in marriage, so as to establish a close bond with the tribe. Livingstone was able to veto the plan because, as he wrote, 'I have a vote in the matter as, having been Sebituane's bosom friend she is called 'my daughter",' but he had to conclude with, 'Ben Habib will probably get her after my departure.'

With such general prestige, and the despot himself in support, arrangements for Livingstone's journey were quickly made, but he was not allowed to start until the rains had come to cool the atmosphere and ground. Consequently, he stayed at Linyanti, living in his old waggon which had been cared for by the people. To this enforced stay, it could hardly be called a rest, we are indebted for entries in the journal and letters to England, to go by 'my Arabian post-office man' from Loanda, and these present his reflections on his great journey and on the Barotse plain he now knew fairly well.

In particular a letter to Dr Tidman, the Secretary of the London Missionary Society in London, is a fine example of a geographical survey of the region. It includes his theory of the trough-like shape of Southern Africa, penned in terms of humility, ending: 'I advance the view to you with the less diffidence inasmuch as I have just ascertained by the perusal of a speech of Sir R. Murchison before the Royal Geographical Society, that he promulgated the idea as long ago as 1852. I cannot imagine how he received that information, but from his eminent scientific attainments it is certain to be a reliable source. And as I reached the conclusion from independent but very jog-trot observation, the view of that gentleman is surely correct.' A truly Victorian style of letter that might have been penned in a comfortable London club, instead of in a decrepit old waggon surrounded by some seven thousand black men in the middle of Africa.

Livingstone goes on to sum up the prospects of the region as a field for missionary effort, and though he admits the prevalence of fever, he explains his own twenty-seven attacks from it as largely due to the circumstances under which he travelled, including the whimsical item—'drenching showers often made me deposit the watch in my armpit—my poor ox Sinbad would never allow "the old man of the sea" to hold an umbrella.'

The most interesting section of the letter, perhaps, is his description of the trouble he had with the inland tribes in Angola, from their holding him up for tribute or toll to pass through their districts: 'In estimating their action it will be but fair to conceive ourselves as placed in their circumstances. They had been encouraged by the half caste traders to make these impositions.' Referring to the occasion when one of the chief's men had counted the guns in Livingstone's party, and had gone back to his chief shouting, 'they have only got five', he goes on: 'The tribes have by this process imbibed the notion that they have as undoubted a right to these tithes as our good bishops have to theirs. Could it therefore be otherwise than utterly disgusting to get the impudent answer from 28 chartists who had only five guns, "We won't pay for treading on the earth of God our common father." They were indignant to behold an unblushing attempt to defraud the revenue, and uttered shouts of most patriotic disgust.'

He concludes the letter with a prophecy on the result of his opening up a route for legitimate trade, which unfortunately did not come true: 'If the movement now begun is not checked by some untoward event the slave trade will certainly come to a natural termination in this quarter.' The untoward events which interfered with this dream were that the missionaries of southern

Bechuanaland were withdrawn rather than pushed forward, the traders who came instead from the south could not face the competition of the Mambari, and, except for the abortive attempt to found a mission station at Linyanti a year later, there was to be no other missionary in Barotseland until Mr F. S. Arnot tried to establish himself there nearly thirty years later.

Livingstone was so attracted by the country at the headwaters of the Leeba, the Lake Dilolo district, that he paid less attention to the Barotse plain, though he realised its fertility and the fortunate circumstances of its inhabitants. His visits being at a time when the Barotse people proper were under temporary subjection to the Makololo, he did not pick them out as the well-defined people they were before and since, and it was his successor forty years later, François Coillard, who finally guided them to the unique position in which they now stand, as a Protectorate within a Protectorate. Nevertheless he fully recognised the potentiality of their flood plain, one which perhaps has not yet been fully realised.

The flood plain in Barotseland is closely comparable to that of the Kafue to the eastward, usually known as the Kafue Flats, and both are destined some day to be the chief food regions of Northern Rhodesia. Both are grain regions and both are cattle districts, that combination which gives reasonable assurance of fertility being maintained by careful management. The Barotse people have gone farther in such management than the Ila people at the Kafue, largely because of the mound cultivation which so impressed Livingstone. The 'mounds' are low islands, partly artificial, only just above flood level, which are occupied for most of the year, but from which the people, led by their paramount chief, migrate to the sand country at the margin of the flood from March to June. The gardens on the mounds are very carefully manured by staking the cattle on them at certain times. The whole economy of life in these two areas is dependent upon the annual flooding, and more particularly on the fact that the peak of the flooding comes two or three months after the peak of the rains.

The geographer in Livingstone quickly noted this fortunate sequence, and prophesied great things for the Barotse valley in the future. Eighty years later Dr Max Gluckman,* formerly director of the Rhodes-Livingstone Institute, studied the economy of the flood plain in detail, and if we transform one of his graphs into a sort of picture-graph as below we can see why it is not only a land of plenty, but one of a balanced diet, which is all too rare in Africa. It shows how the supplies of protein foods are short only when the carbohydrate foods—grain and cassava—are plentiful, and how both are related to the curves of rain and flood. Thus

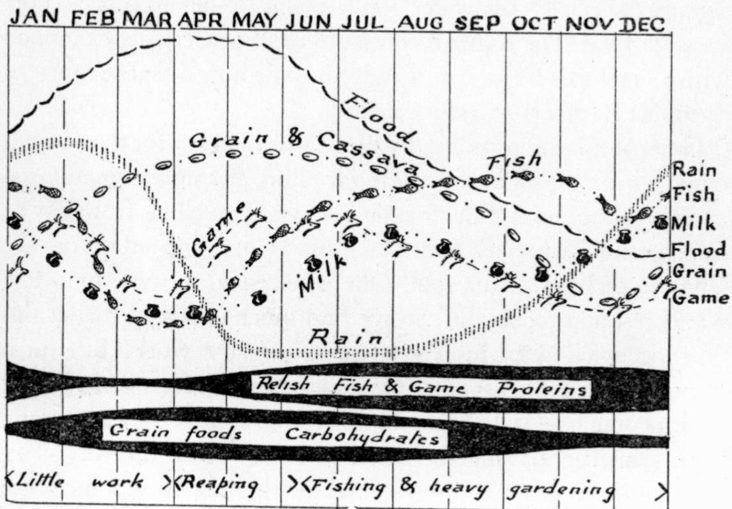

fish can be caught best when the flood has subsided, and least at full flood. The people can supplement the fish by meat in the flood months by killing cattle which have to be moved off the flooded plain to the sandy margins at that season. As the waters retreat, the fish are more concentrated, and fishing goes on apace once more.

Milk, on the other hand, depends on the growth of young grass, so we have two peaks of plenty, one when the floods are receding in the winter months of June to August, and a second one at the end of the year, when the new rains have produced a flush of grass. The curve for game is somewhat similar to that for

* *The Economy of the Central Barotse Plain*, by Max Gluckman, No. 7 Rhodes-Livingstone paper, 1941.

milk, but the peaks in it come when the game is easily killed on islands as the flood is rising and falling; game is widely dispersed by migration when the rains begin. With certain modifications the same picture-graph would apply to the Kafue Flats, though the Ila people put their faith rather more on cattle than on crops.

Livingstone saw plainly enough that, if the floods could be controlled in some way, the production of surplus food would follow, and, if it were associated with improvement in communications, especially by water, both plains could become export areas for food. The Kafue River is already being closely examined with a view to development, and it is to be hoped that the turn of the upper Zambezi will come next.

Livingstone was profiting by his wait at Linyanti for the cooling rains to begin, both in the rest it gave him, and in information on a variety of topics. Of the former he says: 'Travelling from day to day among barbarians exerts a most benumbing effect on the religious feelings of the soul. One is refreshed in spirit by a few weeks rest and reflection.' So we find much of his journal at this time occupied with his views on missionary work. But he is trying also to piece together the geographical information he got from people like Syde ben Habib, who had come to Barotseland from Zanzibar, passing the town of Cazembe on the way. This information is of great interest, because that region was the scene of his last long journey nearly twenty years later, when he again met Syde ben Habib. Thus he was told of Lake 'Tanganyenka', but it was rather misleading information as it was said to be very shallow, whereas it is the deepest lake in Africa.

It was, in fact, rather difficult for him to make sense of these vague descriptions, yet, in reading his version of the raid to the North East by Sekeletu's men, just before he returned, we come upon some interesting news, which I believe has not been noted before. In coming from Cazembe, the Arab had to cross the Kafue, and, in that region, had reached a tribe from whom he got a great deal of ivory, and he noticed that they were very much afraid of the noise of his guns. When he reached Sekeletu he, with true Arab treachery, told the latter he could easily guide a party to this tribe and capture great numbers of cattle. This was the raid for which Livingstone took Sekeletu to task so severely. Livingstone found by questioning 'intelligent persons who went on the late expedition' that this tribe lived in a country much intersected by rivers running into the Bashukulompo river, which is the one for which we have a handier name now, the Kafue. He goes on, in his journal: 'There is a lake there—several rivers flow from it

Map of the Lukanga Swamp area drawn by Dr Livingstone on information from Ben Habib At Linyante about October 10, 1855

into the Bashukulompo and a large river named Lokanga flows into it from the East. This seems to be the river of the Babisa, perhaps Loapula. The lake is named Shuia. Another says the river of the Babisa is called Lohubu.'

These brief sentences are illuminating, as very few lakes have 'several' rivers flowing from them, and there is no doubt the raid took place on the northern side of the Lukanga Swamp, in which there is the lake Shoa. It is an area which was visited by F. C. Selous in his disastrous hunting expedition in 1878 but little was known of it until F. B. Macrae went there and wrote an article on it for the *Geographical Journal* (1934).

Livingstone drew a little map in his journal, incorporating by intelligent guess-work this information, and it is reproduced here as the very first map of the Lukanga Swamp. This swamp is destined in the opinion of some to become a reservoir on the Upper Kafue, by which to regulate its flow, and thereby fulfil the double need of watering the Kafue Flats, and thence passing it on to give hydro-electric power at the Kafue Gorge. The swamp is already a natural regulator for the Kafue, since it takes flood water from that river by at least two channels, which later in the year reverse their direction and empty back into the Kafue again.

A few pages later in the journal Livingstone records an interesting conversation, as follows: 'Machonise, one of the people of the famous chieftain Changamera, informs me that there exists a very high mountain in his country (now that of the Mashona and Machele) called Limilo = a nose. Another named Chica is situated about north of it and 200 miles distant, the latter I may see in going down the Leeambye. Manoa is the country where he was brought up, and he says that there are lofty mountains there having walls built on them by the antients of hewn stone. Those who reared these edifices are said to have attempted to raise a scaffolding up to Heaven but the wood gave way and precipitated them to earth again. Is this a version of the tower of Babel and are these walls the work of those who came to Ophir to search for gold?

'He is very positive the stones were hewn and well fitted together without cement.'

This would appear to be the first information about the stone walls and terraces of the Inyanga mountains of Southern Rhodesia, and evidently Livingstone was so struck by it that he got Machonise to draw his idea of the rivers in the journal to which he himself adds the names as given. Livingstone knew that the area could not be far north of the Limpopo, and that may be why he himself added a rough map of the upper part of that river, on the same page.*

* These maps are in the large journal in the possession of Dr Hubert F. Wilson and a photostat of them would be a useful accession to the Archives at Salisbury.

On November 3rd Livingstone left Linyanti, accompanied by Sekeletu and two hundred of his men, and that very night provided an instance of the regard the chief had for the missionary. A heavy thunderstorm came on; 'wet to the skin we lay down under a bush and Sekeletu kindly covered me with his own blanket, lying during the remainder of the night uncovered himself.' More lasting evidence of Livingstone's standing was the fact that he was furnished with fifteen large tusks of ivory, six smaller ones, thirteen oxen for slaughter and three trained for riding, besides

Ratau, the chief who took Livingstone to the Victoria Falls

hoes and beads for buying food. It took one hundred and fifteen men to carry them.

They left Sesheke on November 13th, the main party going by land, and the seniors by canoe as far as Katombora, where the river falls down thirty feet in a series of very beautiful rapids between a dozen thickly wooded islands. It is interesting to note that even then, long before the hippos were shot at by guns, they were vicious along this part of the river, so that it was necessary to travel near the banks by day and in midstream by night, when the hippos were going ashore to feed.

From Katombora this party went by land to within about seven miles of the Falls, stopping on an island just above the modern Palm Island. The name of the island, Kalai, has now been transferred for some reason to a long thin island only three miles from the Falls, at the lower end of the fine reach which was, for a time, used for flying boats. It was on November 17th, that Livingstone made his first visit to the Falls, after transferring to special light canoes manned by experts: 'We sailed swiftly down to an island situated at the middle and on the Northern verge of the precipice over which the water roars. At one time we seemed to be going right to the gulph but though I felt a little tremour I said nothing believing I could face a difficulty as well as my guides.'

It was appropriate that the first white man to see the Falls should be introduced to them by the most dramatic and awe-inspiring approach possible. The very first sentence of his journal account, written six days later, are a complete epitome of the phenomenon: 'The falls are singularly formed, they are simply the whole mass of the Zambezi waters rushing into a fizzure or rent made right across the bed of the river.' Like a true geographer, Livingstone goes on to give approximate measurements which are very conservative, and indeed from his position on an island in the middle he could not see the full length of the Falls, which he gives as, 'not less than 600 yards', whereas they are 1900 yards. He guesses the depth as 100 feet whereas it ranges from 200 feet at one end to 350 feet opposite its exit. He amended these estimates on his second visit five years later.

There is no feature that he did not notice, including the way in which the streams from the Rain Forest trickle over the edge but never reach the bottom, being whirled up again by the 'ascending vapour'. Any reader who has been lucky enough to visit the 'Cave of the Winds' behind the Falls of Niagara, reached via an elevator, will remember the hurricane of wind he met between the sheet of water and the rocks, and how he had to hang on to the railings to prevent himself from being lifted off his feet. In the Victoria Falls there is rock on either side of the sheet of falling water and the upward rush of air carries the spray up many hundreds of feet, to be seen up to twenty miles away at times. No wonder it was named by the Makololo, Mosi-oa-Tunya,—the Smoke that Thunders.

The whole description is contained in two pages of the journal, and there is not a single extravagant adjective in it. The account in *Missionary Travels*, written in England two years later, is longer, and is so well known that we need only refer to the theories he puts forward in it to explain such an unusual type of waterfall. In it there is a delightful touch of honesty and humility where he speaks of wanting to measure the width of the river: 'In vain I tried to bring to my recollection the way I had been taught to measure a river, by taking an angle with the sextant, That I once knew it and that it was easy, were all the lost ideas I could recall, and they only increased my vexation.' This vexation endured, and when, three years later, he heard from a naval officer of a way of making the measurement without a sextant he explains it fully in his notebook. Here is the method explained with a diagram for the sake of any future Livingstones.

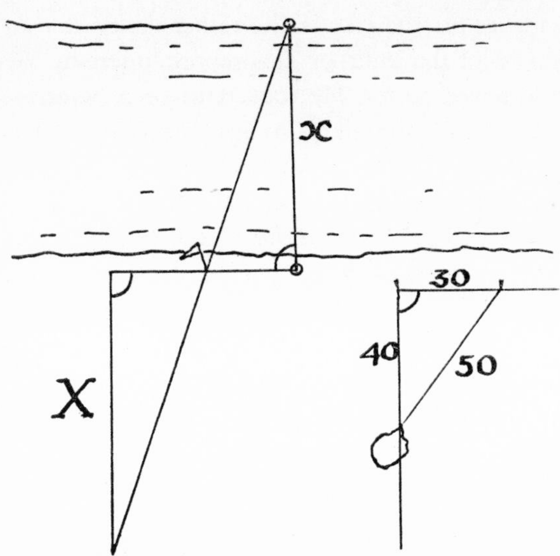

x is the required distance between two trees or other marks on the river banks.

Set out a right angle with your chain, tape or cord and measure out a reasonable distance along the bank, putting up a flag or beacon half-way along it.

Set out another right angle and walk backwards along X *until the flag and the tree are in line.* X *is then equal to* x *and can be measured.*

The right angles are set out by the 3, 4, 5 rule as in diagram for a 100 foot tape or chain. 30 feet are measured and pegged on the first line, and the ends of the chain fastened to the pegs. Holding the chain at 40 and 50 foot marks (with a loop of 10 feet slack) put an equal tension on each part and when taut put in a peg to give the perpendicular line.

A few pages later in his book, Livingstone outlines his theory to account for the whole of the river system he had been traversing for the last three years and, sad to say, it is wrong. And the cause of its wrongness is largely in his choice of a word to describe the Falls, that they disappear into a 'crack or fizzure or rent' in the surface. This induced a line of reasoning which led him to think that earth movements caused the cracks, that their formation was sudden and even catastrophic, and that they drained a very large lake in a comparatively short space of time.

His evidence for the lake is also rather faulty, due to his misinterpretation of the 'tufa' or 'madrepore limestone' over which he had journeyed so far. He took it to be a lacustrine deposit, whereas it is much more likely to be concretionary, that is to say, caused by water percolating through the sand and depositing a matrix of lime and silica at a certain level. We must admit that to formulate such a theory after two visits to one part of the Falls only, was remarkable in itself, and the shape of the 'gulph' into which the water falls has probably caused every later visitor to make the same mistake, taking it for a crack rather than for an expansion of an original line of weakness.

On the true origin of the Falls it is impossible to improve on an article by Dr G. Bond, printed in the *Handbook to the Victoria Falls*, which was edited by Dr Desmond Clark and published in 1952. Had Dr Livingstone been able to see the aerial photograph printed opposite p. 129 of this book he would at once have recognised the lines of weakness upstream of the Falls, and related them to the gorges below.

The basalt lavas, which form the bed of the Zambezi from 40 miles above to 70 miles below the Falls, are perhaps 150 million years old, and the two sets of vertical cracks, only a few inches wide, were formed so long ago that they have been filled

Livingstone's sketch of the Victoria Falls
Photo: M. J. Morris

Garden Island from the air, seen projecting into the gorge of the falls

with material softer than the parent rock. The water could erode such material more quickly and so undercut the harder rock which fell into the crack till it grew to the width we now see. Dr Desmond Clark contributes an article in the same handbook on the evidence of prehistoric man below the Falls, showing conclusively that the cutting back has been going on fairly rapidly. The process goes on in jumps, one of which is now nearly due, and the last one and a half miles of cutting back from the Fourth Gorge to the present First Gorge took a mere ten thousand years.

It is possible that our great-grandchildren in another century will see the bulk of the water rushing down the Cataract at the western end, carving out the beginning of a new gorge along the line of weakness shown in the aerial photograph. If so, it will threaten one of the most abiding memories in the minds of all visitors, the huge bronze statue of Dr Livingstone, brooding over his discovery, and looking along the vast rent to the Africa beyond, where he spent most of the remaining years after his first visit.

And now it was time to say goodbye to Chief Sekeletu and his retinue, and move off to the north-east so as to avoid the very difficult country below the Falls. His guide was Sekwebu, 'a person of great prudence and sound judgement', who had been up and down much of the Zambezi more than once. Sekwebu was his standby throughout the journey, and it was a tragedy that, bound for England with his master, he drowned himself at Mauritius in a fit of despondency. This mental failure on the part of a stout-hearted land traveller need not occasion surprise when we read what the paramount chief of Barotseland, Lewanika, thought of a sea voyage when his tribe was far more sophisticated. We have it from one member of the party going to England in 1902 to attend the Coronation of King Edward VII:

'This being our first time at sea, my colleagues, our King and myself were wonderfully astonished to find that during our voyage we could not trace any view of land. Our presumption was that the sea and sky were meeting together, and for this reason we lost both hope of landing in England or of ever returning to our sweet home.'

In the journal at this point there is a long list of the articles Livingstone was to buy in England with the tusks of ivory he was carrying, in which two items are of special interest. One was a small mill for crushing sugar cane, which grows well in Barotseland, and the other, 'blue naval caps'. It seems an odd part of the world for naval caps, and we suspect that the chiefs were torn between the useful wide-awake hats worn by most travellers in Africa, and the naval style cap worn consistently by Livingstone.

Their route at first was very much the same as that followed by the present road and railway, with the same turn towards the east near the present station of Kalomo, and thence on to Monze, a chief's name. Livingstone was much impressed with the healthiness and comparative fertility of this district, and endeavoured to make friends with the Atonga tribe he found there, as he fancied it might serve as a health station for missionaries stationed on the Zambezi. He crossed the Magoye, which he spells Mokoe, and passes to the east of the present Mazabuka to the head of the Kafue Gorge, indulging in one of his rare prophecies, that the district probably will be the 'point d'appui' for the civilisation of Africa. 'I thank God for honouring me to explore it.'

By climbing a hill near the beginning of the Kafue Gorge, a little below the present bridge, he got an extended view and realised he was near the edge of the escarpment as we now call it, the descent from the lip of the plate in our simile. Here he crossed the river, then at its lowest. He had clearly been expecting much higher mountains in this direction, possibly from reading some of the statements of an armchair geographer in England whose predictions always jarred on Livingstone. There is a page in his journal which, I think, must be a tilt against this gentleman, written after he had viewed the prospect from his climb. Speaking of the ranges he says:

'To my mind it resembles a long ridge made by the plough more than anything else. "Fringe" would do if it were broken up into hills or mountains.

'The hills are not more than 600 or 700 feet high, and yet this is the celebrated cordillera of Africa!

'Those to the south which obstruct the navigation of the Zambezi and are called "Lupata" or "spine of the world" are about the same height.

'It is a very interrupted chain; there is, as surgeons say, a loss of continuity but I must add no more for in addition to spoiling the poetry of the thing for geographers I fear I shall increase the anxiety of the geologists letting them know that their world presents symptoms of being afflicted with "weak spine".'

This is a phrase which would have pleased the late Professor J. W. Gregory who, forty years later, described the Great Rift Valleys of Africa, which are indeed comparable to an inverted or negative cordillera, and certainly are evidence of spinal weakness. He was, of course, overlooking the tangled country which is now traversed by the tarmac road to Chirundu Bridge, and was but a few miles above the site of the present Kafue Hydro-electric Scheme.

Since it is such broken country, it is not easy to follow Livingstone's route, but he mentions the Funswe river, and his course must have been roughly parallel to the great Kafue Gorge but a few miles to the northward of it. It was rough going for his oxen, and they met with belts of tsetse fly, but the people were friendly, the party was healthy, and when he got through the hills, near the lesser Chongwe, he breaks out into unusually rapturous adjectives when he sees his beloved Zambezi:

'The sight of the river as it winds away to the confluence (of Kafue and Zambezi) with the long range of hills on the other side of the Zambezi constitutes as fine a picture as I have seen in Africa. A glorious scene.

'It seemed from hundreds of buffaloes, zebras and lordly elephants feeding majestically to be like what must have been seen by angels when megatheria fed undisturbed in primeval forests.

'I never saw elephants so tame as near the Chongwe . . . we had several times to shout to elephants to get out of our way.'

His journal at this period is written with zest, and, even when he comes to unfriendly people near the Luangwa River, this style persists. At the villages he comes to now 'the women and children are generally out of sight. The ladies, however, are no loss so far as viewing the human face divine with pleasure is concerned, for they pierce the upper lip and draw it out inserting a shell or large piece of reed in it and giving themselves an ornithorhyncous air. What hideousness fashion can make poor mortals perpetrate.'

Pelele lip ring

The party had now reached the zone of influence, evil influence, of the Portuguese, who by their employment of half-castes as traders and slavers, had a name for cruelty and false dealing with the tribes on their uncertain borders. Livingstone was mistaken for one of that race, until he showed his whiter skin and longer hair. Their situation was further complicated by the fact that Sekwebu himself had been one of a party from the south side of the Zambezi which had raided the people at the mouth of the Loangwa. He does not seem to have been recognised. There were consequently some anxious hours at the crossing of that river, with the chief, Mburuma, threatening to attack in overwhelming numbers. Livingstone's attitude to dangers of this kind, many more of which he was yet to face, was to praise the Lord and yet keep his powder dry.

An entry in his journal, which is but partly quoted in *Missionary Travels*, illustrates this procedure rather well:

'14th January 1856. At the confluence of the Loango and Zambezi. Thank God for his great mercies thus far. How soon I may be called to stand before Him, my righteous Judge, I know not.

'What an impulse will be given to the idea that Africa is not open if I perish now....

'*Evening*. Felt much turmoil of spirit in view of having all my plans for the welfare of this great region and teeming population knocked on the head by savages tomorrow....

'I will not cross furtively by night as intended. It would appear as flight and should such a man as I flee. Nay verily, I shall take observations for Lat. and Long. tonight though they may be the last. I feel quite calm now. Thank God.'

And it must have needed a brave spirit and a calm deportment to keep his enemies amused the next day by showing them his watch, burning glass, etc., while his men transported themselves in relays across the river in the one canoe they could hire. When the crossing was accomplished he wrote: 'Perhaps after all they were influenced only by the need to be ready in case I should play them some false trick. They have reason to be suspicious of whites.'

It was no promised land on the other side, for there they saw the ruins of Zumbo, the Portuguese station, deserted for half a century. He had hoped to find easier going, but he saw many high hills ahead, and looked longingly across to the other side of the Zambezi where the plains run far back to the foot of the escarpment which now marks, roughly, the northern boundary of Southern Rhodesia.

Livingstone tried without success to hire canoes with which to cross, but the petty chiefs who owned them were afraid of the 'Lord of the River', chief Mpende, and would not make a deal, though they were ready enough to produce food for his large party, for which he could not pay. As Livingstone says: 'In few other countries would 114 sturdy vagabonds be supported from the generosity of the headmen,' and then follows a curious sentence:

'We have made friends and hope to be able by suitable acknowledgements *on our return* to secure a continuance of their favours.' Here is the first clear indication of Livingstone's decision, which so surprised his friends in England a few months later, that he must take his Makololo back to their home sooner or later.

It was on his next expedition that he showed his interest in the great northward bend of the Zambezi where he now was, and he mentions in his journal then how all the East African rivers seem to wear their left-hand banks more than the right.

He was in fact within an ace of discovering that anything moving in the Southern Hemisphere tends to bear to the left, and vice versa in the Northern Hemisphere, a phenomenon which played some part in the feature now bothering him, that he was on the bank of the Zambezi where it bears against hilly country, but wanted to be on the other bank where the ground was much lower. He noticed the old river terraces, at least three of them, and this no doubt set him thinking of the immeasurable periods of time necessary for the erosion of the great African valleys. There is a significant page in his journal at this point:

'In reflecting on the geological changes which have taken place in this country one gets a better idea of eternity than by any other process I know.

'If we look at the valley of the Quango for instance. We find it about 1000 feet deep and about 100 miles broad. How long I know not. It has been produced entirely by denudation through a solid mass of Keel or clay-slate. . . .

'But though the river carried down as much mud annually as our own Thames what myriads of ages were requisite to bring the hollow to its present depth. The mind becomes lost in trying to fathom it. . . . We come to the time when the enormous mass began first to be deposited stratum by stratum while primaeval seas were performing the Quango work on the rocks, and away beyond that we go again into the hot chrystalizing ages of the earth's history by means of these stepping stones into the past. . . .

We may well bow with humility and a sense of nothingness before the everlasting Jehovah.'

Once again they narrowly averted a fight when they reached Chief Mpende, who finally granted them permission to cross the Zambezi, though he dared not visit Livingstone lest he offend a suspicious prophet in his village, and they ferried themselves across via an island which must be about twenty miles downstream from Zumbo.

They had escaped from the frying pan only to fall into the fire for they now met two Portuguese traders from Tete, José Anselmo and Da Costa, who told them the tribes ahead were very dominating, and would demand tribute before giving leave to pass.

In fact, this crossing of the Zambezi to what was apparently easier country, was the worst thing that could have happened, both for Livingstone and for the fortunes of his next expedition.

Had he continued on the northern bank, he would have seen or heard full details of the Kebrabasa rapids, which were about eighty miles lower down the river, and which were to alter the whole course of that expedition.

It was only a month later, writing from Tete to Dr Tidman, that he says:

'It will be gratifying for you to hear that I have been able to follow up my original plan of opening a way to the sea on either the East or West coast from a healthy locality in the Interior of the continent.

'And now I can announce not only a shorter path for our use but, if not egregiously mistaken, a decidedly healthy locality.

'By this fine river flowing through a fine fertile country we have water conveyance to within 1° or 2° of the Makololo [70 to 140 miles]. The only impediments I know of being one or two rapids (not cataracts) and the people in some parts who are robbers.'

Alas, he was egregiously mistaken about the only part of the river he had not seen, for they *were* cataracts and not rapids.

He was never nearer than fifty miles from Kebrabasa on this journey, having circled round it to the south to avoid the mountainous area, and the same had evidently been done by all other travellers.

An important sentence in *Missionary Travels* but not in his journal, reads: '. . . it may be mentioned that when I reached Tete I was informed of the existence of a small rapid in the river near Chicova; had I known of this previously, I certainly would not have left the river without examining it. It is called Kebrabasa and is described as a number of rocks which jut out across the stream.' Nevertheless it is strange that he did not realise that the difference of height between where he left the river and where he rejoined it again at Tete must be at least six hundred feet over a distance of only one hundred and twenty miles or so, which would either mean a uniform rapid current or else variations between slow current and formidable rapids.

On the subject of altitudes there is a very curious page written in Tete which I cannot explain, yet it may give the clue to some of his abundant hopes about navigating the Zambezi to within measurable distance of the Falls, hopes which were the basis of his next expedition.

When crossing the Zambezi below Zumbo he had measured its rate of flow, making it just under four miles an hour and he uses this figure for a strange piece of calculation:

'The rapidity of the flow of the Zambesi being $3\frac{3}{4}$ miles per hour cannot be adduced as evidence of great elevation in the interior, for according to Dr Arnott 3 inches declivity per mile gives a velocity on a smooth straight channel of 3 miles per hour.

'If we say the Zambesi falls four inches per mile in its sometimes rocky channel in the thousand miles between Quilimane and the Falls we have only $333\frac{1}{3}$ feet. But if we say 5 inches per mile, which is more than the amount necessary for the velocity of $3\frac{3}{4}$ miles, we have $416\frac{2}{3}$ feet to which if we add 100 feet for the falls we have between 500 and 600 feet elevation only.'

The oddity of such an argument does not depend on the rash assumption that the rate of flow of the river was uniform over one thousand miles but on his own very different figures for the height above sea level of the river above the Falls.

He had taken the boiling point of water several times on the journey, though not at the Falls itself but at his first camp to the north-east, which might be four hundred feet or more higher. The figures are entered in the journal but not the heights derived from them.

Reduced with the help of modern tables Dr Livingstone's heights are: for Linyanti 3702 feet above sea level, and for the confluence of the Luangwa and Zambezi, 1537 feet. Both are perhaps one hundred or so feet too high but that is hardly surprising under the circumstances.

Even if he did not reduce his heights at the time, he would still know that Linyanti was over three thousand feet, and the Falls could not be more than a few hundred feet lower.

So the entry in his journal remains a complete mystery, but whatever the explanation, it seems all too likely that it influenced him in accepting 'a small rapid in the river near Chicova'.

The last fifty miles of his journey to Tete (sometimes spelt *Tette*, and pronounced *Tet*) were difficult for precisely the same reason that had nearly halted him at the end of his journey to Loanda.

He could not pay tribute for leave to pass a village, a system which had been submitted to by traders in the past, and the people would not believe he had no goods with which to pay. The party was reduced to going across country, away from the paths, so as to dodge the villages but it was not successful.

The hard going and the anxiety reduced Livingstone to a state of weakness as before, though on this occasion he did not have the added danger of fever and dysentery. Almost in despair, he sent a man forward to Tete with a letter to the Governor, who was as kind as his colleagues on the other side of the continent had been, and sent out two officers with food and a machila (hammock) to carry Livingstone in.

It is very significant of Livingstone's intense interest in the resources of the country that the first two pages of his journal on reaching safety are taken up with descriptions of the coal seams found in the vicinity of Tete, followed by notes, underlined, concerning the most healthy months in which to travel from the coast to that centre. On the same page is the autographed signature of the Governor or Commandant: Tito Augusto D'Aranjo Sicard, who was to be his constant friend and helper in the difficult years ahead.

Both his journal and the book are full of geographical matters towards the end. We have space to mention only those that fit in under the headings of meteorology, medicine and mapping.

There were few days when he did not make notes on the weather, and in particular the temperature and direction of wind interested him, and went down in his daily notebook. But he was never a mere observer, he was always seeking explanations. There is something like an essay on the winds of Southern Africa, written a month before he reached Tete, and a few quotations will show his acumen at reasoning:

'The prevailing direction of the winds in all that portion of Africa north of Kuruman is clearly Easterly and the time of greatest activity and force is between 9 a.m. and 4 p.m. Between four and five the wind falls and the temperature also, so the evenings in and near the valley (of the Zambesi) are always delightful and the nights refreshing.

In Angola a sea breeze was observed to set in every day between nine and ten on the coast. As we receded farther from the coast its activity became apparent later in the day.'

Then comes the explanation: 'The surface of the land heated by the sun's rays, combines with the rotation of the earth to give *one* direction to the air. The heated surface causing an influx of air from the Atlantic meets that from the Indian Ocean but not half way across because the Eastern wind has both the rotation influence and the sun's rarification on its side.' He goes on to describe various special winds and their effects on plants and people.

From first to last all his journals contain medical notes, and there is so much material of this kind that some day a doctor will surely put them together as part of the history of African medicine. He is particularly keen to find out and even try native remedies, and does not hesitate to experiment on himself at times. The lengths to which he was prepared to sacrifice himself in the cause of science are sometimes quite incredible. When he had a bad bout of fever at Sena he writes: 'A large species of bats abounds in all the houses here. Last night while unable to sleep on account of rapid pulse, skin sometimes hot and dry or bathed in perspiration it was interesting to observe . . . that they often hover

Traced from Livingstone's large journal, drawn during his journey to the east coast

close to the face when the eyes are shut and produce a pleasant fanning sensation. I believed they were killing mosquitoes and had no objection to their familiarity. Having bared my thigh I gave them a fair opportunity of playing the vampyre but they did nothing.'

He is constantly trying to probe into the problem of malaria, which at that time was so confused by the use of the word 'miasma', with its natural association of a harmful effluvium or smell. He writes: 'This miasma is a most puzzling affair, it is connected with marshes somehow or other.' At Tete he meets a kindred spirit in a Senhor Candido, and from him he gets much

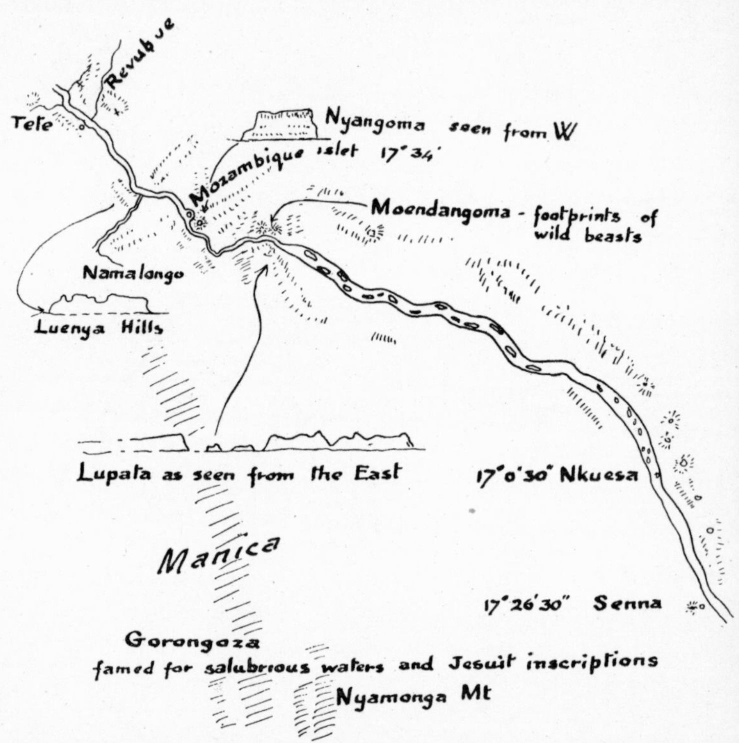

Tracing from Dr Livingstone's map in his large journal, made during his journey to the east coast. Re-lettered by author from Livingstone's notes on the map

information on both medical and geographical matters, but it is to be hoped that his remarks on medicine were more trustworthy than those on geography.

In later years the Portuguese insisted that they were the true discoverers of Lake Nyasa, but if Senhor Candido's evidence is to be cited in proof of that the claim falls to the ground.

That gentleman told Livingstone that he had visited the lake which was forty-five days' journey to the N.N.W., that it had the high mountain Morumbala in the middle, that it was shallow, and that it had a people named Mujao on its north coast.

Very wisely Livingstone gets the doubtfully candid Senhor to draw a map in his journal which, as far as I know, has never been reproduced. It is therefore published here in facsimile, presumably drawn by Candido and the names written in by Livingstone. It is perfectly clear that the lake spoken of was the Shire in flood in its lower plain between Mt Morumbala and the Shire highlands and that native rumours of a large lake in Cazembe's country, which could be forty-five days N.N.W., have been grafted on to an actual eight-day journey to the east.

Livingstone soon cleared up part of the mystery, since he passed Mt Morumbala on his way down the Zambezi a few weeks later. In fact I suggest, from the difference in handwriting, that it was then that he wrote in, on Candido's map, the words 'From six to eight days without wood' to describe the route overland from Tete to Morumbala, and sketched in the map of the Tete district, with the cardinal points put in, referring to that map only.

The information he received of the area to the south of Tete was more trustworthy, and he inserts it on his own map of the river from Tete to Sena (p. 124), the hills of Gorongoza and Nyamonga (which is now called Inyaminga) being correct in direction if not in distance, from Tete.

He made this map on his way down to Quilimane at the end of April, when he was suffering from fever, but that did not prevent him from climbing the hill behind Sena and finding the boiling point of water at its summit, making it four hundred feet high and about five hundred feet above sea level. All this country was to become painfully familiar to him on his next expedition, and it is of interest to read what he thought of it at his first broad view:

'Morumbala with the conical hills on its north appears beautiful. The Zambesi, full of reedy islands winds along a dead flat. West and North is all flat forest which has a sombre appearance.

'It is remarkable how little judgement was manifested in the choice of this situation. Morumbala is lofty and very salubrious. All was completely in the power of the Portuguese yet they place their village on a flat and beside a multitude of low reedy islands.'

Where now, from that same hill, one looks across the longest railway bridge in the world, Livingstone was viewing the stockade of the local rebel, Kisaka, who held the little town in terror, while behind him, where the railway comes now from Beira, the country was in complete subjection to the Landeens (of Zulu race) who 'considered the whites as a conquered tribe', and exacted tribute from them.

When he finally reached the seaboard at Quilimane on the 20th of May, he found letters, one of which, from the Directors of the London Missionary Society, he answered very soberly, but it caused 'the old love of independence, which I had so strongly before joining the Society, to return again'.

His best friend amongst the missionaries at Cape Town was Mr W. Thompson, and to him he wrote more freely about the letter of the Directors, which had said that 'they are restricted in their power of aiding plans connected only remotely with the spread of the Gospel'. There is therefore a tinge of bitterness in his remarks to his friend:

'I had imagined in my simplicity that both my teaching, conversation and travel, were as nearly connected with the spread of the Gospel as the Boers would allow them to be.

'I suppose that it is intended to send me to some of the tried, near, and easy fields where I may wax fat and kick like Jeshurun.

'I shall not boast of what I have done, but the wonderful mercies I have received will constrain me to follow out the work in spite of the veto of the Board. If it is according to the will of God means will be provided from other quarters.'

He therefore prepares 'to withdraw from pecuniary dependence on any Society', but without rancour, for he adds, after saying

'I am poorer considerably than when I landed in Africa sixteen years ago,' 'yet I shall leave you without abuse of any sort. The Directors have always treated me well and I shall remember you all with affection.'

Bashukulombo headdress

DEBITS & CREDITS

CHAPTER FIVE

Besides, I must tell you, all our Country rings of him, there are but few Houses that have heard of him and his doings, but have sought after and got the Records of his Pilgrimage: yea, I think I may say, that his hazardous Journey has got a many well-wishers to his ways.

JOHN BUNYAN

After sixteen years of Africa, much of it journeying to the tune of two thousand miles in a year, Livingstone stepped ashore at Dover at the latter end of 1856, acknowledged by all as an explorer of the first rank. Yet he felt a stranger because, of actual friends outside the family, there were but a handful in England, of whom the three principal ones were Oswell, Steele and Vardon, the 'Indian gentlemen' whom he had helped with their big game hunting. That was quickly remedied since every one from the Prince Consort downwards was anxious to make his acquaintance.

We cannot detail the list of honours which came his way, receptions, dinners, honorary degrees, freedoms of London and Glasgow and Edinburgh, and the crowning honour of being made a Fellow of the Royal Society. In truth he became a great national figure, and one result was an easement in his financial resources, both from subscriptions and from the proceeds of his best seller book, *Missionary Travels*.

The process of being lionised is no doubt pleasant to the lion,

* The headpiece shows the *Ma-Robert* passing Mt. Morumbala.

The Statue at the Falls

Sculptor: Sir William Reid Dick, K.C.V.O., R.A.

Photo: Northern Rhodesian Information Department

Oblique air photograph of the Victoria Falls, taken from a point almost over the Hotel, showing the line of weakness where the chasm of the future will be

but it can easily interfere with his roaring and spoil him for future hunting. That it did not do so with Livingstone is a tribute to his character, but he was never at ease in a large concourse or on a platform and it undoubtedly put a great strain on him. What pleased him most was the fact, apparent to him at last, that his labours had attracted 'a many well-wishers to his ways'.

Having severed his official connection with the London Missionary Society very gently, with many compliments from both sides, he was free, as it were, to pursue his dual purpose of combating slavery and opening up Africa in his own way. At least, he thought he was free, but he soon found that his own reputation was to bind him and coerce him in directions he would not otherwise have taken.

His new and important friends would not hear of his going off alone again as he would have preferred, and before long he found himself being edged into commanding a large Government expedition, as one of Her Majesty's consuls, and under the ultimate authority of the Foreign Office. It could not well have been otherwise, but it is clear from his own letters that he had misgivings, both as to his own capacity for leadership, and even whether that was the best way to open up Africa.

There were melancholy stories of the failure of Government expeditions on the Niger to give him pause. On the other hand, there were his hundred or so Makololo at Tete waiting to be taken home again in fulfilment of his promise, and that necessitated haste. He had every help from his grand friends, and, in the end, he was practically given *carte blanche* by the Foreign Secretary, Lord Clarendon, so that he became responsible for the plan, the organisation and the personnel of the expedition. He himself drew up the charter of instructions for the Expedition. Indeed as his biographer, Sir Reginald Coupland, wrote, 'The Expedition *was* Livingstone.'

The published aims of this Government-supported Expedition were plain enough, if a little puzzling to the Government at Lisbon, but Livingstone had more in his mind than was allowed to reach the Press. It is best explained in a private letter to Professor Sedgwick of Cambridge written a few days before he left England, from which I am allowed to quote by the courtesy of the Director of the Rhodes-Livingstone Museum:

'That you may have a clear idea of my objects I may state that they have something more in them than meets the eye.

'They are not merely exploratory, for I go with the intention of benefiting both the African and my own countrymen.

'I take a practical mining geologist to tell us of the mineral resources of the country—an economic botanist to give a full report of the vegetable productions—an artist to give the scenery —a naval officer to tell of the capacity of the river communication —and a moral agent to lay a Christian foundation for anything that may follow.

'All this machinery has for its ostensible object the development of African trade and the promotion of civilisation but what I tell to none but such as you in whom I have confidence is this. I hope it may result in an English colony in the healthy high lands of Central Africa—(I have told it only to the Duke of Argyll).'

As it turned out, the first colony was not to be on the highlands of the Kafue region as he expected, but in the more accessible ones of the Shire district. It is therefore clear that Nyasaland owes its establishment as a Crown Colony, even more definitely than most historians suppose, to the dreams of David Livingstone, who concludes his letter with 'in the course of time, say when my head is low, free labour on the African soil may render slave labour, which is notoriously dear labour, quite unprofitable.'

In this book we are concerned with David Livingstone mainly as a geographer and not as a leader, nevertheless, we must take some account of him in the latter capacity since it so seriously affected his work in the former. It must be realised that he had never been in command of white men before and it must be admitted that he had grave shortcomings in the three essentials for leadership of an exploring party. A leader must select his men wisely, he must see that his equipment is sound and finally he must weld his party into a team.

He made two mistakes in his choice of men, in the persons of Commander Bedingfield, the naval officer, and his own brother,

Charles, eight years his junior, but moulded in a very different pattern from himself.

He quickly recognised he had made a mistake in selecting Bedingfield as soon as they reached the Zambezi. He seems to have impressed Livingstone so deeply that the latter did not even inquire into his record with the Navy, which was not good.

He was dismissed soon after their first voyage up the river in the *Ma-Robert* and in a letter from there soon afterwards Livingstone wrote: 'Bedingfield turned out an unmitigated muff, thought we could not move a mile without him and thereupon assumed all manner of airs. I mounted the paddle-box and sent him home to nurse his dignity there.' His error in selecting his brother, and for such a queer post as 'moral agent', he did not discover until much later and even then he did nothing to remedy it.

As far as his equipment was concerned, there was perhaps only one mistake, but it was a vital one. Whether it was the fault of the allegedly philanthropic ship builder, Mr Laird, or of Captain Bedingfield who approved of the vessel after trials at Liverpool, the *Ma-Robert** was a failure almost from the beginning. In this matter Livingstone was certainly let down by his technical advisers. He was to become a first rate seaman himself ere the Expedition was over, but steam launches were an entirely new field for him, and we can hardly blame him for this unfortunate failure in his transport.

For the last and most important element in leadership—the ability to pull a party of individuals into a harmonious team—we must admit a grave lack in this otherwise most remarkable man, however much we may make excuses of one kind or another. Part of the trouble was, perhaps, that he never recognised the necessity for doing so, but the major part was that he was not built for it, he could not make friends and confidants of them. He was too shy to praise a man, and equally too shy to blame him until too late; he was content to give them general orders and leave them to work out the means and supply the zest for doing what was indicated.

* Named after Mrs Livingstone, who, in the fashion of the Bechuanas was called 'Mother-of-Robert', her eldest son.

It was not till two years later, that his very objectionable young brother took him to task on this matter, telling him 'that the members of the expedition did not get orders what to do—and were always at a loss how to act'. In answer to this, to himself and in the privacy of his journal ,he adds: 'On principle I abstained from multiplying orders believing that it is more agreeable to men to do their duty in their own way. It is irksome to most men to be in any degree driven as soldiers and sailors are.'

With the exception of Bedingfield and brother Charles he had, I submit, a very promising team indeed. John Kirk, the young Scottish doctor, only twenty-five years old, Thomas Baines, ten years older, and a seasoned traveller, and Rae the engineer, all did well in their later careers. Even Richard Thornton, for all his youth and inexperience, was sound enough, and only needed some patient teaching as to what was required of him.

With all these elements of promise, it would have been fairly easy for a man accustomed to have white men under him to achieve harmony and arouse enthusiasm, but I doubt if Livingstone saw his duty in that direction at all, in fact he would probably have called it either molly-coddling or interfering with their freedom of originality.

There is no avoiding the fact, that this large expedition fell so far short of its plan and its promise that it must go down in history as a failure, or, if that be too absolute a verdict, as a great disappointment.

Livingstone himself constantly snatched partial success out of failure by his own superhuman efforts, but in the end he really had no one of his own calibre but young Kirk to help him. He was in fact a failure as a leader, and he would have been the first to admit it, all the more bitterly, because he knew his expedition could have been a success if he were working alone with his Makololo.

Their first geographical problem was, strangely enough, to find the Zambezi itself, or rather, a feasible entrance to it. This, however, was the work of an able and energetic naval surveyor, Lieutenant Skead, who joined the *Pearl* at Cape Town.

The expedition did not truly begin until the *Pearl* had left them on an island, some forty miles from the bar at the mouth of the river, where stores were landed, an 'iron house' put up and a base formed, from which to move the bulky impedimenta upstream by relays in their inadequate transport, the eighty-foot *Ma-Robert*, a large pinnace and a whaleboat.

The lower half of the delta of the Zambezi was a part of the river he had been unable to see when he went by canoe from Tete to Quilimane in 1856, in a time of high water, since the latter port is not strictly on the delta at all. It was ill fortune for Livingstone that the two sections of the river he had missed were each to turn out to be far worse than he expected, but some member of the expedition should have been put on to making enquiries, since the Portuguese had been on or near the delta for centuries, and at least one British ship had been some distance up it.

Livingstone had put it in writing that he even hoped to get up as far as Tete in the *Pearl*, which was optimism in its most dangerous form, because the health of the party depended on getting up river as soon as possible. In the *Narrative* he makes hardly any mention of this first setback, and probably he did as he had often done before, set his teeth, and got to work overcoming it.

In a very few days the *Ma-Robert* went off with the first lot of freight up river, and after only thirty miles they found that they were running into, or rather, through, a minor war, which had already lasted six months. The Portuguese were trying to destroy a nest of rebels who had established themselves at Mazaro, a village close to the entrance of the channel, Mutu, which at high water gave a passage to their provincial headquarters, Quilimane. As usual the rebel was a half caste Portuguese, one Mariano, but, as he was in prison at Mozambique, it was his brother Bonga who was literally holding up trade and traffic on the river which the Portuguese were supposed to command.

Thanks to the skill which Livingstone always displayed in his dealings with Africans, he managed to get into the good graces of both sides, which he sums up by saying, 'Henceforth we were recognised as friends by both parties.' Nevertheless they did manage to come under fire in peculiar circumstances. They landed at the Portuguese H.Q., having heard that the Governor was seriously ill, and Livingstone went to his hut to attend the patient. Baines had also landed, and was making the sketch which appears opposite p. 28 of the *Narrative*, while Bedingfield and Rae stayed by the launch. Just then the rebels renewed the fighting, and 'musket balls began to whistle about in all directions'. The behaviour of the four Englishmen was, I think, characteristic of each. Baines calmly went on with his sketch, Bedingfield told Rae that they must go off in the launch, Rae refused to do so until the Doctor rejoined them and was kept busy pushing frightened slaves from seeking refuge on the launch. Livingstone himself was fully occupied carrying down the stricken Governor to the launch, at first unaided. The whole affair occupies only fifteen lines in the book and these details come from diaries of other members. The Baines' sketch shows a dead body or two and the Portuguese slave-soldiers streaming down to the *Ma-Robert* and escaping in canoes.

We may say at this point that the *Narrative* is a disappointing book in comparison with his *Missionary Travels*. It was written by David Livingstone at Newstead Abbey in the winter of 1864–65, but it also bears the name of Charles Livingstone in order to allow Charles to enjoy the profits of the American edition.

It is written throughout in the third person and in a rather strained objective style, with a minimum mention of names, with little either of praise or blame, and with the obvious intention of glossing over unhappy memories. It is not a day-to-day narrative as was much of his first book, and it is difficult to follow the sequence of events at times. The somewhat distant, almost aloof, style convinces the reader that this strange man was more truly alone in this series of journeys than he was in his earlier one-man travels.

There is the same indomitable spirit shining through the pages, but now it is tinged with bitterness, which is liable to affect his judgment. Where, in his earlier book, a difficulty or threat was the will of God, it now became a plot by man against his purpose.

The first effect of the poor performance of the *Ma-Robert* was that the party had to move in relays and was constantly separated into small groups, and it is not at all easy for readers to follow the sequence of journeys, or appreciate the difficulty of the leader in having such a dispersed command.

Livingstone's real base of supply was the Kongone entrance to the Zambezi, and his means of supply was an occasional steamer passing up and down the East Coast on other business. His line of communication was therefore tenuous and almost accidental. The delta was no place in which to keep a section of his party waiting for fresh stores, yet it had to be done occasionally. Hence the frequent journeys up and down, and delays of a few weeks on the unhealthy and incredibly dull Expedition Island. Forty miles farther up was a second depot, Shupanga, far more interesting, but only slightly more healthy, and liable to be very exciting because there was intermittent fighting between the Portuguese and 'rebels' on the opposite northern bank, or trouble with the Landeens in the country to the south. It was, nevertheless, a favourite spot for members of the Expedition, because there was a comfortable stone house there and usually some hospitable Portuguese officials; and there was a distant hill to be seen away to the north-west, Mount Morumbala, overlooking the junction of the Shire River (pronounced *sheeray*) which they were all to know so well. Sixty miles up river from Shupanga there was the first official centre of the Portuguese, the town of Sena on the southern bank of the river, with a hill behind it and a view of higher hills to the north.

Here lived a good friend of the expedition, Senhor Ferrano, always kindly, though he was the owner of some six hundred slaves. Indeed, Livingstone says that the only redeeming feature of Sena was that Senhor Ferrano lived there, the sentence before that remark being, 'one is sure to take fever in Senna on the second day if by chance one escapes it on the first day of a sojourn there.' The town of Sena has now been moved back somewhat from the river and shares the honour and the traffic of the long railway bridge with Dona Ana, the station at the northern end of the bridge on the steeper bank. So steep in fact, that the trains often have to run back half a mile on to the bridge itself to get up speed enough to rush the steep incline. On the next one hundred and fifty miles of river up to Tete the navigation hazards were less frequent and the scenery distinctly more interesting. There was no permanently deep water, however, until, at two-thirds of that distance, the narrows of Lupata were reached beyond which the Luenya entered from what is now the Southern Rhodesian highlands and Tete was another twenty-five miles beyond it.

For the expedition, able to be friends with both sides, the river was comparatively free as far as human obstruction was concerned For the Portuguese, however, there were really only two centres of comparative safety. Sena and Tete. They had to run the gauntlet to the first past the sphere of influence of Mariano and Bonga on the northern bank, and nearing Tete, a second bottleneck through the country of another 'rebel', also called Bonga.

It was no wonder, therefore, that the Portuguese knew next to nothing of the Shire River, or of the lakes beyond, which were to be the major discoveries of the English. It is necessary also to point out, with some emphasis, that, although this expedition is usually regarded as an anticlimax to his former one, it was even more important in opening up Africa. We are prone to assume that, because its advertised purpose of finding a route by water to the Upper Zambezi was a complete failure, its subsidiary, or rather, its alternative discoveries, were of minor importance. The consequent deflection of their exploration from the more or less known west to the completely unknown north-west did far more towards discovery than if the expedition had been able to follow its original plan.

It was soon after their first journey over the Shire Highlands to the first of the lakes (Shirwa) that Livingstone had news of the discovery of Lake Tanganyika. He may have felt slightly forestalled, and says little about it in the *Narrative* yet Kirk's reception of the news may have been a reflection of his leader's when he says in his own journal: '. . . we heard of the splendid discoveries of Burton and Speke inland from Zanzibar. This will pull us up to do something more. The Lake Tanganyika is surely the source of the Zambezi, but we have no particulars.' Livingstone must have been sorely puzzled, because, up to that date, he had heard from Syde ben Habib of Lake 'Tanganyenka' as a large shallow lake which was crossed in three days by punting canoes, and from

Senhor Candido he had heard of a lake in very similar terms. No sooner had Speke and Burton discovered a long and very deep lake instead of a shallow one than he himself, later by only a year, discovered a companion to it in Lake Nyasa, almost as long and nearly as deep.

If we are bent on comparisons on other aspects of African exploration, we may as well remember the disharmony amounting to complete severance, which was the result of the Burton-Speke partnership, and note that Livingstone and Kirk never ceased to be friends, even when relations became strained through the ineptness of H. M. Stanley.

Meanwhile, Livingstone's first duty was to pursue the plan of surmounting the rapids he had not seen. He had soon become an efficient skipper of his *Ma-Robert*, whose behaviour had already earned it the description of a 'tin can' and the sobriquet of *The Asthmatic*. He and Kirk were becoming river-wise in their methods of avoiding sand banks or getting free of them when they had run aground. If only the bottom plates of the tin can had been an eighth of an inch instead of a sixteenth it might have served their purpose long enough. As it was, every grounding was an agony, as it meant further damage to the hull of their craft. Rae did his valiant best with the engines but they, too, were rapidly degenerating. It was a great pity that the leader and second in command had to spend so much energy in navigating, but there seems no doubt that, secretly perhaps, they rather enjoyed the piloting, of which Livingstone writes, 'The work of being skipper is not very hard but it demands constant attention.'

It is very strange that Livingstone made no use of Baines in this or a similar capacity, for he had had far more experience of boat work than any other member of the expedition, including Bedingfield. Not only had he sailed nine hundred miles in an open boat in the Arafura Sea north of Australia, but he had roughed it on land to a degree only inferior to Livingstone himself.

However, the work of transporting people and goods up river went on fairly steadily, and included making some kind of a map of the channel with soundings, and measurements of cross sections and velocities. Baines and Thornton were to the fore in this work.

The twelve Kroomen whom Livingstone had picked up from Sierra Leone on the way out were not very satisfactory, but they did provide some amusement at times. There was an occasion when, through their carelessness, one of the whaleboats got adrift and Tom Toby was nearly drowned in swimming for it. The accident was observed by Tom Jumbo who jumped in and saved him, also by Tom Coffee, a bosom friend of the swimmer, but he pretended not to notice and hurriedly went down into the cabin, coming out duly surprised when the affair was over. This was at Sena, which the party had reached about eight weeks after they had begun the move upriver.

Livingstone went on with Baines, who had been ill with sunstroke, towing the pinnace and the whaleboat heavily loaded. But now the engines of the *Ma-Robert* began to complain in earnest, and there are entries in the journal such as, '*Ma-Robert* has no power—excessively useless' as well as severe strictures on Mr Laird for supplying second-hand cylinders and boilers.

Progress was so slow that, after ten days and only sixty miles on their way, Baines volunteered to stay behind with the pinnace while the launch went ahead to Tete.

Never in the whole book is Thomas Baines mentioned by name, though he was with the expedition for eighteen months. Surely that is carrying resentment rather far, especially as the book contains several drawings by him, with no mention of their origin except in the list of illustrations, and acknowledging the kindness of Lord Russell in allowing him to use 'the drawings taken by the artist who was in the first instance attached to the Expedition'.

The arrival at Tete was naturally a major event, for not only had the native inhabitants never seen a steamer before, but here Livingstone met once more his 'faithful Makololo', though we must remember that all were not faithful and only three were true Makololo. Still, of the 114 he had brought there 3 years before there were nearly 80 left, 30 having died of smallpox and 6 having been killed by the chief Bonga while on a friendly visit to his village to show off their dancing skill.

The meeting with them was most certainly an emotional one

on their part, and probably for Livingstone also, though his account of it in the *Narrative* is bald enough. In the journal he quotes them as saying, 'Now our hearts will sleep—we have seen you again.' They had done fairly well for themselves in the three years of their sojourn there, and Major Tito Sicard had been true to his promise of assisting them, though the Portuguese Government gave them no aid in spite of reports that they would do so.

After getting stores ashore and shipping a ton of coal from the Revubu mine for the *Ma-Robert*, he goes quickly back to Sena, finding that Baines had made shift to sail a few miles further up the river and 'had arranged the pinnace tastefully'.

Thence down to Shupanga, where he heard that H.M.S. *Lynx* was at the Kongone mouth with stores for him, so off he went to meet her, Kirk having gone down already in hired canoes. While waiting for Livingstone, Kirk assisted some of the naval officers in making a survey of the creeks and channels of this entrance.

Two of the ship's officers volunteered to fill Bedingfield's post, but Livingstone was by this time thoroughly scared of naval officers, and he took two petty officers instead, Walker and Rowe.

Having got everything and everyone up to Sena, Livingstone, restless as ever, took a short trip across to the Shire with Kirk and Thornton, and climbed nearly half way up Mount Morumbala. They saw the hot spring near its base, the first of many he was to see before he had finished with this part of the Great Rift valley of Africa.

In the journal at this point there is a characteristic medical remark, which runs: 'Quinine daily for the sake of the effect on the imagination. It is decidedly curative but questionably prophylactic if we deduct the effect on the imagination. A much more important precaution than quinine is constant employment and sufficient bodily exercise to produce perspiration every day.' He himself said to his dying day, and possibly not always wisely, that the best thing to do when you have fever is to get up and march.

They proceeded on to Tete with the help of hired canoes but, anxious as he was to visit Kebrabasa and settle the doubts about it, he paused in the Lupata Gorge to make a measurement of the discharge of the Zambezi at this, its low stage. It was done in professional style, choosing a base nine hundred feet long on the bank, and sounding frequently across the two sections chosen. It is at this point that he quotes the method of measuring the width of a river which he got from a naval surveyor, the method mentioned in the last chapter. Livingstone was nearly always in a hurry, but rarely missed a chance such as this of doing sound geographical work.

As soon as he reached Tete he made plans for the crucial trip to the rapids, taking with him Kirk and Rae in the *Asthmatic*. He must have had some misgivings about what he was going to find, because, whatever may be the explanation of the mysterious calculation in his journal, as described in the last chapter, he had fairly trustworthy altitude figures. These, in fact, were published in the *Geographical Journal*, while he was in England, and they were all too plain. When he left the river to cut across the big Kebrabasa bend he was 1400 feet above sea level, and when he joined it again at Tete he was only 800 feet above sea level. That 600 feet drop had to come in somewhere in the 100 mile gap about which he knew very little. Such a drop means about 6 feet per mile instead of the 5 inches per mile assumed in his calculation, and, therefore, should mean anything from a uniformly fast current to prodigious rapids or even waterfalls.

The lower part of the gorge was somewhat deceptive, the river at low water being enclosed in a chasm some twenty yards wide incised in a broader valley which would take some of the flow at high water. Livingstone describes the scenery as: '. . . quite remarkable. A series of lofty hills among which those of a conical shape predominate most, encloses a dell . . . which is the bed of the river at high water, and it is a strange mass of huge rocks containing a deep chasm winding from side to side along it. This fizzure or cleft is at first not more than 20 feet deep but it soon becomes 80 or even 120 feet deep. We saw evidence that the water in flood rises more than a hundred feet perpendicularly.'

This was not utterly impassable, but Kirk urged that they should go on farther to see if there were other rapids above and there certainly were. They slept on the sand in a little cove and returned to the launch the next day.

Apparently he concealed his disappointment from Kirk but he confided to his diary: 'Things look dark for our enterprise. This Kebrabasa is what I never expected. No hint of its nature ever reached my ears. The only person who ever saw the river above where we did was José St Anna and he describes it as fearful when in flood. This I can very well believe. A Governor sent down two negroes in a canoe and neither they nor canoes was ever again seen. What we shall do if this is to be the end of navigation I cannot now divine.'

Livingstone himself contracted *herpes*, an irritating skin disease, on this little trip, which perhaps rendered him sharper in temper than usual, but whatever it was, the next essay to reconnoitre further was an unhappy one. A few days later they set off again from Tete, taking the whole party. 'Do them good,' says Livingstone in his diary, using his own remedy for fever and lassitude.

From the different accounts of this sortie we get an unhappy picture of the inequality of the party. Kirk, the soundest in health and most balanced in kindly judgment, wrote in his diary, wishing that 'the Doctor would explain more fully what he wants' and defending Baines who was taken to task over some omission—'Baines, too, is scarcely off the sick list and has been, I should say, the hardest worked member of the Expedition.' Baines at all events did not delay progress, nor did Thornton, but Charles Livingstone did. He may have had fever upon him but there are significant entries on the subject. In Livingstone's journal the entry is merely 'One European knocked up by the heat'.

In Kirk's diary it is longer: 'Mr L. has become so tired with the walk as to be fit for little more than sleep. More than half the time is occupied allowing Mr L. to have a snooze every half hour or so. At each of these rests Baines and I practise at the hippopotami.'

It was strange that, as early as this after the start of the Expedition, everyone recognised the weak link in the party except the leader himself. And it was so even three years later, when it took Dr Stewart only a month or two before he wrote: '. . . that there is an evil genius in a very bodily shape connected with the expedition no one who has any acquaintance with its affairs will doubt. His tongue seems to be against every man and what his occupation is would be very difficult to say.'

The slow progress evidently exasperated Livingstone, whether he diagnosed the root cause or not, and, after a day or two, they returned to the main camp, where they heard there were worse cataracts beyond the point they had reached.

In his own journal he writes: 'Next morning announced my intention of returning to see the upper falls as it had never been my custom when alone to leave a matter unfinished.' And it is quite likely that he did put the proposals in some such tactless language. He continues: 'Dr K. thought it would be considered an insult to the expedition if I went alone so I gave consent to his forming one of the party—with 4 Makololo.'

The incident improved the relations between the leader and Kirk, however ungracious were the words Livingstone used in saying he could come if he liked. In fact the description of it by Kirk shows that he alone of that party could take an unprejudiced view: '. . . all felt their honour rather touched by the insult, which, after all I believe, was not meant for anything more than that he could do it himself and was doubtful if any one else could . . . as it turned out, I stood the work which he said was the hardest he ever had in his whole lifetime quite as well as he.'

The clamber along the sides of the gorge to the uppermost cataract Morumbwa was really a desperate affair, and at one point the Makololo had to be left behind. 'They declared', wrote Livingstone, 'that they always believed I had a heart until now—that I had become insane surely as they had shown me the broken blisters on their feet in vain.'

The cataract was indeed the end of their quest and of the leader's hopes for it was 'a fall of about 20 feet in 30 yards' according to Livingstone and 'falling about 30 feet at an angle of 30 degrees' according to Kirk. As they all returned painfully to the launch they met Baines coming up with provisions for them and Livingstone notes that he was 'sketching as he always does indefatigably'.

So the major plan of the whole expedition had been wrecked on 'the small rapids' that he had been told about, there was no 'God's highway' to the country of the Makololo, they had reached 'the end of navigation'.

We are not told in the journal of the leader's reflections but clearly there were two alternatives, either to transport all their goods to the river above the cataracts by the route he had followed

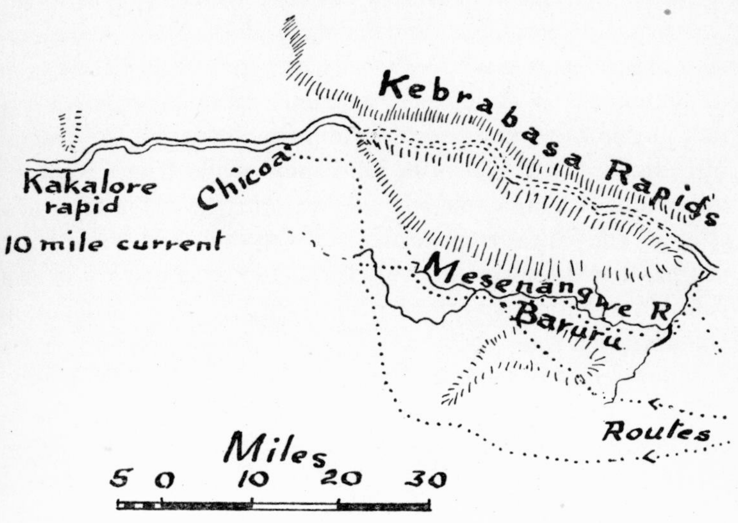

From Major Gibbons' map of his routes round the Kebrabasa Rapids in 1898

before, or to see if there was another way into the interior via the Shire River. It was as well that he chose the latter course because forty years later it took Major Gibbons seven weeks to portage two smaller boats over the land route, using nearly five hundred porters, with seven white men to supervise the move.

So, within a fortnight he was off in the launch, with Kirk and Rae, to examine the Shire, a river which was rumoured by the Portuguese to be impassable for boats. He left his brother in charge of affairs at Tete, with instructions for Charles to explore the country to the south, for Thornton to examine the Revubu coalfield thoroughly and for Baines to pay a visit to the rapids again when the river had risen high enough to smooth out some of the rapids.

These three geographical asides had each their own degree of importance but only one was properly carried out. The 'moral agent' decided to collect local birds instead of exploring the country of the Landeens, and Thornton's examinationof the coal was piecemeal.

The further visit to Kebrabasa was done with care, as although Charles was in command, Baines did the work. They went along the southern bank this time, and Charles soon went back to the camp by the boat while Baines with one Makololo continued. As they got near the uppermost Morumbwa cataract his companion was exhausted and had to be left behind while Baines went on for two days more alone and saw the critical sections from the opposite side of the river to where Livingstone had been. Their trip had lasted a fortnight, and Baines' report must have been a valuable one for Livingstone who, however, does not mention whose work it was.

Meanwhile, the reconnaissance journey up the Shire was going well. Livingstone was always at his best when establishing relations with suspicious natives and Kirk saw him for the first time at that kind of tricky operation.

They climbed to the top of the four thousand feet Mount Morumbala and found cultivation right to the top, a likeable chief and a cool climate with no fever. No wonder Livingstone wrote 'What fools the Portuguese are, not to have a sanatorium here'. The flood plain of the Shire spread out before them was described by him as 'the very picture of an amphibious animal's paradise.'

They steamed on, warily, passing the 'considerable population' of the plain, Manganja people who were very nervous and forward with fingers on drawn bows at times, 'trigger-happy' to use a modern phrase. In spite of these difficulties and such a shortage of wood that in one place they had to use elephant bones as fuel, they got to the junction of the Ruo and the Shire in a week, the site of the modern Chiromo and the railway bridge.

They were impressed by the Elephant Marsh there of which

Kirk made a coloured sketch of their encounter with elephants but they recognised it as malarious 'exhaling at sunset a very offensive smell'.

In another five days they reached the head of navigation at rapids which Livingstone named after Murchison, and they had discovered over one hundred and twenty miles of unknown river in that short time. It was good going on the part of the *Ma-Robert*

Elephant Marsh, a black and white rendering of Kirk's coloured sketch

because a modern stern-wheeler does the same trip in only two days less. That journey was one of the happy occasions when the writer felt he was following in the footsteps of that stern, implacable explorer as there had been no change in the physical surroundings since Livingstone's day, but he did it in such comfort that there was no true comparison.

Seated all day at a table on an upper deck, making a compass survey of the river, with no greater nuisance than sparks from the funnel occasionally burning holes in my coat, I could see over the fringe of reeds to the cotton lands on either side, overshadowed by the steep escarpment of the Shire Highlands in the east. The elephants had gone but the palm trees were still there and the crocodiles and waterfowl, and the occasional dug-out canoe.

It was not difficult to picture the 'asthmatic tin can' wheezing its way slowly round the frequent bends for the very first time, with Livingstone and Kirk sketching and observing and wondering what they would see round the next curve, while the dependable Rae was nursing his engines to cope with the occasional four-knot currents at narrow places.

Such places were interesting enough going slowly upstream but they became exciting coming down again, when our stern-wheeler, with a five-ton barge lashed to each side was waltzing down stern first much of the time and bumping from side to side, crashing its way into the dense bango-reeds at each side and literally bouncing its way round bends. The *Ma-Robert*, with its hull of one-sixteenth inch steel, could not carry on in that care-free way and it must have been nervous work for pilot and engineer.

Where we saw smiling villagers clapping hands and lullilooing to us as we passed, Livingstone saw flights of women and children and 'two men flitting from bush to bush taking aim at them with drawn bow'.

It is the habit of Africans to name their villages after the head-men resident there, and the villages themselves are often moved, so it is difficult to recognise where they stopped on this pioneer journey. At the village of the Chief Chibisa, they were well received and were told of a small lake a few days away and a large lake beyond that, so they pushed on another ten miles when they came to the Murchison cataracts. Once again rapids were to limit the navigation prospects on which Livingstone had based high hopes.

He was much impressed by the high sandy terrace just above Chibisa's on the west bank where now the boma of Chikwawa stands, looking down over the swirling waters which have now (1954) undercut the first house built by the District Commissioner.

The pontoon ferry which now takes cars across is worked in a way which shows how rapid was the current for the weak *Ma-Robert* to prevail against. The pontoon with the car on it is held on the far bank while a small boat towing a rope is rowed across the furlong or so of fast water as quickly as four Africans can pull, as they are swept down a couple of hundred yards. The rope is then fastened to a stout wooden pillar and the pontoon is swung across by the current on the end of the rope. Much depends on the strength of the rope for when it breaks as it did during my first visit, the pontoon goes downstream for eight or ten miles till it catches on some sandbank.

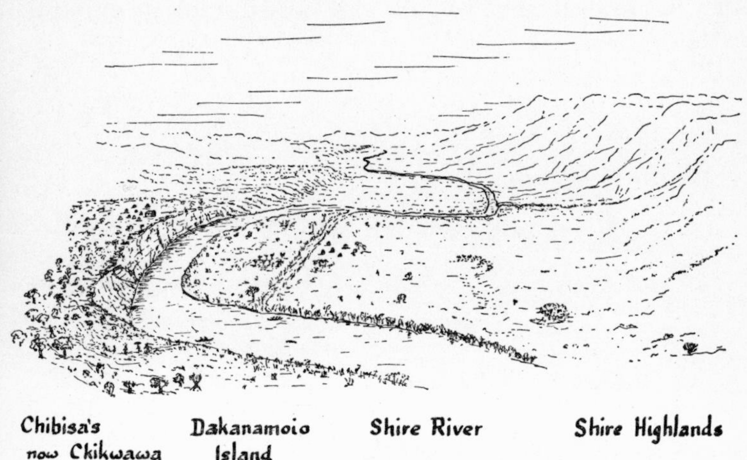

The famous Chibisa's village, now Chikwawa

The rapids of Mamwera, the lowest of the series, have not altered in the least discernible way from the sketch of them given in the *Narrative*. One can still shoot from a high bank on the west side at a crocodile on a rock in midstream, but the red paint with which they recorded their visit on a rock face at the far side 'V.R. Jan. 10 1859' has long since been removed by floods and weathering.

Livingstone hurried back to Tete, and though he does not say so openly in his journal he must have realised that the Shire and the lakes beyond provided the chance to retrieve his failure to ascend the Zambezi. So by mid-March he and Kirk, with the two petty officers to look after the launch, set off again and duly arrived at Chibisa's, to receive a friendly welcome from him.

The unhealthy season, just after the rains, was beginning and

Kirk's remark on it shows how thoroughly he had adapted himself, in six months, to the hazards of low country travel: 'Bad health and a touch of fever is nothing, were it not for the bad humour it puts anyone in, and sickness is a thing with which the Doctor has no patience, either in himself or anyone else.'

They acquired a very untrustworthy guide to the 'small lake' and later had to discard him and trust to their compasses after they had made their way up the long ridge towards the site of the

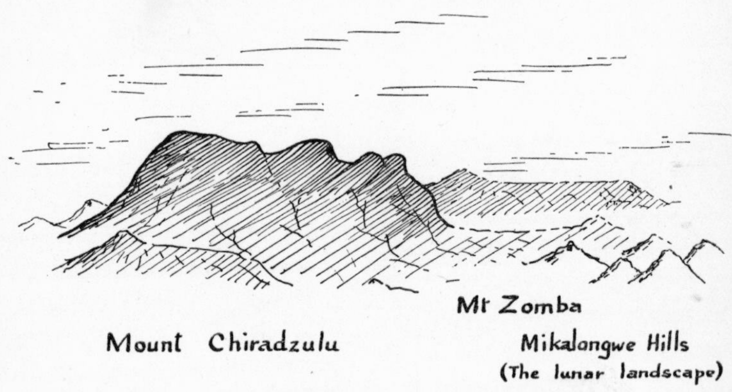

View looking north from Cholo

present Blantyre. Here their guide kept veering to the right towards the Elephant Marsh far below them and the party must have got near the Cholo district before they realised his error.

From here their view to the north must have been of Mount Chiradzulu, looking like the head of a sleeping negro, with the long line of Mount Zomba, seven thousand feet high, behind and to the right the odd collection of bare rocky hills of Mikalongwe looking like a lunar landscape. From the foothills of Mount Chiradzulu they 'got a fine view of what we were in search of. Before us was a long line of blue water; between us and it a wide plain . . . we have seen the LAKE.'

Needless to say, these words of relief come from Kirk not from Livingstone who never indulged in such high spirits.

The plain was only sparsely inhabited then, where now there are over 300,000 people, and without trouble they reached the lake to find it shallow and brackish. They were naturally much struck by the great granite mass of Mount Mlanje to the south, capped as it usually is by masses of cloud in ever varying mood.

Nervous about the petty officers' health down in the hot valley Livingstone turned back from the lesser lake, leaving the larger one for a later visit, and none too soon as the naval seamen were in a bad way, the healthier one not daring to use any of the strange medicines on the one stricken with fever. The journey back to Tete by mid-June and then down to the Kongone entrance to receive supplies from an expected cruiser showed up the wear and tear on the *Ma-Robert* all too clearly, the hull being riddled with rust holes, requiring constant patching by Rae. Water from below through the leaks in the hull and from above from leaks in the cabin roof destroyed most of the botanical specimens so carefully collected by Kirk.

But the cracks and leaks in the launch were not nearly as serious as those in the social structure of the expedition: Kirk takes as balanced a view as he can of the rifts between Charles Livingstone and the others, and even recognises that the post of 'moral agent' was not a simple one: 'Mr Livingstone has made a good collection of Birds of which I am right glad, as Botany keeps me well occupied. He has had an unenviable post, and being on no good terms with some of the others it has been doubly so. I am very glad I was not tried in his position.'

Baines and Thornton were left at Tete, both under a cloud, but doubtless much relieved that brother Charles went with the main party, down to the entrance.

When the *Persian* did arrive Livingstone shipped all the Kroomen off to the Cape and exchanged the fever patient, Quartermaster Walker, for a young seaman named Hutchins. The Kroomen had no doubt become spoiled but their own reasons were the treatment to which they had been subjected by Charles Livingstone. They were replaced by some of the Makololo.

It must have been Charles' recital of events at Tete while he and Kirk had been absent for four months which determined the leader to get rid of both Baines and Thornton, because he handed to Baines, as he left Tete for Kongone, a letter which Baines had not even time to read before the launch pushed off. It contained charges of which Baines had hitherto not heard, of going off 'skylarking with the Portuguese, of taking the whaleboat without authority' and of spending 'expedition time and materials in painting Portuguese portraits'. Before Baines saw Livingstone again the latter had written a letter of dismissal with fresh charges including that of 'making away with large quantities of public property'.

We cannot follow this melancholy matter further here, but it must still be a puzzle to all admirers of Livingstone that he could not only believe the word of his malevolent brother but could also be unjust and ungracious to an incredible degree towards a man who was never allowed to call witnesses in his defence. It is a sad blot on the Livingstone scutcheon and we gladly return to his third trip up the Shire, this time with Kirk and his brother, and no less than forty men to act as carriers on the march beyond the cataracts.

They stayed for a night at the village of Mboma, which was where Port Herald now is, a day after one of their men had been drowned from the capsize of a boat towed behind in the dark when the launch ran on to a sandbank. Needless to say, Livingstone is most assiduous in taking the latitudes of all the principal stopping places. He is quite susceptible to the scenery and speaks of 'the majestic mountain, Pirone, to which we have given the name of Mount Clarendon', while a little further up river he mentions 'the southern end of the grand Milanje range rising in the form of an unfinished sphinx, looking down on Lake Shirwa'.

Having arrived at Chibisa's village they left the launch, and the cavalcade (or *ulendo*, to use the local name) of forty men set off for the Shire highlands once more, this time keeping to the valley of the Likubula, a tributary which rises a little to the north of Blantyre. They kept to the west of their former route over the highlands and came down on to the upper Shire somewhere near Liwonde. They marched up the east bank till they came to Lake Malombe where they were mystified on being told that there was no other lake or *nyansa*. The mistake was due to the local people regarding Malombe as part of Lake Nyasa, which is more or less correct. On September 16th they reached Lake Nyasa proper (which Livingstone always spelt with a double *s*), just two months before the German Dr Roscher reached it about half-way up on the eastern side.

Here they discovered that they were camping on the high road

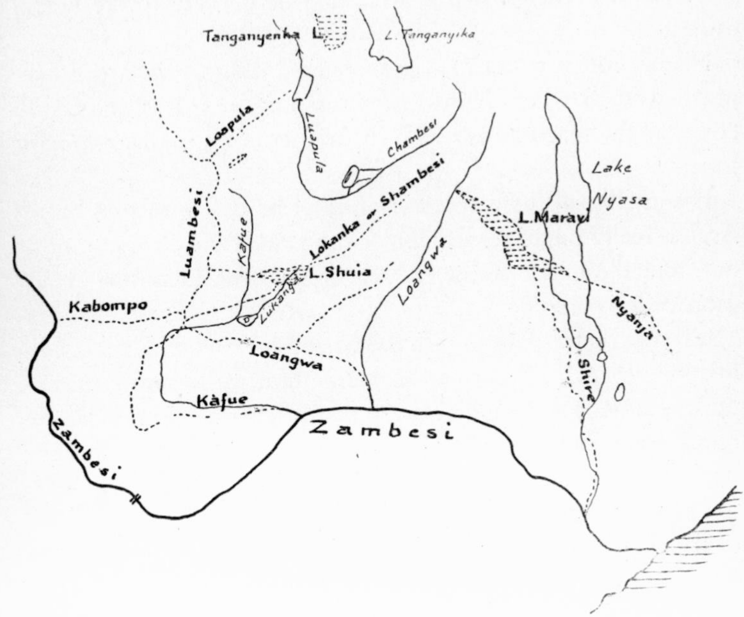

From Livingstone's map of 1857—dotted lines, heavy lettering
From modern map—continuous lines, thin lettering
Comparison of modern map with Livingstone's intelligent guesswork from Arab accounts

for Arab slave gangs being brought from the far interior round the southern end of the lake on their way to Kilwa on the coast. In fact it was on the lake shore that they saw the first slave gang they had met, and one which was afterwards captured by their friends on H.M.S. *Lynx*.

After eighteen months of stress and disappointment here at last was a geographical discovery of real importance. And how it must have puzzled the explorer! In the map published in the

Journal of the Royal Geographical Society after his trans-Africa journey he had done his best to reconcile a series of reports he had collected during his trip. The two he regarded as of most value were those from Syde ben Habib in Barotseland and Senhor Candido in Tete, and it was now clear that he should have given more credence to the Arab and hardly any to the Portuguese.

His last journey, yet to come, covered most of the area to the north-west of where he was now standing, so it is of interest to compare the map of 1857 with the modern one, in diagrammatic form.

His intelligent interpretation of what he had been told by the Arab is really rather remarkable. Thus Lake Tanganyika is not far out, and the upper Kafue, which he calls the Luambesi is also more or less correct.

It is true that he fails to turn the Chambezi round to become the Luapula, for which no one can blame him so he runs it into the upper Kafue. The Luapula was to be his *bête noir*, because later he removed it from the Zambezi system and tried to connect it with the Nile instead of with the Congo.

The Lukanga and its small lake Suye are badly magnified of course. His joining of the Kafue to the Kabompo represents, I take it, the impression he had that the divide between those rivers was marshy and indefinite. He was badly out over the course of the Luangwa, but he had no information at all about it.

Lake Maravi, as reported by Candido, was long and shallow and with a mountainous island in it called Murumba. Livingstone may have had doubts as to whether this was not just the flooded Shire north of Mount Morumbala, but he evidently decided to give Candido the benefit of the doubt, so it appears with two impossible outlets, the Shire and the Nyanja.

He was not the man to be worried about post mortems, inquiring who had given him the wrong card and where his finesse had gone astray, and he was extraordinarily calm over the fine new deep lake he had found which certainly was not the fabulous Lake Maravi. He may have dimly recognised that he had discovered the entrance to Africa he was seeking, not exactly a water route perhaps but one which would cut the slave trade roads much more directly than would the Zambezi route.

His chance meeting with the slave gang on the shores of the Lake was an omen indeed, both for him and the missionaries who followed him, and most certainly for the Arab slave-traders. His two recent journeys had done more than that, for his plan had always been to find a healthy locality for the missionaries and traders who were to undercut the slave trade, and he recognised the Shire Highlands as exactly what he wanted for that.

On the journey back from the Lake all the white men got ill from eating badly cooked cassava. This wonderful plant is the greatest safeguard against famine that Africa possesses. It is easily propagated by sticking short lengths of the stem slanting-wise into the soil, preferably raised in a mound and it more or less looks after itself, the tubers forming underground after a few months' growth and continuing to swell for another two years. The dark green leaves can be used as a salad or relish, locusts will not touch them and the tubers can be gathered at almost any time of the year. They are up to eighteen inches in length and occur in two varieties, one bitter and one sweet, the main difference being that the bitter one has a larger amount of prussic acid in it than the sweet, and requires more care in preparation. Most of the poisonous principle resides in the skin which is peeled with a knife leaving dead-white sticks of the consistency of potatoes. These may be pounded and sieved to a white flour in which form most of the poison evaporates or they may be cut up and boiled in two or three changes of water. Livingstone used to be careful in asking only for the sweet kind of cassava, which needs less preparation but on this occasion they seem to have been given the wrong kind and their cook was either ignorant or feckless.

It must be remarked here that Livingstone, in spite of being a doctor, was always rather careless about the food he used and the way it was cooked, and even about the water he drank. This is the more curious because he suffered far more from digestive troubles than from any other form of illness. The fact is that once camp was made in the late afternoon he was always so busy talking to the local headman, or preparing for astronomical observations or entering up notes in his journal that he left all cooking matters to his men, and indeed he rather prided himself on being able to manage on native foods.

Whatever the cause on this occasion the whole party were ill, and when they got to the *Ma-Robert* they were a sorry lot of invalids, with Livingstone heading the list.

I would like to refer the increase of carping criticism in his journal at this period to his ill health, but whatever the cause he is very bitter in his remarks, about some of his companions, about the Portuguese, about his ill-fated 'tin can'. Some of his orders at this time reflect his unhappy, almost disordered state of mind. For instance, he sent Kirk and Rae overland to Tete, a very dangerous journey for sick men and one which they barely survived, with orders to search Baines' boxes for goods he was suspected of stealing. Only a man with Kirk's tact could accomplish such a disagreeable task without lasting offence, and in fact he found nothing to sustain the imputation. Baines seems to have been an untidy storeman but nothing worse than that. In fact, some of the things he was accused of stealing were afterwards found. There is a note in Livingstone's journal some months later, 'found the box of fine powder which he had supposed lost', but even in the privacy of his diary this strange man could not add that it was one of the items he had accused Baines of taking.

Another trouble at this time was the changing attitude of the Portuguese, yet here again he failed to realise that his own strictures on them were the root cause. There is a great deal of moralising about slavery and he was speaking very plainly to the officials about it with the very natural result that they began to withhold assistance.

When Kirk and Rae brought Baines down to the delta in canoes Livingstone cross-examined the latter in what appears to have been an ungracious manner, and he seems to have been at odds with every member of his party. Even the sturdy Petty Officer Rowe who had done so well in a station rather above his training comes in for sharp criticism: 'Rowe is growling because he did not get beer, porter, etc., and seems inclined to shew us we are dependent on him.' However, Baines went off in the *Lynx* to

Cape Town, as full of rancour as such a kindly little man could manage to be and Rae went off to England to superintend the construction of a steamer for the lake, though he was to be shipwrecked on the way and have endless trouble later in getting compensation for what he had lost.

Livingstone, at this time, seems to have had a genius for doing the right thing in the wrong way. It was no doubt right that Baines should go because his consistent ill health, added to Livingstone's strange distrust of his capabilities, prevented him from being a useful member of the expedition. Kirk would certainly have agreed to Baines being invalided home, but that idea never seems to have occurred to the leader.

Thornton, too, had been of little use, partly through youth and inexperience, but also because he had been left too much to his own devices. His dismissal too was probably the best thing but it was brought about in a most awkward way and with accusations tainted by Charles' malevolence towards the youth. To say 'he has joined himself to the Portuguese, attends their feasts and plays shy with Dr Kirk and Mr Rae' is a very ill-defined reason for dismissal, though it is obvious that Thornton really did not know what he ought to be doing.

The party in fact was crumbling and as a last shock to Livingstone came quarrels with his brother, which opened his eyes to some of his own shortcomings as a leader. These unsavoury details are mentioned here because they show how, with disruption of one kind or another encircling him Livingstone could still do the right thing, and at the moment the thing to do was to redeem his promise of taking the Makololo back to Sekeletu.

The one thing he failed to do was to get rid of his brother, yet he knew in his own mind that that was what he ought to do, for in his journal he writes: 'I am at a loss how to treat him. As an assistant he has been of no value. Photography very unsatisfactory —magnetism still more so. In going up with us now (to Sekeletu) he is useless as he knows nothing of Portuguese or the native languages. He often expected me to be his assistant instead of acting as mine.' It was in this unhappy frame of mind that they prepared for the major land journey up the Zambezi, and the start was ill-omened because many of the Makololo did not want to go. There was the strange spectacle of these men coming to refuse and Livingstone consenting 'to three only staying and they on account of sickness. The Makololo have learned no good of the Portuguese', but a further sentence gives the best reason for this reluctance of being taken 'home'. 'Many of the deserters were captives (slaves) of Sekeletu but were regarded as free men at Tette.'

In the end about ten remained, several deserting on the first few marches, which were very short indeed owing to Kirk and Charles Livingstone having severe attacks of fever.

Crested Crane

CHAPTER SIX

When he came at the Hill Difficulty he made no stick at that: nor did he much fear the lions; for you must know that his trouble was not about such things as those.

JOHN BUNYAN

The members of the expedition had now dwindled from seven down to three, with two naval ratings to look after the *Ma-Robert* while the three officers went off to fulfil the promise to Sekeletu to bring back the men Livingstone had taken five years before. To many men the toilsome journey back on his old track would have been a dull routine, especially after all his hopes had crashed of a route by water—a 'God's highway' as Sir Roderick Murchison incautiously called it —to the great Interior which was always Livingstone's aim.

He did not view it that way at all, and he took all his paraphernalia, sextant, chronometer, etc. just as if he were exploring a new route. Moreover, he determined not to miss any more vital sections of the river so he skirted the Kebrabasa rapids on the north side instead of going by the customary route to the south which he had followed before.

But before they started, in May after the rains had ended, there was an instance of the curious way in which this shy, rather uncouth and infinitely reserved leader treated his followers. Kirk's term of service, two years, was up in January and, as he wrote in his diary: 'The two years are accomplished. But there is work to be done, and the sooner the better. . . . I should not think of leaving the Doctor alone at this time—that is, if he wishes me.' But no wish came from the Doctor, he just never mentioned it. Three weeks later Kirk questioned him on future plans so as to get some indication of his wishes, but his leader said nothing: 'He did not continue the conversation but only remarked that he was ignorant of the intentions of the Government.'

Kirk's biographer, the late Sir Reginald Coupland, gives us the choice of two alternatives in explanation. Either they were both too shy to risk an answer which might have been a disappointment, or else, Livingstone might have been secretly wanting to do the journey alone. That he was ready to do it with his brother is negatived by what we have just quoted, nor can one easily believe that he still did not realise that Kirk was moulded in the same pattern as himself, as one who would strive to seek and not to yield.

The start of the journey was inauspicious, with fever prostrating his two white companions, and the children they had left behind them calling back his black companions, so that there were desertions reducing the party by one quarter of its proper size.

He left the *Ma-Robert* at Tete in the care of his two English sailors, but he hardly expected it to last until his return from the interior. In a breezy letter at this stage he wrote:

'Our steamer is done—a sham at best. We leave it on the river at Tette to be swept away by the next flood. . . . I am tired of being skipper, I engaged in it only not to be beat. . . .

'Got the loan of two donkeys, there being but three in the country. The Portuguese cultivate skin-diseases and drunkenness more than horseflesh and are asses themselves.'

Nevertheless, the account of this journey in his *Narrative* is the best part of the book, as though Livingstone felt more his old self, away from the Portuguese and with a minimum of white men in his party. For a while his style is that of *Missionary Travels* and there are long descriptions of the country they are passing through interspersed with pleasing anecdotes about the incidents of the way, the mode of pitching camp and so on.

They had to find a route away from the river, by-passing the terrible country they had clambered over in their reconnaisance of the Kebrabasa rapids. They met reasonable civility from the few villages they passed through, as there was plenty of food from a good season. His men killed an elephant, there was beer for all and the party began to pull together after losing the waverers. There is a short dissertation on food, from the gelatinous richness of elephants' foot, cooked in native style, to the sour grittiness of their Kaffir corn porridge, always insufficiently cooked and 'a failure, at least for a Scotch digestion that has been impaired by fever'.

Every traveller in Africa will, to this day, marvel how his cook-boy can prepare reasonably tasty meals for his *bwana* (master) and yet himself prefer the stodgy stiffness of his par-boiled meal, thrown into boiling water and stirred with a stick till it is of a doughy consistency to be rolled into balls, scorching hot, dipped into some relish and popped into a mouth which can endure as high a temperature as would scarify a European tongue.

As usual, Livingstone was concerned to question the headmen closely about their area, where their rivers ran to and whence they came, all to be sifted in his mind and set down on the sketch maps he kept adding to his notes.

They reached the river again at the rapids called Morumbwa where he measured the velocity of the water as about four knots. Incidentally, he logs it as '4 knots per hour', a curious mistake for a first-class geographer to make, a knot being a rate and not a distance.

He gives a graphic description of this critical point in the river, which had so wrecked his hopes, but he is still determined to prove it is not utterly impossible to pass and therefore is inclined to under-estimate rates and levels. Thus he made the difference in height between these rapids and Tete only a hundred and sixty feet by barometer, but adds 'it must be remembered that we had no simultaneous observations at the two stations'. The true difference of level appears to be about twice that figure.

Nevertheless, Livingstone was right in suggesting that at the height of flood the rapids are smoothed off and a passage might be made with a full powered craft. The portals of this 'Iron Gate' of the Zambezi are the onion-shaped mountain of Zakavuma, its smooth surface facing 'the more castellated form of Morumbwa across the broken water of the rapids rushing down a deep gorge between them'.

It is at this point in the *Narrative* that we get the best account in all of his writings of the kind of travel he used for all his journeys, so well described that one can understand the charm it had for him and for many another African traveller since. From it we can picture the long line of carriers passing along the native paths, each with bundle or box on head and a spear or two in hand, winding along at about 2½ miles an hour.

Each man's sleeping mat goes atop the load, tied at any angle and it is the first sight one has of a caravan, bobbing along above the tall grass which in early winter is often the height of a man. They seldom marched for more than five or six hours a day and Livingstone gives reasons for that measured progress: 'To hurry over the ground, abuse and look ferocious at one's native companions, merely for the foolish vanity of boasting how quickly a distance was accomplished, is a combination of silliness with absurdity quite odious.'

They were usually on the march by sunrise making a halt for breakfast about nine and another break for rest at mid-day. Camping early in the afternoon there was time for the white men to hunt for meat, for writing up journals, interviewing the local headmen and so on—a procedure still followed almost exactly by administrative officers going on tour round their districts.

By the time the short twilight has put an end to such occupations, the fires are lit, and cooking is afoot, and, Livingstone's description of the evening may spur other people to taste the delight of travelling in Central Africa:

'After the great business of cooking and eating is over, all sit round the camp-fires and engage in talking or singing. Every evening one of the Batoka plays his *sansa*, and continues at it until far into the night. At times animated political discussions spring up and the amount of eloquence expended on these occasions is amazing. The mis-government of Chiefs is an inexhaustible theme. "We could govern ourselves better," they cry. "so what is the use of chiefs at all, they do not work; now this must be bad, unjust and wrong." All shout to this a loud "ehe", equivalent to our "hear, hear!" Next the headman, Kanyata, and Tuba with his loud voice, are heard taking up the subject on the loyal side.

' "The Chief is the father of the people; can there be people without a father, eh? He is wise, but his children are fools."

'Tuba goes on generally till he has silenced all opposition; and if his arguments are not always sound, his voice is the loudest and he is sure to have the last word.'

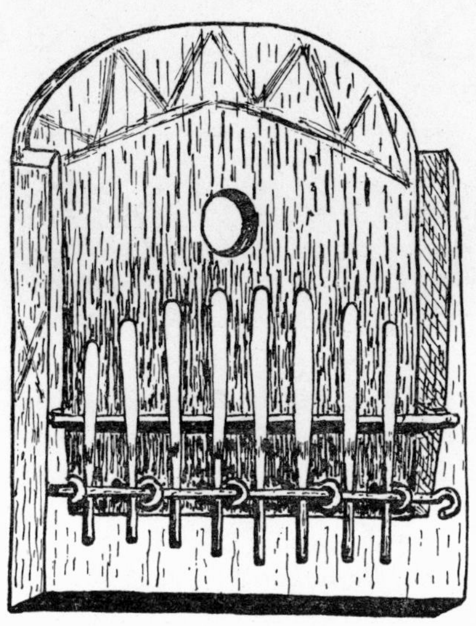

Sansa: musical instrument

Can we not see gatherings similar in essentials to this in every 'local' in England and realise that black and white are brothers under their skins?

The sansa is the most pleasing of the native African musical instruments, small and portable. It is made of strips of flattened native iron resting on a metal bridge and fastened down at one end, the other ends projecting over a miniature sound box. The instrument is grasped by the fingers of both hands, the thumbs being free to flick the ends of the strips producing notes something

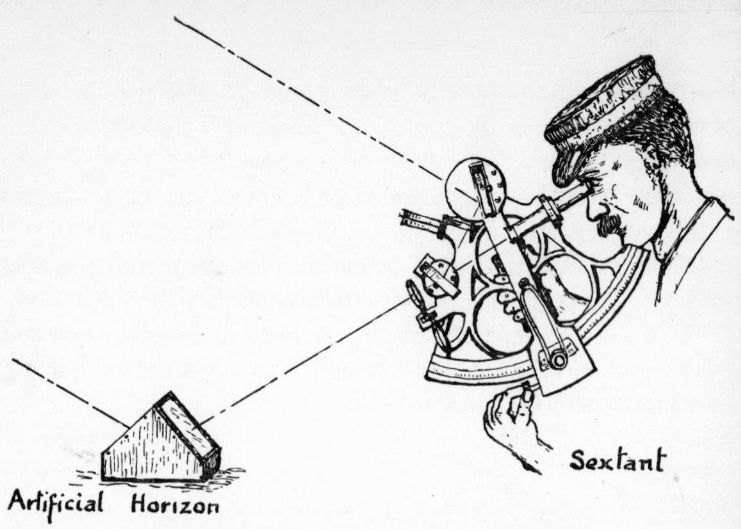

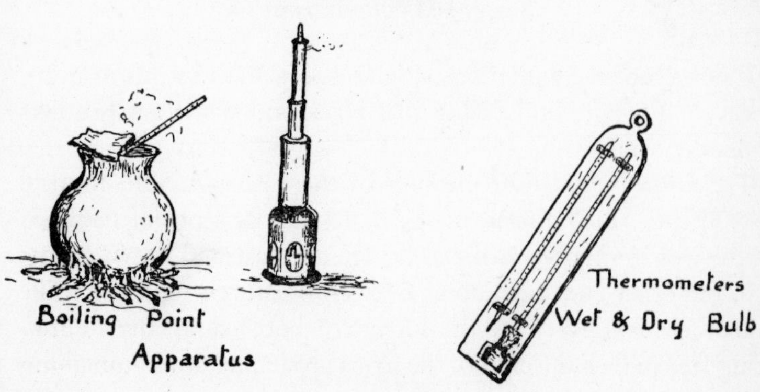

An impression of Livingstone's instruments

like those of a Jew's harp, set mostly in a minor key. The tinkle of a sansa to the low musical recitative of the player's voice is a fine sound for inducing sleep under the starry sky however hard the bed and coarse the blanket.

We cannot help feeling that as he wrote in this vein Livingstone was back in his early years of travel when he felt perfectly at one with his Africa and his Africans. He was usually the last to bed, for on most nights he was at work with his star sights or his journal and always first awake for his was the duty of rousing his companions.

This is perhaps the proper occasion to say something about his ceaseless work in navigation, as it should be regarded as an ever-present backcloth to all his travels. His three instruments were a sextant, a chronometer or watch keeping Greenwich Time and an artificial horizon, the originals of all of them being on view at the Scottish National Memorial Museum to Livingstone at his birth-place, Blantyre, near Glasgow.

Readers will be familiar with the appearance of the first two instruments but the horizon may need explanation. It is literally a shallow, rectangular iron tray which is filled with mercury to give a reflection of sun or stars from a perfectly level surface. To prevent ruffling of the mercury by the wind a cover of glass is set over the tray and the whole apparatus, together with the mercury carried in an iron bottle, is as heavy as the sextant itself in its solid mahogany box.

The operations connected with these instruments were, of course, a source of awe to his men and of superstition to those villagers who happened to see him at work, and the memory of what he did was so clear in their minds that it was a means by which, years later, Commander Young recognised the white man being described to him as being none other than Livingstone.

It was when Young came out to Nyasaland to find out whether the rumour that Livingstone had been killed was true, and he met a headman who lived on the route the explorer had taken. Asked to describe the boxes that this white man had with him, he said: 'There was one, a little one, in it there was water which was white. When you touched it by placing your finger in it, ah, behold it would not wet you, this same white water; I lie not.' When asked how the white man used it, he replied: 'He used to put it on the ground, and then he took another thing in his hand to look on the sun with.' The old chief gravely took up a stick and mimicked the action of pointing it to the sun and bringing it down to the artificial horizon.

Livingstone was a first-class observer with the sextant as any practised person will admit when he sees from his note-books how quickly he measured angles between the moon and a star. Some-

Jambala vil. 12 April 1859

Mer. Alt. Saturn 2)109 43 30 + 20 = 50

54 51 55 - 40" = 15

90

35 08 45

19 44 31

15 24 14

Facsimile of typical sight for latitude

times he managed to average one observation per two minutes, which is very good when the observer has to read and book the chronometer times himself and make the sextant readings by the poor light of a candle lamp. This in itself accounts for the scrawling figures to be found in his navigation note-books of which the above is a facsimile of a star sight for Latitude.

Those readers who have some notion of how a sight for latitude by the meridian altitude of a star is taken may like the following explanation of the simple sum. The altitude as measured by an artificial horizon is twice the true altitude so he halves the sextant reading, having first added on his Index Error of +20″. From this he subtracts the correction for Refraction, which he gets from a simple table and is 40″.

This figure is an altitude and he wants its complement, the Zenith Distance of the star, so he subtracts it from 90° to give him

35°08′45″. He then looks up the declination of Saturn in his Nautical Almanac and as it is northerly he subtracts it from his zenith distance to give him the Latitude 15°24′14″. Livingstone took literally thousands of such latitude sights in his twenty years odd of exploration and they are practically always accurate to within a mile.

For longitudes he had to use his chronometer and take altitudes of sun or stars to east or west of his meridian just as is done at sea. But this depended on his chronometer keeping an even rate, and this, with the shocks of land travel, could not be relied upon. So he also used the method of occultations of a star by the moon passing in front of it, and the somewhat similar method of lunar distances. Occultations were simple to observe, with a small telescope, but complicated in the computations involved. Lunar distances were tricky to observe with the sextant and also to compute.

It was his practice to send his figures to his friend Sir Thomas Maclear, the Royal Astronomer at the Cape, to re-calculate with more accuracy before he finally used the longitudes in his maps. His industry at this astronomical work can best be illustrated by saying that on his journey of three weeks to discover Lake Shirwa he took ten latitude sights, three observations for longitude by lunar distance and one by occultation. Further, his astronomical work-book for the first six months of that year, 1859, contains one hundred and ninety pages of his figures and calculations.

Such remarks will hardly interest the non-astronomical reader but they may convey an idea of his determination to have his maps correct whatever the hazards of the journey, the weather, his own health or occasional hostility from chiefs. Yet his navigation work was but a small part of his instrumental work, for he worked his thermometers and barometers harder than any traveller of those days.

At the Rhodes-Livingstone Museum there is one of his daily note-books used on this journey in which page after page is full of meteorological entries. Even to readers who find weather data uninspiring and unintelligible the thoroughness of Livingstone's work must be astounding. We can best illustrate it by quoting what observations he took on October 20th, 1860—the very day when they took that 'considerable risk' of shooting the rapids of Kariba Gorge, when two of the canoes were half swamped.

One would imagine that the day was full enough of other things to do, but here is his weather log for the day:

20 Oct 1810	*Time*	*Wet Bulb Thermometer*	*Dry Bulb Thermometer*	*Clouds*	*Wind*
Kariba	6¼ a.m.		80	0	Calm
	7		82	0	Calm
Zambezi Water 83.5					
	8		87	0	E
	9	68	88.5	0	E
Zambezi Water 86°					
	12	68	94.5	0	N E
	3	70	95	0	N E

Wind strong. In strong blasts it rises to 97.

The entry that accompanies the figures is equally laconic and barren of the personal incidents of the day. It reads: 'Went on 3 hours through the gorge, strange contorted rocks dip generally N and N.E. but it varies. Mid stream sluggish. A few people near lower end with patches of maize and tobacco. Wind rose and entered the gorge with great force . . .' and then, almost in parenthesis: '. . . waves half filled my canoe and swamped Charley's but being near shore nothing was lost.'

On a more normal day, such as five days earlier, he takes nine dry bulb temperatures and three wet bulb, between 5.30 in the morning and 6 at night. Ten days earlier still he had a field day with his thermometer, the record being as follows:

Shade	1 p.m.	102
In sun	3 p.m.	137.5
In shade	3 p.m.	103.5
Blood of Dr Kirk		99.5
Native blood		98.2

If this was his standard for meteorological work no wonder he had deposed his indolent brother from that duty long before and took all readings himself. It was the same in all his journeys even up to the last, for when he was within a month of his death in 1873 he was recording the rainfall each day, setting up his rain gauge at each halt and recording the amount before going on.

The natural question arises as to what use these myriads of figures have been. Livingstone himself never had the time to make more than broad deductions from them. It is to be hoped that some day a climatologist with that taste for statistics which distinguishes that breed of scientist will come along and analyse these masses of data, which are all to be found in Livingstone's daily note-books, all carefully dated, though not always clearly legible.

So they journeyed slowly along giving time for Livingstone to exercise to the full his extraordinary faculty for geography. He is delighted with the fertility of the plains near Chicova but he does not stop at that for he discerns two distinct river terraces of which the lower is the best soil while the upper is the habitat of either a grassy plain or a thorny jungle, or in clayey places, a *mopane* forest. He finds ample evidence of another coalfield, and to the amazement of the local people shows them that it will burn. He describes it as bubbling up in an open fire, giving out gas 'like good domestic coal, or like toasting cheese'.

Near the Kakolole rapids above Chicova they have to halt for two days, for the usual reason, that one of his men had shot a hippo and it must be consumed or made into a sort of temporary biltong, to last for a few days. True biltong needs a longer time, the meat being carved into long strips about half an inch thick and hung in the full sun for several days. The rather dry flesh of most African game glazes over in a few hours and resists the onslaught of countless flies, while if salt and saltpetre can be rubbed into it the meat lasts for months and preserves its flavour perfectly.

The enforced stay enabled Livingstone to muse at great length in his journal on such varied topics as game-pits for trapping hippo and what it is like to fall into one nine feet deep: on the habits of white ants and their enemies the black ants and the men's enemies, the red ants. It is not generally realised that Livingstone's party was preceded in this part of his journey by young Thornton who had gone nearly to the Kafue junction about a year earlier.

In justice to him it must be mentioned here, that he made the journey after he had received notice of dismissal from Livingstone and it was, therefore, a private venture of his own.

He had told his friends amongst the Portuguese, with whom Charles Livingstone had informed the leader that he was 'sky-larking', that he would like to see the country inland and two of them, Senhor Manuel and Senhor Clementina invited him to accompany them on a trading journey they were to make in the the late winter of 1859.

Part of his diary concerning the trip is in the Rhodes-Livingstone Museum and a study of it is enlightening in several respects. He was only twenty years of age at the time that he was more or less wished on to Livingstone by Sir Roderick Murchison, who evidently had a high opinion of his promise, but could not have had much personal contact with him.

Perusing this and other diaries of his, one is forced to the conclusion that his worst fault lay in his lack of experience, he just did not know what to do and no one told him what to do except in general and possibly unsympathetic terms. He would, in fact, work like a Trojan if he knew what to work at, a statement which is admittedly rather different to that of Dr Stewart three years later who wrote in his diary: 'Thornton is young and clever rather than able, opinionative and active, would work if one but knew how to get the work out of him,' To get work 'out of' a member of an expedition is not, of course, the right basis on which a leader should have to proceed, the urge to find out must come from the man himself, inspired perhaps by the leader but not blue-printed for the man.

Without the tale-bearing of Charles Livingstone, Thornton might have gradually become a useful member of the party, but it was unfair to expect of him what Murchison and Dr Livingstone undoubtedly did. Though trained, or perhaps only partially trained, at the School of Mines, Thornton was rather a free lance geologist, preferring to dodge from one aspect of the subject to another than to become as master of any section. He rather pottered about with his examination of the rocks he found, just as later on Stewart spoke of him as more fond of sailing a boat back and forth on the Zambezi than of getting anywhere with his sailing.

His diaries show him to be lethargic, the term that was used of him by Kirk, but that again was largely due to his lack of incentive or real interest in his work. Early in the expedition Livingstone praised him for his surveying of the lower river and he put in a tremendous amount of work at this, though he was only learning as he went along.

The style of his writing is dull and his spelling is so atrocious that one begins by thinking he was uneducated, where perhaps it was that he had no visual memory for words. Here are three sentences taken from a few pages of his diary to show what marvels of orthography satisfied him: 'My sissors were stolen tooday but I climbed to the pike of the volcanic crata. After that I shot at a guse on the bank of the river and followed a heard of babboons. I was ill with diorea last night.' Even with native names, which generally follow phonetic principles, his interpretation of sounds is so widely different from that of Livingstone's that it is very difficult to recognise place names from Thornton's diary as the same in his leader's.

He was adventurous enough and seems to have jumped at the chance of going with his Portuguese companions, who were indeed kind to him, though no doubt they profited by having an Englishman with them.

They left Tete on July 19th, and took the by-pass route to Chicova which all the traders used. He took quite an assortment of instruments with him; theodolite, sextant, compass, etc. and he used them all constantly and laboriously, if perhaps without great discretion. There are 'rounds of angles' at nearly every camp, but without any sketches to help him to recognise features at the next station. Nevertheless, with his memory to help him no doubt the maps he made subsequently, which the writer has not been able to see, were of value, and as detailed as the one which Livingstone commended. In between the copious angles the brief notes of each day's incidents are heavy reading. We have space for only one excerpt which is more interesting than most: 'Off early, went alone with only stick, compass and notebook. Fell into a large pitfall. It was round abt 9 or 10 ft deep, the sides were smooth. I hurt myself somewhat with the fall and at first almost despaired of getting out again. I searched my pockets for my knife but I had not it with me. Then I tried to work myself up putting my shoulders against one side my feet spread out against the side and my hands pressed flat against the side. At first I got up pretty eesily but the pit widened towards the mouth and my legs are short but I saw some sticks across the mouth to support the grass, they looked rotton but I carefully reached 2 with each hand and putting them near the edge carefully worked myself up a little more so that I saw a young tree which was growing close to the mouth. this I carefully laid hold of and then got easily out—very thankfull I felt when once again on the surface.'

However one may smile at the style and the spelling one must admit that this young man was learning the job of the explorer the hard way and without complaints. Nor was it any light journey to have almost reached the Kafue and when turned back by threats of attack by the Matabele, to have gone up the Loangwa with a few men and no Portuguese to help. He appears to have got as far up as the present Beit Bridge but the native names he uses have changed and he took no latitudes on this journey.

There is no mention of this journey in the *Narrative*, which even though Thornton was no longer a member of the expedition deserved some credit from his former leader. When Livingstone reached the ruins of Zumbo they found that two half-caste traders had, under orders from the Governor of Quilimane, re-established the former outpost there by putting up a small stockade and by making a murderous assault on a friendly and trusting chief.

They were still following their former route and came to the abundant game lands below the confluence of the Kafue River, so that they were rarely without meat for the whole company. They crossed the Kafue in canoes and were now passing through unexplored country; a little beyond the present Chirundu bridge over the Zambezi they bore westwards to avoid the hilly country round the Kariba Gorge. Needless to say, Livingstone was mapping all streams and other prominent features as he passed and compiling a map which has even now not been fully superseded.

They left the Zambezi at the large island of Mpande at the confluence of the Zongwe stream, which they followed up to the high Batoka plateau. Here, in July, they had frosts and a bracing winter climate and Kirk is very downright in saying, 'These Batoka lands are the only ones suited for Europeans between the coast and the interior along the Zambezi,' a prophecy which came true because they were then not far from the zone or belt of white occupation along the present railway line.

The party took much the same route along the divide as does road and railway and they were much impressed both by its fertility and the industry of the Batoka people.

They saw the spray-clouds of Victoria Falls at a distance of twenty miles, and on August 9th they reached it. Here they camped once more opposite the island of Kalai and went down to the Falls in canoes guided as before by Tuba Makoro—the 'Smasher of Canoes', and Livingstone rather spreads himself in his journal on the dangerous passage. They did hit a rock and half fill the canoe before they reached Garden Island.

So many people have visited Garden Island since that time, and usually with a certain amount of trepidation, that it is worth recording Livingstone's feelings, as, for the second time, he trusted himself to the local guide or genius of the Falls. Tuba was a very large impressive man and he took care to live up to his reputation as the only man who had the proper medicine with which to ensure safety amidst the rapids immediately above the Falls:

'To confess the truth, the very ugly aspect of these roaring rapids could scarcely fail to cause some uneasiness in the minds of newcomers.

'Before entering the race of waters we were requested not to speak, as our talking might diminish the virtue of the medicine, and no one with such boiling eddying rapids before his eyes, would think of disobeying the orders of a "canoe smasher".'

Tuba in fact belonged to the age-old race of showmen, and, as Livingstone divined, his patter about silence had a better reason than medicine:

PUBLIC LIBRARY, PLAINFIELD, N. J.

'He doubtless thought that talking on board might divert the attention of his steersman at a time when the neglect of an order, or a slight mistake, would be sure to spill us all into the chafing river.

'At times it seemed as if nothing could save us from dashing in our headlong race against the rocks, which, now that the river was low, jutted out of the water. Never was canoe more admirably managed: once only did the medicine seem to have lost something of its efficacy.

'We were driving swiftly down; a black rock, over which the white foam flew, was directly in our path; the pole was planted against it as readily as ever, but it slipped just as Tuba put forth his strength to turn the bow off.

'We struck hard, and were half-full of water in a moment.

Livingstone's sketch of passage to Garden Island

Tuba recovered himself as speedily, shoved off the bow, and shot the canoe into a still shallow place to bale out the water.

'Here we were given to understand that it was not the medicine which was at fault, *that* had lost none of its virtue; the accident was owing entirely to Tuba having started without his breakfast. Need it be said we never let Tuba go without that meal again?'

Livingstone knew that he was a poor hand with the pencil or paint brush, but he could not let this second visit to the Falls pass without attempting some pictorial record. In his sketch book, now at the Rhodes-Livingstone Museum, there are several examples of his art, relating to this visit. One of them seems to be a memory sketch in pencil of this perilous passage and we reproduce a careful tracing of it.

It is not labelled so we are permitted to allocate names ourselves to these tense figures, so juvenile in style of drawing but so dramatic in their pose, and showing such economy of line. Surely the vast figure at the stern must be Tuba himself even though he seems to be at the wrong end of the canoe, towering above his two assistants. The bearded white man must be either Kirk or his brother Charles and the bent back and attitude of taking it easy inclines me to guess that it is Charles Livingstone.

It is very revealing to compare this rough pencil scrawl with the beautiful sketch by Thomas Baines facing p. 176. The honours of artistry lie with Baines, of course, but truth has forsaken him: even the skilful Batoka canoemen do not stand up when negotiating the rapids, nor do they use graceful pointed dugouts for

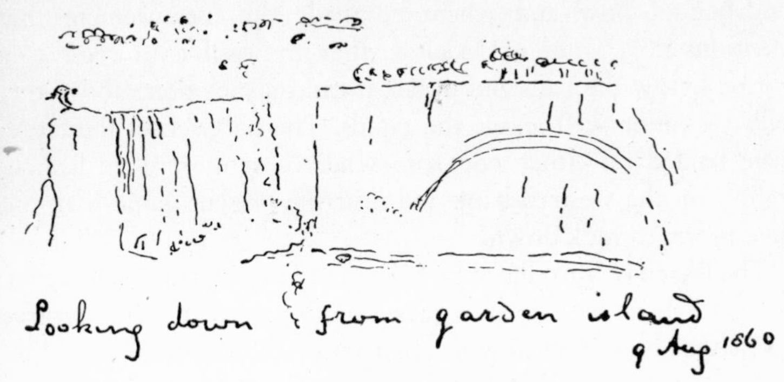

Livingstone's sketch from Garden Island

that service. Nor, one imagines, would Baines and Chapman recline in that *dolce far niente* fashion, for they were just as anxious as Livingstone when they made the same passage two years later.

Garden Island, now renamed Livingstone Island, projects slightly into the vast 'fizzure' and therefore permits a view along most of the mile-long trough when the spray clouds are not too dense. Looking across the gulf you have the main falls to your right and consequently the highest of the spray clouds is usually there, beyond which can be seen the densest part of the rain forest, and, in the morning, the best of the rainbows.

Below, you may get glimpses of the turmoil at the bottom, and the ridge of rock which there runs down the centre. To the left you can see where the water from each end of the Falls 'unite midway in a fearful boiling whirlpool and seek an exit and find an outlet' into the Boiling Pot and the First Gorge. An outline of all these features can be recognised if we once more call upon Livingstone's sketchbook for the first drawing ever made of the scene described above, including a suspicion of one of his companions peering over the cliff. The perspective is somewhat awry and there is no nonsense about putting in the difficult spray clouds but the essentials of the scene are there, which is all that Livingstone cared. 'Into this chasm', he writes, 'of twice the depth of Niagara-fall, the river, a full mile wide, rolls with a deafening roar: and this is Mosi-oa-Tunya or the Victoria Falls.'

Another of his sketches, this time in a colour wash, is the only evidence of how and where he made the measurements he mentions in a letter to Maclear. It is impossible to cross the gorges below the Falls and in fact it can only be done above the Falls by canoe well above the rapids. The party must therefore have landed on either side, somewhere near the present launch station on the western bank and near the present game park on the eastern, to walk down.

The sketch is reproduced facing p. 112 for two reasons, the first being to show how little regard Livingstone had for its artistic merit that he uses it to enter his routes and measurements. The second reason is to show how thoroughly he did it; the 1180 yards along the rim of the chasm through the rain forest would be quite a task for chain-men even now when there is a path and no chance of meeting buffaloes, as Baines did a few years later.

The figures show that he measured to the first sharp bend, just below the Falls Hotel where one now takes a stroll after dinner, and on the other side to the second bend where now one can descend on a trolley to the Generating Station. Garden Island is the patch of trees about the centre of the Falls themselves and just above the entry '130 feet' is where he took his companions down the eastern end of the Falls, that figure referring apparently to the width of the promontory leading to the Knife Edge.

Having added the 1180 yards on one side to the 650 yards on the other, he writes, at the bottom of his sketch, 'Say 1860 yards' since that was the year of his visit. It is actually 1900 yards.

He was even more profoundly stirred than before by the

grandeur of the great Falls, and in a letter to Sir Thomas Maclear he is severely practical over measurements and whimsical over its appearance:

'We found the depth to be 310 feet and the breadth we call 1860 yards by way of assisting the memory though it is a little more. The sextant gave 80 feet as the width of the fizzure at Garden Island but we could not throw a stone across so it may be more, but it is not more than 80 yards.

'If you come to the other side of the columns of vapour you have the strangest sight conceivable (now for my exquisite drawing to enlighten the darkness of the observatory): the crack is prolonged in a most remarkable zig-zag manner, the promontories formed thereby are of the same level as the bed of the river above the falls.

'If this isn't a lion worth seeing, aye, that and all. Nothing but a painting in oils could do it justice.

'Between ourselves I perpetrated the mad freak of going down the end of the fizzure at X and Dr K. and my brother followed.'

He measured the depth of the Falls by lowering a line, weighted with bullets and a square of white cloth, over the edge, a member of the party watching the cloth to see that it did not catch on a ledge. This operation must have been very mysterious to his black companions because when Arnot got there twenty years later they told him what a wonderful magician the Nyaka (doctor) had been, for he lowered a line and brought up a white fluttering bird from out of the clouds of spray, and some pearls (bullets). Others went so far as to assert that Livingstone crossed the falls with the aid of some string and calico.

There is a good description of the first three gorges in the *Narrative* but his appreciation of the nature of erosion deserts him here since he says: 'In this gigantic, zigzag, yet narrow trough, the rocks are all so sharply cut and angular, that the idea at once arises that the hard basaltic trap must have been riven into its present shape by a force acting from beneath.'

The gorges were, of course, formed by erosion following lines of weakness in the rocks, which are difficult to trace on the surface but are easily recognisable in the oblique air photograph facing p. 129. In this, taken from above the Falls Hotel, the road and railway are seen curving round to the bridge which Cecil Rhodes insisted should be built within sight of the Falls past the rain forest to the left. It was taken at a time of exceptionally low water so that the lines of weakness referred to above should be apparent. As Dr Bond points out in his paper on the origin of the Falls, the directions of the Falls and the first gorge are exactly paralleled in

Kudu

these lines seen through the water above the Falls, showing where the Falls will be by, say, A.D. 3000.

Such incipient cracks can be simulated closely if you take a slab of junket or jelly and place it on a wet slab or table. If you then push it gently over a low ridge on the table and then over another ridge inclined at a slight angle to the first one, two sets of cracks will form and close again as the slab reaches a level surface again, forming lines of weakness without appearing as obvious cracks. The lavas which formed the platform for the Zambezi here were of the kind that flow slowly and for great distances and the cracks which led to the formation of the gorges one by one may have been formed in some such way as described for the junket.

One sentence of Livingstone's is so graphic that it deserves remark here: 'The whole body of water rolls clear over, quite unbroken; but after a descent of ten or more feet the entire mass becomes like a huge sheet of driven snow. Pieces of water leap

Baines and Chapman on the Zambezi, 1862
from a painting by Thomas Baines
Photo: Central African Archives

off it in the form of comets with tails streaming behind, till the whole snowy sheet becomes myriads of rushing, leaping, aqueous comets.' This is a simile which should appeal to millions of television viewers in England since the B.B.C. occasionally uses a film of part of the Victoria Falls as an 'interlude' item, though, for some reason, viewers are not told that it is from Central Africa.

They found that the hippos had destroyed the plantation of young trees on Garden Island that he had planted in 1885, but he planted more, with little hope of their survival. When a party came there three years later they had once more disappeared. To the 'D.L. 1855' that Livingstone had carved on a tree his brother Charles added C.L. 1860, but the tree had gone by 1880, or more probably the bark had overgrown the initials.

Marching on to Sesheke where Sekeletu was residing he found the state of the Makololo kingdom somewhat parlous. Not only was Sekeletu suffering from a loathsome skin disease and remaining hidden from his people but the true Makololo were decreased in number and in so obvious a minority that their hold over Barotse and Batoka was dwindling, to disappear altogether about four years later in a wholesale massacre of the last remnants. As Livingstone said, 'Sebituane's grand empire was crumbling to pieces,' and, when he heard of the *débâcle* later on, he wrote, 'This fate we deeply deplore, for whatever other faults the Makololo might justly be charged with, they did not belong to the class who buy and sell each other, and the tribes who have succeeded them do.'

In spite of these impending events hanging over the Makololo, Livingstone was obviously happy to be amongst his pet tribe again and the *Narrative* is full of anecdotes about them and their ways. They pressed him to come, with Mrs Livingstone, to establish a station on the healthy Batoka highlands to which they would then remove, no longer in fear of the Matabele. Sekeletu offered to set aside a section of his country for the special use of the English, and desired above all to have Dr Kirk, whom he took to at once.

Livingstone does not vouchsafe his own opinion on these offers and that perhaps is a clear indication that the explorer and liberator had overcome the missionary in him. With equal justice, however, we may assume that he thought he could do more useful work round Lake Nyasa where he would be astride the path of the slave trader.

On the other hand, in a letter from Tete after he had returned from this journey he says what he can about the Makololo people as suitable material for a missionary to deal with: 'The Makololo are a noisy set of blackguards, but live in a jolly, careless way and have plenty of time, and some inclination to be taught as an amusement. There are numbers of young men of good sense who would attach themselves (to an English missionary), noisy boisterous rascals but intelligent and respectful.' This sounds very much like what Pope meant by damning with faint praise and even had the Makololo survived as a group the London Missionary Society might well have paused before sending anyone to amuse them by teaching them.

The fact is, no one except Livingstone ever did have much good to say for the Makololo though we must add that only Oswell ever had the chance of meeting them in their disciplined days under Sebituane.

His terms of very much qualified approval of them are much the same as one can hear any day from administrative officers in Africa who have been in charge of tribes such as the Masai, the Turkana and many others who live in a jolly, careless way but are very respectful to those who like and understand them.

Livingstone was lent his own old horse, now twelve years old, to go one hundred and twenty miles across to Linyanti to fetch medicines etc. from his old waggon which had been standing for eight years, inviolate all that time to all except white ants. He did the journey in three days each way, which says much for Livingstone's stamina and even more for the horse.

On September 17th, 1860, the party began their return march, and as they could not again take carriers all the way to Tete, they were escorted by the Makololo to the Zambezi below the Falls, where they could purchase canoes for river transport. Two of the escort were to go right through to Tete and bring back medicines for Sekeletu, but it was later found that they did not go back, for lack of companions to make a sufficiently large party. One of these two, Ramakukane, became a chief on the Shire and was of doubtful value when the white men came there twenty years later.

Livingstone was determined not to miss seeing any important features of the river this time and he took his party over the very rough country just below the Falls. With a few men he made a special digression to see the Moamba Falls or rapids, which are some twenty miles to the East.

He did not climb down the cliffs here to inspect them closely, perhaps because they were not very spectacular to a man who had just been surveying and even climbing down to the base of the Victoria Falls. Indeed his main object was to find out where the river first became navigable by canoes.

Nevertheless, these Chimamba Falls, as they are now called, are very impressive and deserve fuller mention. Even now only a handful of Europeans have ever followed Livingstone into this difficult country, but fortunately one of them was the distinguished geologist, W. G. Lamplugh, from whom I was privileged to hear some account of the falls in 1919. In his printed description he says: 'Insignificant in height, it is true, but when one stands on the brink of the lower cataract and sees the whole volume of the great Zambesi converging into a single pass only fifty or sixty feet in width, shuddering, and then plunging for twenty feet in a massive curve that seems in its impact visibly to tear the grim basaltic rocks asunder, one learns better than from the feathery spray-fans of the Victoria Falls, what force there is in the river, and one wonders no longer at the profundity of the gorge.' A breathless sentence worthy of what must be a breath-taking scene.

They crossed the Kalomo about twelve miles from its confluence and marched on till they reached the Zambezi again at the large island of Chilombe where chief Sinamane, a vassal of Sekeletu was to provide canoes. They could purchase only two canoes and borrow three others so some of the party had to continue marching along the banks, where they fared very well at the hands of the friendly villagers. The canoe party seem to have had few adventures with the rapids which caused such delay to Major Gibbons, coming up river forty years later, with their steam-powered boat the *Constance*, two months later in the year.

A comparison of the experiences of the two expeditions shows the enormous difference between coming down a river and going up. At the Kariba Gorge Gibbons had to dismantle his boats, boilers and all, and portage them by land, taking four days of very hard labour. Only two miles above their new launching they encountered the Kaiungwa rapids, called the Nakabele by Livingstone, which caused more trouble, while just above the junction of the Sanyati river they took two days to negotiate the Nakansala rapids.

Waterbuck

In the *Narrative* one page suffices for all three of these rapids though they had to land and inspect those of the Kariba before entrusting themselves to the swift water, and Livingstone admits that they were taking a considerable risk.

It is interesting to note his remarks on the country just below the present Chirundu road bridge, which has recently been set aside as a Game Reserve, through which every car between the two Rhodesias will pass: 'An hour's walk on the right bank, morning or evening, reveals a country swarming with wild animals: vast herds of pallahs, many waterbucks, koodoos, buffaloes, wild pigs, elands, zebras and monkeys appear, with the fresh spoor of elephants and rhinoceroses which had been at the river during the night.' He is usually far more interested in birds, and particularly in their song, than in the quadrupeds, but where, as in this district, he is surrounded by all kinds of game he makes a few notes on them.

He is much interested in the way in which the Lord of the Forest, the elephant, pushes down trees and sweeps through dense bush as though it were not worthy of notice, and the noise of the blind, blundering, thundering gallop of buffalo when alarmed, crashing their way to safety. The way in which the different kinds of buck carry their heads attracted his notice as it does that of every one who sees them, and the variations in their type of horns.

No doubt he wondered why the heavily-built but slim-legged kudu lays his spiralled horns along his back as he charges through the thorn bush which is his habitat, while the noble waterbuck with horns curved forwards carries his head high through the reeds he favours as his haunt.

That heraldic beast, the sable antelope, on the other hand, curves his neck and takes the brunt of the branches on the stout lower portion of his ringed horns, keeping the sharp points, his weapon of defence, safely just above his shoulders.

He remarks elsewhere upon the curious loping gait of his own discovery, the swamp-loving lechwe, carrying head and horns low and out of sight until pursued, when he raises them high and jumps in the air as do wild dogs when hunting, to catch a glimpse of his enemy as he flees from him.

In spite of Major Gibbons' difficulty in coming up from the Kebrabasa rapids his opinion of the navigability of the Zambezi was much the same as Livingstone's for this eight hundred stretch of the river. He writes: 'I venture to predict that for at least six months of the year steamers will make this passage without encountering any current exceeding five knots per hour and seldom more than half that rate.'

The author would venture to suggest that the large native canoes would be better than steamers unless heavy freight were to be carried. These furnished with the type of outboard motor which has its propeller on a long shaft will move a thirty-foot canoe at four knots and if a second one is clamped to the other side, at six knots or more. The propeller can be instantly lifted out of the water and when swung at right angles will turn the craft in its own length. It is worthy of note too that hippos dislike the noise and will not attack a dugout which has a motor.

At the Karivua rapids a few miles above Zumbo they measured the highest velocity of current, six knots, and but for the presence of mind of his men there might have been disaster. 'The canoes entered (the rapids) without previous survey, and the huge jobbling waves of midcurrent began at once to fill them. Without a moment's hesitation two men lightened each by jumping overboard.' They swam alongside and steered the swamping canoes to the foot of the rapid. At the next rapid they carried the goods overland for about one hundred yards to avoid a second swamping, and the total length of these narrows is about thirty miles.

They were now in a hurry, as it was November and the rains were due to begin, and they reached the gateway to the Kebrabasa Rapids by the 11th of that month. They hoped to save some miles marching in the bad country by running the first few rapids. It not only proved impossible but it was by nothing less than a miracle that Kirk and his two paddlers were saved from drowning, with the loss of precious things such as all Kirk's note-books and botanical drawings.

So the whole party had once more that weary climbing up and down the huge hills on the north side which they had suffered from before, during which an incident occurred which finally rounded off Kirk's opinion of the character of Charles. The two doctors were separated from the party and were without food for thirty-six hours. They were very exhausted and fired shots to attract the attention of Charles and the others. He heard the shots but took no notice of them. Livingstone turned on his brother and there was yet another open quarrel between them, in which it was revealed how much Charles had slandered all the members of the expedition. The ineptness and unsuitability of the expedition's 'moral agent' had been clear even to the leader long before this of course, and yet he would not get rid of him, presumably for family reasons.

For Kirk the whole journey had been ruined by this friction between the brothers and now that he had lost all his notes he wrote rather bitterly to Sir Roderick Murchison, 'We have kept faith with the Makololo though we have done nothing else.'

They had, in fact, done a great deal else, including a survey of the whole of the Zambezi and full knowledge of its potentialities, in the six months' trip. When they reached Tete they found important news awaiting them which cheered them up, and their two sailors, left in charge of the *Ma-Robert*, had made shift to pass the time with good humour if not exactly with profit. They had ideas on farming, so they bought sheep and fowls and two monkeys, and they sowed vegetables and cotton.

Hippos robbed their vegetable garden, the monkeys ate all the eggs, the sheep ate the cotton, crocodiles ate the sheep and the natives stole the fowls. Livingstone was much pleased with them in spite of their ill success as farmers, and his own anecdote of their manner of trading is worth repeating from the *Narrative*: 'They had invented an original mode of settling a bargain; having ascertained the market price of provisions they paid that but no more. If the traders refused to leave the ship till the price was increased, a chameleon, of which the natives have a mortal dread, was brought out of the cabin. The chameleon settled every dispute in a twinkling.' One can only reflect how much happier the journey to Sekeletu would have been if Livingstone had taken these sailors with him and left his brother to look after the ship.

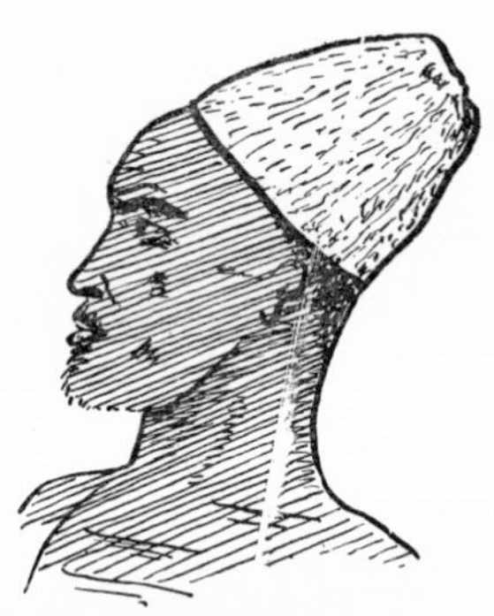

An Arab slave-raider

CHAPTER SEVEN

In the doorway stood many men in armour to keep it, being resolved to do to the men that would enter what hurt and mischief they could.

JOHN BUNYAN

It must be clear from the last chapter that the morale of the expedition was at a low ebb when they reached Tete. Kirk himself was resolved to terminate his extended commission on it, indeed he writes quite bluntly in his diary, 'I have no desire to be any longer on it.' What Livingstone would have done had his only good officer retired at this point can only be guessed, but he would probably have done what he did two years later, gone all alone to further the exploration of Lake Nyasa.

As it turned out, the news waiting for them in their mail at Tete revived the party and Livingstone at last made a direct request to Kirk that he should stay and help in the re-casting of their plans, which were consequent on this news. The main items were that the new vessel, the *Pioneer*, for which they had asked, was on the way out, that the Home Government approved of Livingstone's plan to try and reach Lake Nyasa via the Rovuma river, and finally that a large party of missionaries was also on its way. The latter was the answer to Livingstone's concluding words in his missionary propaganda speech at Cambridge in 1857: 'I beg to direct your attention to Africa. I know that in a few years I shall be cut off in that country, which is now open; do not let it be shut again. Do you carry out the work which I have begun. I leave it with you.'

He had heard before he left for his journey to Sesheke that plans were shaping for a mission from the English Universities and in fact in a letter written on the way up the Zambezi he had stated that it was 'the best news we have got since we came to Africa'.

So the moral barometer for Kirk and Livingstone began to rise again, and this is reflected in their letters, but not, curiously enough, in the *Narrative* written four years later. In the chapter concerned with their arrival at Tete there is not a single word of the news that had sent them hot foot down to the mouth of the Zambezi to await the new ship and the new missionaries. No reader of that book is ever allowed an insight into either the hopes or the fears of its strange author, which would have made so much better reading than the faults of the Portuguese or the horrors of slave trading or the veiled criticisms of his companions.

The prospect of a new ship did much to reconcile the party to the loss of their own craft. In a letter Livingstone said with grim humour that they started from Tete in both the leak-ridden 'Asthmatic' and the worm-eaten pinnace 'intending to stick to that which swam longest'. The pinnace gave up the ghost at Lupata Gorge so they used her as fuel to keep the launch going, but she too sank about a day above Sena.

They reached the Kongone mouth in hired canoes at the beginning of 1861 and had to wait a month for the arrival of two cruisers and the new expedition vessel, the *Pioneer*.

The story of Livingstone now becomes very involved since he was in conscience bound to look after the new mission party and yet his prior purpose was to prosecute his inquiries about the interior and measures for combating the slave trade. He tried hard to weld the two aims together, and in a measure he succeeded, until disaster overtook the missionaries.

The leader of the latter, Bishop Mackenzie, and Dr Livingstone had a very good opinion of each other to begin with, but two strong-willed men can rarely work smoothly in double harness when the prime objects are different. The Bishop was all for taking his party at once to the Shire Highlands where their work was to be but Livingstone did not dare to let them go alone into such country and therefore had to persuade them to go to the island of Johanna in the Comoro group, between Africa and the northern end of Madagascar while he himself undertook the duty, for which he had instructions from Lord John Russell, of testing the navigable capacity of the Rovuma river, the only one outside Portuguese territory which gave any promise of a reasonable route to the interior. The Bishop came too and they found that they could not get the *Pioneer*, drawing five feet of water, more than thirty miles up the Rovuma and after several fever-laden weeks they had to return to the Zambezi. The real testing of the new route had therefore to be postponed but the preliminary excursion had brought Livingstone out in a new light, as a ship-master, to take the place of the fever-stricken officers.

He himself mentions the matter slightingly and humorously: 'The habit of finding geographical positions on land renders it an easy task to steer a steamer with only three or four sails at sea, where if one does not run ashore, no one follows to find out an error and where a current affords a ready excuse for a blunder.'

We cannot follow in detail the struggle to get the *Pioneer* up to Chibisa's, the village eight miles below the Cataracts of the Shire which became the starting point for the march up to the highlands four thousand feet above. One or two sources of trouble became apparent, including the fact that when hauling over sandbanks was to be done the Bishop and two of the missionaries willingly lent a hand but the others were content to sit in the cabin reading. In fact the party were selected in as great a hurry and with as little care as had been the case with the expedition itself. Nor can we detail the circumstances under which Livingstone freed the whole eighty-four of a slave gang from being marched off to Tete, and the inevitable consequences when the Bishop and Livingstone had military action forced upon them.

There is a pleasing picture of the march in one of the Bishop's letters written just after they had passed old Chiradzulu and were nearing Zomba Mountain on the left and on the right 'the distant peaks and precipices of the Mlanje Mountains', which provide the finest scenery in all Nyasaland. 'We were a strange party,' wrote the Bishop, 'Livingstone tramping along with a steady heavy tread which kept one in mind that he had walked across Africa.'

The mission station was placed at Magomero, rather farther from the Shire than was wise, but on a well-chosen site as far as water supply and defence were concerned, and there Livingstone left them to go back to his long deferred plan of carrying a boat up to survey Lake Nyasa.

This was a real geographical journey and deserves our close attention.

We can best understand what he wanted to do on this and indeed his next two visits to the lake region if we visualize the topography by means of a block diagram, that is to say, a perspective view of the lake and its surroundings as seen from the south. It shows more clearly than a map how his routes were determined by the shape of the lake and its steep shore lines, for it is a typical example of the Great Rift Valley system of Africa, which is unique in the world.

Livingstone's path was up the cataracts from the Lower to the Upper Shire, overlooked, particularly on the east, by the escarpment or shoulder of the Shire Highlands, and this again is overlooked by the remarkable mass of Mlanje Mountain and the more central one of Mount Zomba. Magomero is on the line between them but much closer to Zomba.

The long line of the Lake itself shows the full Rift, though its true depth, to three hundred feet below sea level, is not apparent. The diagram shows too the characteristic feature of the rift valleys, the gash itself flanked by higher mountains, so that the drainage is away from the rift valley except where, as on the western side, river erosion has extended the lower land well back from the rift proper.

In the far distance are to be seen the three major mountain areas on the flanks of the rift, the Livingstone Mountains on the east and the Nyika plateau overlooking the longer lower Vipya plateau on the west of the Lake itself.

They started on August 6th, that is to say, in the coolest part of the year, all three officers and a seaman with a score of their Makololo who were to be a land party, marching parallel to the boat along the shores of the lake.

The boat was the lightest they could come by, a four-oared gig

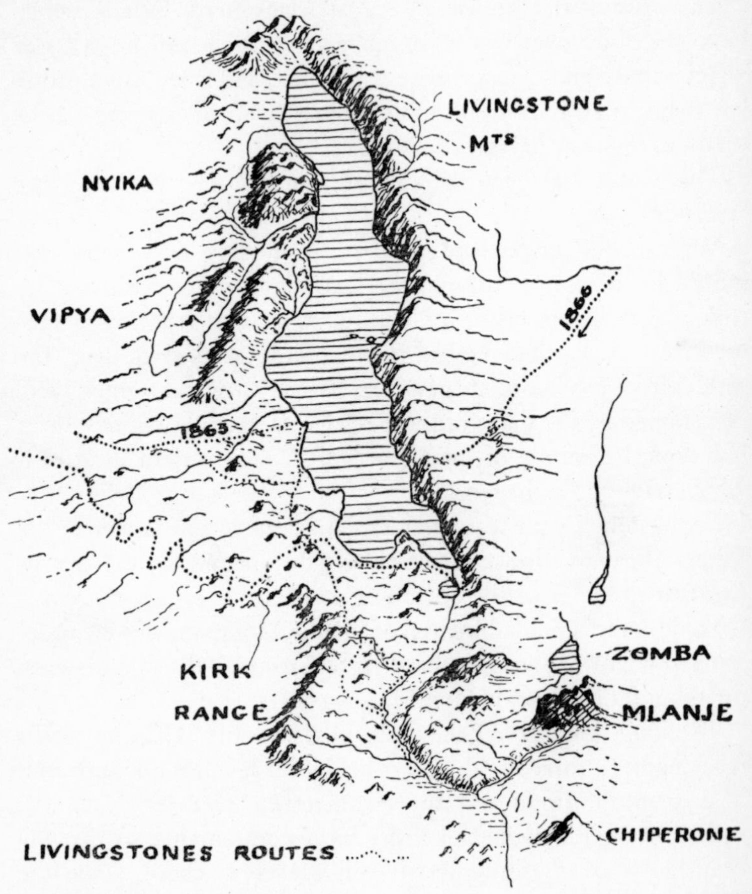

belonging to the *Pioneer* and the first job was to carry it past the cataracts, for which they hired carriers, each village providing men for the next stage.

The first 'carry' was three miles done in one day, up the path which became so much used in years to come that it is very clearly marked to this day, and from there they were able to track the boat for about a mile. Livingstone called these first rapids the Kapachira Falls but they have now been named after Livingstone himself, reserving the name Murchison for the whole series of cataracts, covering some thirty-five miles.

By August 12th they had reached the most scenic of the waterfalls, which he calls the Pampatamanga, the modern usage being to omit the first two letters. These falls are just below the present road-bridge from Tete.

The work went steadily on; sometimes carrying, sometimes tracking, or even rowing a mile or two. There was one place where the hippos had such a bad reputation for attacking canoes that the party landed and carried the boat a hundred yards to avoid tempting them.

He took the latitude at every important rapid and made many notes about the fall in feet, checking with his boiling point thermometer.

By the 27th, that is to say, in three weeks, they reached the village of Matope and had finished all the portaging. For the next forty miles, up to Lake Malombe, they found the people fleeing across the river from raids by the Ajawa (Yao) led or at least incited by slaves from Tete collecting other slaves for their Portuguese masters.

They sailed to the western end of Lake Malombe, making soundings from nine to twelve feet but shoaling westward to six feet. They wanted to contact their land party, and had much difficulty in getting ashore through the heavy belt of papyrus in this corner, which can still cause much delay unless one can find a fisherman who knows the right passage.

The countryside was so demoralised by the slave raiding that his land party had been threatened more than once so Livingstone walked with them up the western side of this lake. He noted the prosperous inhabitants, 'tall, well-fed people, growing some rice' and the large fig trees and baobabs which still adorn their villages, serving as the council meeting place in the heat of the day and the dance arena at night.

They reached the outlet of the lake on September 3rd and sailed along keeping to the west shore, Livingstone still going overland to lend his carriers the prestige of a white man, the first ever to reach that region. He named the rocky promontory, which they rounded, after his friend Maclear, and took extra care to fix it by astronomical sights, and then sailed a few miles down the shallow bay southwards so as to meet his land party. This necessity delayed the boat party rather seriously, but the small boat could not carry crew and provisions as well.

They therefore crept up the western densely-populated coast of the lake at a rate of little more than seven miles a day, taking sights on every possible occasion and making extensive notes about the coast, the people and the products for a whole month.

They had many adventures, especially from the stormy character of the lake, and on one occasion had to ride out one of the '*mweras*', the sudden southerly gales, for a whole six hours anchored a mile from shore, expecting every moment to be swamped. Livingstone's description of this storm is, for once, vivid and personal:

'We were caught one morning and anchored a mile from the shore in seven fathoms. The waves most dreaded came rolling in threes, with their crests, driven into spray, streaming behind them. Had one of these white-maned seas struck our frail bark nothing could have saved us; seaward, inshore, and on either side of us they broke in foam but we escaped. For six weary hours we faced those terrible trios, any one of which might have carried the end of the Expedition in its hoary head.

'The natives and our land party stood on the high cliffs looking at us and exclaiming, as the waves seemed to swallow up the boat, "They are lost, they are all dead!" '

The people were suspicious of them but their curiosity overcame their instinct to be unfriendly. When they were nearing Kota Kota they were robbed one night of all their spare clothing, kept in bags, and Livingstone exclaims, 'This is the first time I have been robbed in Africa,' which was not strictly true.

Their white skins became an embarrassment to them, both from the curiosity it excited and because it restricted their bathing, as the leader wrote, 'One feels ashamed of the white skin;

it seems unnatural, like blanched celery—or white mice.' This is a comment which has been echoed by every traveller since, especially when he sees one of the rare albino Africans, who are invariably ugly and often half-witted and half-blind. They often had to refrain from a proper bath and merely soap head and the upper part of the body because of the crowd of spectators. When his grandson, Dr Hubert Wilson, was on that coast some fifty years later he met an old man who had seen Livingstone. His most vivid memory of him was when, with another ten year old urchin, he had crept into the reeds to see whether the white man disappeared into the lake whence he had come, as was commonly believed by the people. He did not do that but he petrified the small boys by 'taking something in his hand, dipping it into the water and rubbing his head till his brains came out'.

In spite of these embarrassments Livingstone was revelling in the new and untouched field for observations under every possible heading. He was busy the whole day long, sounding depths, measuring heights, noting the productions, especially the fish, logging the weather, while Kirk was not far behind him, collecting plants and noting their uses.

At Kota Kota, then just becoming a slave centre, they missed by one day a dhow fully loaded with slaves transporting them to the other side. They rounded the long sandy spit which protects the shallow harbour from the south east but on this occasion did not go to the large town where the coastal Arabs were in actual control, and the paramount chief, the Jumbe, was only nominally in command yet profiting hugely by the slave trade.

At the mouth of the Dwangwa, which he calls the Loangwa, they shot an elephant and acquired merit thereby. Livingstone was most anxious to find out whether any big river entered the lake, suspecting that if there were such it might be the overflow from Lake Tanganyika which could be only a few hundred miles from their position. He hears much of a large river, called 'Rofu' in his field notes, which may well have been the Rukuru, the largest but not the longest stream of all those entering the lake and he presses on hoping to reach it. He may even have wished it might be the Rovuma.

But he reaches an area where there had been a recent raid by the Mazitu (i.e. the Angoni, a tribe of Zulu origin) graphically described by Kirk: 'The borders of this land are deserts, all the people have been killed and it has been a dreadful slaughter; for the shores are covered with skulls, and where a foraging party has passed fresh bodies beginning to decompose lie scattered on the sand.'

The land party refused to go on unless Livingstone came with them, but a note in his journal reveals that brother Charles was showing signs of funk: Kirk, as always, was ready to go wherever his leader went, however much he thought it unwise.

As a result of this separation and the very hilly country that delayed the land party the two parties lost contact and Livingstone showed his diplomacy and utter fearlessness when a party of the Mazitu attempted to hold them to ransom. The *Narrative* deliberately understates the dangers they met in that four days of separation, but the daily note-book does so even more, since the most prominent entry, beyond the bare facts, is 'Cow-itch very annoying', and then, 'Met some Mazitu who seemed much afraid but demanded a goat.'

'Cow-itch' was their name for what is now known as the Buffalo Bean, or Hell-fire Bean, a climber which bears velvety beans and is the scourge of damp places at that time of year. The bean pods are covered with fine silky hairs of a reddish brown which if touched cause a worse irritation than anything else ever met by the author, a combination of itch and burn which is almost unbearable for an hour or two, leaving large white weals and blisters. The 'velvet' can also blow off the pods on to one's clothing and soon work through to the skin. To call it merely 'annoying' is quite masterly understatement.

Kirk in the boat was having his own troubles; he and their seaman, Neil, were prostrated with fever and the weather was very stormy. Kirk, too, was catching the habit of understatement for he records, without comment, the reunion of the parties as 'Dr L's salutation on meeting was, "What on earth made you run away and leave us."'

When Livingstone met the Mazitu he had only two of his men

with him and was almost defenceless. One cannot help feeling that he had something magnetic about his personality, for this was only one of many occasions when he was within an inch of being speared. Or, if readers prefer a less psychic explanation, it may have been his complete fearlessness. Or was it that these savage men of Africa detected in his clear gaze an utter absence of

The Buffalo Bean or 'Cow itch'. One of the minor horrors of African travel

enmity yet guessed from his firm chin that provocation could reach a limit?

They had to turn back about thirty miles short of the large river he had hoped to find and forty short of the bold hills of the Nyika Plateau from which the great Livingstonia mission of to-day surveys the lake three thousand feet below, and looks across to the majestic Livingstone Mountains on the far side, in the territory of Tanganyika.

Unfortunately for the explorers it was the season of grass fires when one cannot see clearly across even that narrow lake for the dense blue haze so caused, and they could only record that side as 'mountainous'. In fact they were misled more than once by the swarms of the *Nkungu* fly which look so like the smoke from grass fires and, nowadays, even more like the black smoke of a hull-down steamer. Livingstone's first meeting with them is worth recording in his own words: 'We sailed through one of these clouds, and discovered it was neither smoke nor haze, but countless millions of minute midges called "kungo" (a cloud or fog). They filled the air to an immense height, and swarmed upon the water, too light to sink. Eyes and mouth had to be kept closed while passing through this living cloud.' He might have added 'the nose also', in a very dense cloud, because the writer has seen a canoe on the Victoria Nyanza which had been found derelict a few days before with the corpses of four fisherman who had been choked to death by clotted masses of the flies in their noses and mouths.

Livingstone goes on to describe what a strange harvest the lakeside dwellers have from them. 'The people gather these minute insects by night and boil them into thick cakes, to be used as a relish, millions of midges in a cake. A kungo cake, an inch thick and as large as the blue bonnet of a Scotch ploughman, was offered to us; it was very dark in colour, and tasted not unlike caviare or salted locusts.'

On the return journey they were detained by gales at the mouth of the Bua River and there met a party under Arab command bringing ivory and copper from the Katanga region, now centred round Elizabethville in the Belgian Congo.

He did not know it, of course, but this meeting was a presage of future events for him, since the men belonged to an Arab who had been for many years at Cazembe, and was almost certainly the Mohamad bin Saleh who was so kind to him at Cazembe's seven years later, but who was himself more or less a prisoner of that chief. They puzzled Livingstone once more by telling him that the Luapula flowed north-east, which it does near Cazembe's town, but which Livingstone thought must run into the Zambezi.

The Yao raiding of Manganja villages for slaves was going on still more vigorously as they passed down the Shire again, but poor Livingstone began to lose heart when he found that the Manganja were themselves selling each other to those he called the 'black Portuguese', half castes from Tete. They heard rumours of plans by the Yaos for an attack on the missionaries.

They got back to the ship after a very strenuous and hungry three months to hear that things were quiet with the missionaries, but the Bishop had taken sides in two fights, against the advice of Livingstone, and there was at best but armed neutrality between black and white.

Livingstone does not, either in the *Narrative* or in the private journal, review the results of the trip, which were immense from a geographical point of view. Poor Kirk on the other hand, travelling entirely in the boat with the 'moral agent' for company had no doubts as to his opinion: 'Sitting in the stern of that boat, exposed all day to the sun, has made an impression not easily forgotten. The inactivity and the pains in the bones and the joints from the sun, the gradual emaciation, the fevers and the starvation of that Nyassa journey combine to make it the hardest, most trying, and most disagreeable of all our journeys. It is the only one I have no pleasure in looking back on.'

More delay was to come their way for in attempting to get the *Pioneer* down the Shire, now at a low stage, they ran aground for no less than five weeks, apparently at a point a little above the present cotton 'port' of Alimenda where there are several sandy islands and the currents run between them at up to three knots.

The worst of fortune met them here, for they not only lost the carpenter's mate from fever, but they got away only two or three days before the Bishop and Mr Burrup, a new recruit from Oxford, reached the same point, fever stricken, and both had died of it before the Expedition people came up-river again.

At the mouth of the Zambezi they met more reinforcements for both missionary and expedition party and the next few months is well documented from the published diaries of Dr James Stewart, who had come out to reconnoitre a station for the Scottish Church, and of Lieutenant Devereux, a breezy naval paymaster who must have brought considerable entertainment to the flagging spirits of the Zambezi veterans. The reinforcements were profoundly counter-balanced by the women folk. Mrs Livingstone, had she lived, might have been of the greatest moral value to the expedition but of the others we may as well hear what Devereux thought.

Mrs Livingstone he describes as 'a motherly looking lady about thirty eight or forty', and Miss Mackenzie, sister to the Bishop as 'a pleasant, humorous, good natured elderly Scotch lady'. He does not mention the young Mrs Burrup here but says of the two maidservants or lady's maids that 'they are rather fond of dress but a little steadied by being attached to the mission'. Then he, rather naturally, speaks wrathfully of the University Mission, 'which is not content to push a part of their people blindfold and almost purposeless into the wilds of South Africa, but adds to their distressing position by allowing a lot of helpless females in their blind devotion to accompany them.'

Livingstone always wrote very freely to his brother-in-law, John Moffat, now a missionary in the Matabele country, and in a letter to him we learn, by inference, that he was not very hopeful about the combined party:

'The bishop is a very good man but lacking in decision of character. Of his associates Waller, the lay member, is low church. Proctor and Scudamore tend that way, if any way at all, while parson Rowley is red hot high church. We have five of the parson tribe (altogether), one carpenter—a poor stick—one shoemaker, one gardener, one printer—Europeans—and three black men, two of them noted blackguards. The Bishop's sister goes up to join him now. She has more sense than many, but is a confirmed invalid. Mrs Burrup, a laughing English girl of 21, accompanies her and so does Jessie Lennox, school teacher, and a maid.

'Mary (his wife) has, I am happy to say, joined me at last. The missionaries wish her up with them, and if she gets fever, up she must go.'

And then comes the only snapshot of Mrs Livingstone herself that we can get for this book, for above the last sentence in the letter she wrote 'Do not believe him', following this defiance with a swift sketch of her own head, in profile, putting the thumb of derision to the nose of scorn as Professor J. P. R. Wallis, the editor of the letters, puts it.

Rae the engineer, that stolid tower of strength, had rejoined them with the twenty-four sections of the new ship, the *Lady Nyassa*, which Livingstone had hoped would have sailed out to him, so that both vessels could have transported the tons of goods and supplies brought out for the Mission, about which Devereux is so eloquent. He was a paymaster so must have been a reasonable judge but he writes:

'It is impossible to look on the mass of goods strewn on the shore which we are obliged to leave behind, and the quantity to be disposed of at considerable loss, without wondering at the short-sightedness of the people who have had the direction of their affairs. Nearly every conceivable kind of goods, wearing apparel, household furniture, provisions, agricultural instruments, cooking utensils, nick nacks of every kind, are to be seen half buried in sand, exposed to chance and weather.

'I never saw people so superfluously provided. They are gorged with luxuries, "regardless of expense". There seems to have been an utter want of geographical knowledge.'

Perhaps a serving paymaster is not quite the best critic of a mission venture, nevertheless, it all meant a great deal of extra responsibility for Livingstone, who could not avoid the duty of getting what he could up to the mission on the highlands. Captain Wilson of the *Gorgon* was ready to help him with no less than seventy of his men, but there was danger in the divided command. Devereux, who was devoted to his own captain, was trenchant in his criticism of Livingstone and writes, 'I never saw such constant vacillations, blunders, delays, and want of common thought and foresight as is displayed on board the *Pioneer*.'

No doubt Devereux was as kindly disposed towards both expedition and mission as a momentary helper could be but I decline to accept these strictures for the simple reason that the junior man in a venture can never know fully what the leader has in mind and I have heard the same kind of remark from junior members of modern expeditions whose final results were proof that the leader did the right thing.

My sympathies are entirely with Livingstone at having to take charge of all this collection of human and material reinforcements for the mission, much of it superfluous. His calculations were entirely upset by the discovery that the engineer of the *Pioneer* had neglected an essential part of the machinery so that what she should have accomplished in a few weeks took nearly six months.

Dr Stewart's note on this defect is that 'Hardesty (the engineer), I suspect, is a muff of some sort. Mr Geddie, the mate or master, is also off work, and there seems to be something wrong'. Everyone seemed to be expecting all things from Livingstone, for Stewart complains of the 'woeful want of arrangement about this ship' and later asserts 'It is not enough that a man in Dr L's position be passively unselfish: he must be actively so: he must see that the actively selfish, of whom there are likely to be many, do not take advantage, that the lazy do their work and the willing be neither overtasked nor their labours be unrecognised.' The next sentence is perhaps a left-handed apology for such sentiments, reading, 'I was not at all in a sweet or amiable mood this morning.'

Viewed at a distance of nearly a century the scene on the Zambezi is a melancholy one. Discontent and mismanagement in all directions, fever rampant amongst all the Europeans and for Livingstone the crowning disaster of the death of his wife at Shupanga.

Though born and bred at Kuruman, Mary Livingstone had been away from the more feversome parts of Africa for many years and no doubt had lost the immunity to fever she had possessed in her younger days. She had only just begun to make her influence felt, both by her practical commonsense and her pleasant equable temper, when she took a virulent form of fever and died in a few days, despite all the two doctors could do for her. The heavy blow quite prostrated Livingstone and yet our sympathy tends rather towards the gentle wife of the great explorer who, for obvious reasons was very rarely permitted to be his companion as well. Of the eighteen years of their married life she had been with him for less than half the time but she had never failed to give him her moral support in his ventures far away from her and the children.

It was especially hard that just as she was about to share in his travels once again she should be cut off. Of all the women who came to the Zambezi she was the one with the best claim to be there, yet she alone was taken. She was not of the mental calibre of her husband but there is reason to believe that she had a calming influence on him and as a housewife she seems to have been the true daughter of her famous mother, able to create comfort where few others could have done so.

Mrs Livingstone's tombstone at Shupanga. The large baobab tree had fallen a few years earlier and broken the original tombstone

from a photograph taken in 1898

It was perhaps as well that Livingstone himself was so occupied with expedition affairs that he had not time to grieve too deeply over his loss; his public responsibility gave him no leisure for private sorrow.

Circumstances had forced him into a situation for which he was peculiarly unfitted, the management of affairs for a very dispersed set of parties over whom he had no official authority but who depended on him for succour and for whose sins of omission or commission he was saddled with blame.

From the time when all these duties came upon him, January 1862 until early in the next year, he had hardly a moment for his own purposes, and was become the servant of all the unequal crowd of missionaries for whom he was, indeed, morally responsible.

There is space only for a quick review of what he did in these busy and anxious months.

The *Lady Nyassa* had to be put together at Shupanga, but it had taken three months to bring up all the parts from the Kongone bar and a total of six months before she was assembled under the direction of Rae, who never seems to have been accorded due credit for the job.

Provisions were running short so then Livingstone had to go in the *Pioneer* to Johanna island for more, attended by the other three members of the Expedition, with Kirk still the only whole-hearted one of the party, ready to stand by his leader, though he saw his faults clearly enough.

On this voyage Kirk made the oft-quoted note about Livingstone's manner when at sea: 'When the weather gets foul or anything begins to go wrong it is well to give Dr L. a wide berth, most especially when he sings to himself. But the kind of air is some indication. If it is "The Happy Land", then look out for squalls and stand clear. If it is "Scots wha hae" then there is some grand vision of discovery before his mind.... But on all occasions humming of airs is a bad omen.'

At Johanna, Livingstone made one of his characteristic quick decisions, which often were wise, but were just as often disconcerting to his companions. Few things are so important in leadership of one's equals in intelligence as that of sharing plans in full with the followers—a thing that Livingstone could rarely bring himself to do.

He decided to go and tackle the Rovuma again, by boats and, escorted by the cruiser *Orestes*, off they went to the mouth of that river.

It was apparent almost at once that the water was far too low to enable the whaleboats to get very far, but it was, quoting Livingstone himself, 'never his custom to leave a matter unfinished', and they hauled their boats over sandbanks and through sloughs of mud until even Kirk has to write 'His determination seems to amount to infatuation'.

This persistence gives occasion too for a very striking and very sage remark of Sir Reginald Coupland in his book *Kirk on the Zambezi* which runs:

> 'It was indeed the first demonstration of that relentless, unreasoning, almost defiant force of will which, a few years later, was to spur Livingstone on, mile after mile, through the maze of Central Africa, till he died.
>
> 'And the key to it must lie in that conviction of a predetermined fate to which he had given such dramatic expression at Cambridge. From now onwards that mystic note begins to sound again in his journals and in his letters to intimate friends, and of course it intensified his desire to be alone.'

In defence we may recall that exploring the Rovuma was one of the duties laid upon him by the Government; someone had to do it and who better than the man who didn't know when he was beaten. At a cost of two Africans killed in a river fight in self defence, and, it may be added, of the last atom of confidence in him clung to by Kirk, they got one hundred and fifty miles inland, to a point at which a fortnight's march on foot would have taken them to the lake had they had food and carriers.

It is hardly fair to call it 'a miserable and fruitless month' as Coupland sums it up. Miserable it may have been, but it had much to do with the decision of the British missionaries and traders that, after all, the Shire was the only practicable approach to Nyasaland. Much as I hesitate to differ from such an able historian of East Africa I would go so far as to say that the Nyasaland of to-day is largely the result of that negative but supremely important journey and that in his uncouth way Livingstone showed finer qualities of leadership in pressing on against the wishes of all his men than in most of the other subsidiary journeys of this period. The eye of history is all too likely to be partial, to look upon positive discovery as the supreme aim of geographers and to neglect those negative results which usually cost more in human misery to attain, but are often the means of guiding future advance in the right direction.

His *Narrative*, however, does scant justice to this journey. It mentions the attack by the natives on their boats but omits or suppresses the fact that poor Kirk and a seaman, in the second boat had to kill two of the most persistent attackers, an incident which Kirk felt very deeply ever afterwards.

This was to be Livingstone's route to the interior on his final journey, a plan decided upon before he actually finished writing the book and he may have decided that it was politic not to mention the killing, however fully justified it had been.

The complete suppression of the names of those who did valiant work is part of the objective attitude chosen for the *Narrative*, which may have been forced on him by his outward sharing of authorship with his brother Charles, of whom no good thing could be said.

The party got back to the Zambezi in late November, bringing oxen from Johanna, for Livingstone's major plan to get a steamer up to the lake was as much in his mind as ever.

But little could be done until the river rose and there were wearisome delays until in mid-January the *Pioneer* started off towing the *Lady Nyassa*, but with the usual groundings and waiting for shallow places to deepen it was not until mid-April that they reached Chibisa's. And a very melancholy journey it must have been for all hands since the almost happy and populous valley of the Shire which they had first penetrated three years before was now laid waste by slavery and famine, so that they saw 'four or five dead bodies floating down daily'. The mission party too, had not found better health by going up once more to the highlands where two more of them died of fever, one other being saved by Kirk, sent for post-haste.

Thornton had rejoined the expedition more experienced but as carefree and independent as before, and his spirits and his sailing boat did something to relieve the gloom for at least four members of the expedition, Kirk, Charles Livingstone, Meller and Rae, all of whom were anxious to get home to England and all were suffering from their long stay in the unhealthy lowlands.

Thornton, unfortunately, died from fever after over-exerting himself on behalf of the missionaries.

Meanwhile, Rae was busy dismantling the *Lady Nyassa* which was to be carried in sections past the cataracts to the Lake.

Late in April Livingstone came to the conclusion that his brother and Kirk had better leave, and even now after their five years of companionship his mode of agreeing to Kirk's departure was about as ungracious to Kirk and absurdly flattering to his brother as it could well be. Kirk writes: 'Dr L. said that his brother had requested to go home and that he had consented as it would be selfish in him to keep him longer; and that as I had desired to go, he would feel the same in my case.' Truly he must have been physically incapable of ordinary courtesy to have so dismissed his worthiest member as a sort of afterthought to parting with his brother, the real black sheep of the party.

But Kirk could not go until Livingstone had been looked after by him for another three weeks during his most sudden and most serious attack of fever with dysenteric complications. With the going of these two on May 19th there came the official recall of the Expedition by the Foreign Office which however, did not reach the leader until July 3rd, and which was not unexpected.

The unconquerable man within a month after his illness started up the forty miles of cataracts again, proposing to mend and launch the boat they had left up there in a tree two years before, only to find that it had been burnt about three months earlier either by their enemies the Yao, or possibly by a chance grass fire. On their return to the ship they found the despatch from Lord Russell recalling the whole expedition.

It was impossible to get the *Pioneer* down river until the floods of December so while the *Lady Nyassa* was being screwed together again Livingstone determined to carry yet another boat up the Cataracts, using the six oxen he had brought from Johanna for the purpose. They proved insufficient so he got his Makololo who had settled at Chibisa's to do the carrying, together with some Ajawa (Yao) and some Manganja. His opinion of their relative capacity is plainly stated in an entry in his journal on July 24th went they had been nine days on the way. 'Three

Manganjas went back this morning—inveterate skulkers and when told so took their leave. The Ajawa men are far finer specimens and run with the boat.' But once again Fate spoiled his plan for when they had passed most of the rapids the men tried to row the boat and it was capsized and lost. His note of the incident reads: 'Lost the boat, it went over the cataracts. The Shupanga men went into it without leave or orders, to try where the Makololo had failed—it puts a stop to our journey I fear.'

This was, I submit, an occasion when the grandeur of his persistence had one of its finest hours, for, apparently in an hour or two, he had determined to go on foot for as long as time permitted and had sent the culprits back to the ship for provisions and equipment for such a journey.

While under sentence of recall he had tried twice to repeat his boat journey and when twice foiled he calmly decided to go afoot.

Rae came up with the men from the ship and reported that the putting together again of the *Lady Nyassa* was progressing, and here at last in the *Narrative* is there public mention of praise for his helpers 'as fine steady workmen as ever handled tools' and with a half apology to his readers he prints the names of the carpenter and two engine room artificers.

Livingstone, of course, wished to go alone with his black carriers, but presumably Rae got in a word at last, for in the book there is the sentence 'as all our party had earnestly advised that at least two Europeans should be associated together on the journey, the steward was at the last moment taken'.

An entry on August 19th when the party started, puts his aim in a few words: 'Our object in going forward still though deprived of our boat is to take up the slave-path westward from the south end of the Lake—to get information of the sources of supply, its connection with the ivory trade—prices—routes—the situation of the malachite (ore of copper) as this may be the means of inducing merchants to establish lawful trade.'

The time of year was the best for a seven hundred mile walk but the circumstance of war was hardly favourable, for the Yao were raiding across the Shire from the East, and they had walked only three days up the Rivi Rivi river to the north-west when there is the note: 'We passed as large a town as ever I saw in Africa—quite deserted—skeletons everywhere.'

They got into tsetse country and had to kill their ox, the two white men got separated from their carriers for three days, they passed up the beautiful valley which now leads to the administrative centre of Ncheu, and on over the tableland towards the present hill station of Dedza.

They were warned of raiding parties of Mazitu (the tribe of Angoni, whose fathers had come north all the way from Zululand) whose habit of war was to receive the arrows of the local people on their broad shields of ox-hide and then attack with the stabbing assegais, and they saw that they would have to pass down to the lake to avoid them. In his inimitable way he made great friends with a chief Chinsamba who had only just beaten off an attack from them a day earlier. Here he met the Babisa traders from the country west of the Loangwa River, whom he was to know very well in his last expedition, and whose muskets had been chiefly responsible for defeating the assegais.

They marched along the lakeside to Kota Kota which had grown immensely in the two years since they had last been there and the coast Arabs had now made it into a main depot for passing slaves across the lake to the coast.

Their halting place here was under the very large fig tree which is now the central feature in the court yard of the U.M.C.A. mission, and there he heard that he had just missed by one day the Syde ben Habib he had met at Linyanti eight years before, who had sailed across the lake in one of the Arab dhows which had been built on the Lake.

From Kota Kota, now the centre of Mohammedanism in Nyasaland for the above reasons, they marched due west and found the going heavy because of the altitude and cold. They suffered from occupying native huts infested by 'tampans', that special form of tick which induces a relapsing fever. These ticks are so prevalent in this part of Nyasaland that the villagers regard them as a necessary evil from which some degree of immunity is possible if you stick to the same set of ticks. Quite logically therefore they take their own brand of ticks with them in a section of bamboo when going to live elsewhere and 'transplant' them to the new home, on the principle of 'Better the tick you know than the tick you don't know'.

For these and other reasons they were rather an ailing party on the highlands and one man died before they reach the large village of Muasi (modern form, Mwase), the name of the paramount chief then, and now, of the large section of the people known as Chewa. Livingstone said they called themselves Matumboka, as they may well have done as they were allied with the Tumbuka people somewhat to the north of them. Mwase had compromised with the Mazitu raiders by paying tribute but the Tumbuka remained as independent as they could until twenty years later when they rebelled and were all but extinguished in the siege of Mount Hora, some hundred miles further north. The writer heard the story of that siege recited by the descendants of the Angoni who won it, every detail of the story being cherished in much the same way as the English recite the story of the Spanish Armada.

Muasi's village is still in precisely the same place, 'about 2 miles south west of a high hill called Kasungu', where in 1952 I was kindly received by the present Mwase, inside the remains of 'the stockade embowered in very tall euphorbia trees, whose height shows that it has been inhabited for at least one generation'. More interesting still, one of the counsellors present was Vidzumo, reputed to be over ninety years old, who was therefore a very small boy when Livingstone visited Muasi and found that chief 'as frank and straightforward as could reasonably be expected'.

I could use precisely the same expressions about the present Mwase, who was quite the most intelligent and friendly chief I met in Nyasaland but who was, at the time, much embarrassed by the intrigues in his tribe concerning the topic of the day, the proposed Federation of the three Central African territories. Vidzumo did not, naturally enough, remember Livingstone but he remembered the slave-trade well enough and no doubt took part in it, though now he is a valued ally to the administration.

Livingstone noted the prevalence of elephants in the district, which is still a route for them migrating from the Loangwavalley, where they are still abundant, over to the lake side of the long ridge, where they are liable to be shot at.

Mwase described to me very graphically an incident of the year before when he saw a furious elephant passing below his office window and killing a woman a few hundred yards away before it was shot by a hunter. The elephant's fury was then explained since it had a festering wound from spears which had been delivered down by the lake sixty miles away.

Livingstone pressed on for another three days to the west, reaching the tributaries of the upper Luangwa and wishing he could spare the time to go on and reach Lake Bemba, which he was told was only ten days distant. This was Lake Bangweulu where he was to end his days but it was really three hundred miles away. There is no doubt that what he heard of the country in that direction at this time directed his plans for his next and last journey, and he met men who knew the chiefs, such as Shinte, whom he had met on his way to Loanda in 1854.

He turned back at this point as he was under orders to get the *Pioneer* down to the mouth of the Zambezi by the end of the year and it was now the end of September. They returned by a shorter route, crossing the Bua River a little lower down than the present bridge on the Great North Road and remarking on the prominence of Mount Ngalla which overlooks the bridge.

A few days later they had a dramatic meeting with a band of the Angoni Mazitu who chased a laggard of the party up to the main body. Livingstone and his head man walked back and faced the Mazitu calling out 'What do you want?' Either the sight of the white man or that of his Makololo kneeling down and taking aim frightened them off and they were troubled no more. This encounter was exaggerated into a rumour that he had been killed which reached England before he did, so that he was able to write to a friend in his whimsical manner, 'Don't go pale on receiving a letter from a dead man.' But the interesting thing about the rumour is that the incident giving rise to it occurred not far from where the deserters on his next journey turned back and said they had seen him killed by Mazitu, to check which an expedition was sent out from England led by the very Lieutenant Young, who was in charge of the *Pioneer* down at the base of the Cataracts at that moment.

They stayed again for a few days with the friendly Chinsamba and then followed their outward tracks almost exactly till they reached the Lesungwe river. A pleasing note occurs in the *Narrative* when, puzzled by finding no native name for the high range of mountains bounding the western side of the Shire Valley, Livingstone writes 'our wish to commemorate the name of Kirk induced us afterwards to call the whole chain "Kirk's Range".'

That was as much as one could expect, perhaps, from a man who paid so little attention to that kind of matter that he never mentions the name of the ship's steward who did this march of seven hundred and sixty miles with him, at an average of twelve miles a day. He records his practice of carrying his chronometer cushioned in a box full of clothing and how he checked its 'travelling rate' by taking time sights at a series of places on the journey out and repeating them at the same places on the return. He illustrates the necessity for this procedure by stating that the *ship's* rate of the chronometer he carried was a daily loss of eleven seconds, whereas the *travelling* rate was a daily gain of one second.

They reached the ship on November 1st, and in spite of attacks of fever for most of them, Livingstone is able to say that 'the steward, after having performed his part in the march right bravely, rejoined his comrades stronger than he had ever been before'.

In a note at the end of the journal from which we have quoted occasionally, kindly lent to me by Dr Hubert Wilson, there are two significant items. The one concerning the slave trade reads, 'From all I can see in this present journey on foot one steamer on the lake would have compelled the Portuguese to give up the slave trade altogether. Five fathoms (of cloth) for a large tusk! We could have given twenty and driven a brisk trade. It is the ivory from which the chief profits are drawn.' The other is rather a growl on his part: 'The Europeans in our expedition, except Dr Kirk and Rae, were the *impedimenta* of the enterprise; carrying their food and enduring their growling while doing most of the hard work myself was uphill labour.' This latter is an excellent example of the accusation indirect because the only European, other than Kirk and Rae, who accompanied him on long journeys was Charles Livingstone, to whom it applies all too accurately.

If proof were needed to persuade us that Livingstone did best when alone, except for a nameless steward, this excellent geographical journey over new country is ample.

He returned to the ships to find his able technicians, under the command of Lieutenant Young, ready with them both and anxious for the rains to raise river level so that they could all get away from the Zambezi. But again there was delay, this time on the part of the river, which did not rise sufficiently until mid-January when both ships got easily down to the Kongone mouth by mid-February where they met the *Orestes* and the *Ariel*, two of Her Majesty's cruisers.

The Expedition was officially terminated but adventure was not, for the *Lady Nyassa*, while being towed to Mozambique by the *Ariel* ran into a hurricane, the tow-ropes parted and the tiny vessel, built in sections for lake transport, stood up to the strain so well that the naval officers in the *Ariel* pronounced her to be 'the finest little sea boat they had ever seen', while those of the *Orestes* which in the same storm had split eighteen sails were quite certain that the *Lady Nyassa* must have gone to the bottom in such weather.

It must have been her splendid behaviour which impelled Livingstone to take the enormous risk of a trans-ocean voyage in her, and being unable to sell her in Zanzibar, he decided to take her across himself to Bombay, the only market they could reach.

This voyage, while having little to do with Africa, was such a remarkable feat on Livingstone's part that it must claim some space in this chapter, and it certainly deserves fuller notice than it has yet had. The *Narrative* deals with it in under two pages.

He had some difficulty in getting a suitable crew and he finally left Zanzibar as master and navigator with three Europeans, a stoker, a sailor and a carpenter, with seven 'native Zambesians and two native boys'—Chuma and Wikitani—of whom we shall hear again. They only had fourteen tons of coal aboard and their first contretemps was to find that the engines used four tons of fuel a day, whereas Rae had assured him they could do much better than that, as they probably could in his hands.

Livingstone had hoped to do the voyage in eighteen days but it took him forty-five , and Collyer the carpenter with Pennell the sailor were each incapacitated by sickness for a time. Three of the 'Shupanga' men were taught to steer and most of them became handy with the sails.

Unable to steam since the coal had to be reserved for emergency and experiencing many calms they had only done about 1000 miles out of the 2500 after being four weeks at sea. The 'waiting for a wind' proved just as exasperating and depressing as it has done for a great many other voyages and Livingstone very honestly entered in his diary that all the crew, including himself, were feeling very 'ill natured'.

In fact Livingstone as a skipper seems to have had the same faults and the same virtues as he had already shown as leader on land. He was apt to feel and speak more kindly to the black men than to the white, he never shared his thoughts or plans with anyone, he was liable to be haphazard over discipline and regularity. On the other hand, he would ask no one to do anything he would not undertake himself, he was utterly fearless and he was a better navigator than most ship-masters.

Somewhere east of the island of Socotra, he decided he must make for Aden instead of Bombay but when the wind did come it was against him, and there was too much of it. One prolonged squall tore the ship's sails and she 'nearly rolled quite over: it was terrible while it lasted'.

They were still eight hundred miles from Bombay when he found that their supply of water, severely rationed, would only last for ten or twelve days, and so far they had had nearly twenty days of calms.

June came in blustery, however, the preliminaries to the dangerous south-westerly monsoon, and though squalls split their square sail to ribbons they made fair progress. His landfall was absolutely exact about one hundred miles southward of Bombay, as he had been pushed southward more than he had wished, and he had saved enough coal to steam into the harbour of Bombay in a dense haze, unpiloted and almost unnoticed.

The customs authorities were incredulous for here was a man who was an owner-skipper, with no cargo, in a vessel which was much too small to have come far, saying that his last port was Zanzibar, 2500 miles away, and that he did not know a single soul in Bombay.

So ended this much advertised expedition of six years' duration and there is no doubt that, at the time, its affairs, its members and its achievements were under a cloud. It had cost the Government far more than was intended, there had been much disaffection in the party and no one was very clear as to whether anyone at all had benefited, except the map maker.

The leader had certainly lost the immense prestige with which he had commenced the venture and his strange impersonal narrative did little towards creating a reputation for those, like Kirk, who had earned one.

There was no lack of criticism, much of it of a sweeping character, such as that of Dr James Stewart, who was a spectator of its last year's doings. He wrote in his journal, at the time, but it was not published till 1952 (in *The Zambezi Journal of James Stewart*, edited by J. P. R. Wallis, as Number Six of the Oppenheimer Series): 'It was a grand scheme and a magnificent enterprise, having for its object the amelioration of some of the most degraded of our race. But no part of it has been fulfilled, so far at least as the moral and permanent results are concerned.'

He continues in the same vein and becomes so jaundiced in his judgment of all Livingstone's doing that we suspect there was something wrong in their relations. So there was, and it robs his assessment of most of its value. It would have been difficult for two such aloof men to have got on well under any circumstances but when Stewart insisted on remaining a spectator, doing little or nothing to help the expedition, particularly in the way of manual labour, it 'shocked and offended the strenuous Scot', as Stewart's editor so neatly puts it, and the effect was to intensify the reserve and the barely concealed aversion of the leader.

The egocentric attitude which led Stewart to glory in his

disillusionment shows that he had a long way to go before he could reach the calm judgment and sound ability with which he was to assist in piloting the great missionary venture of Livingstonia some twelve years later.

An entry just before he left the Zambezi is illuminating in this respect: 'In the afternoon I went down the river-bank a short way and threw with all my strength into the turbid muddy weed-covered Zambesi my copy of *Missionary Travels in South Africa.* The volume was fragrant with odours of and memories of the earnestness with which I studied the book in days gone by. How different it appeared now! It was nothing short of an eyesore, the very sight of its brown covers. I disliked the book and sent it to sink or swim in the vaunted Zambesi.'

Such theatricals vitiate any opinion from this witness and we turn therefore to Horace Waller, who saw a great deal more of Livingstone than did Stewart and who was a practical man where the latter was a visionary. In a letter to Stewart himself a year after their return he says: 'I have not heard a word from the doctor since he has been home to make me think he is "cool" towards you. With all his grand qualities those who know him make allowances for the unrounded corners of character. His heart's in the right place and he's the bravest man I ever saw, or ever expect to see, which, for one who has longed to have a tithe of his pluck, is a go-and-do-likewise object to gaze upon and not pick to pieces.' But such contemporary views of Livingstone himself are no sure guide to the judgment of history itself, nearly a hundred years later. It is indeed essential to take a long term view because a short term one alone would, superficially stated, ruin the name of Livingstone and his men altogether.

It is not generally recognised that the immediate consequence of Livingstone's journeys up the Shire was that the Portuguese slave traders used his information to open up that virgin field for their foul exploitation. To that extent Livingstone was responsible for the slaughter or slavery of scores of thousands of Africans, if one is short-sighted enough to be satisfied with such a *post hoc propter hoc* statement.

In a letter to Stewart from the devastated area Kirk says: 'You have no idea of what we found the country on our first visits: then there was peace and plenty, inhabitants everywhere; now you have seen the country burned up by drought and scourged with famine and war.'

So in a manner of speaking the consequences of, or more precisely, the sequence to, Livingstone's labours on the Shire was diametrically the opposite of what he had hoped.

I think, myself, that he was all too conscious of it and that it was largely responsible for the change in his character noted by Coupland, from that of a practical philanthropist to a mystical fatalist of which we shall see plenty of examples in his next and last journey.

Truly we may say with honest John Bunyan that in going down into the Valley of Humiliation Livingstone had taken slips by the way.

We shall cling to the opinion that although this expedition was a moral failure it was a geographical triumph, and in the long long run it made Nyasaland the most advanced and contented of all our mid-African protectorates.

We should note that the signal for Recall came just a month too early. Had they succeeded in getting the *Lady Nyassa* up to the lake, the history of Nyasaland might well have been put forward by twenty years. Her presence on the lake would have, as Livingstone predicted, altered the tactics of the slave traders entirely. But, we must add, she would have needed a firmer skipper than Livingstone, who was so apt to spare the whip and spoil the child.

Dr John Kirk

CHAPTER EIGHT

I am made to tread those steps thrice over, which I needed not to have trod but once: yea, now also I am like to be benighted, for the day is almost spent.

JOHN BUNYAN

David Livingstone came home, overland by the isthmus of Suez (so soon to be opened by the canal), all alone and, one would think, despondent. But there is no evidence to that effect, partly because he was already devising plans whereby he could 'tread those steps' in Africa for the third time and partly because of the reception he had from his circle of friends in England. The general public may have been interested but was certainly cool yet his friends gave him a warm and sometimes a commendatory welcome.

What a contrast there is in the entries in his journal over a bare eight weeks. In mid-May, when delayed by calms off Socotra he wrote: 'I shall have nothing to do at home; by the failure of the Universities Mission my work seems vain. I have been unprofitable enough, but may do something yet in giving information.'

Now in late July his entries, one within a few hours of arrival in London, include: 'Sir Roderick took me off with him, just as I was, to Lady Palmerston's reception. My lady very gracious. Spoke to Duke and Duchess of Somerset. All say very polite things and all wonderfully considerate.'

For the next day: 'Got a dress suit at Nicol & Co's (evidently the Moss Bros. of the period) and dined with Lord and Lady

Dunmore, very clever and intelligent man and lady very sprightly. Thence to Duchess of Wellington's reception. A grand company —magnificent rooms. . . . Ladies wonderfully beautiful—rich and rare were the gems they wore.'

And on the third day: 'See Lord Russell—his manner is very cold as all the Russells are. Received an invitation from the Lord Mayor to dine with Her Majesty's Ministers.'

All that, except the cool manner of Lord Russell, sounds like 'roses, roses all the way' but it did not deceive Livingstone, and no doubt he rated the coolness of some as more important than the warmth of others.

It was, doubtless, not very good for him, and there is a slight and pardonable air of snobbery in some of the entries, but once he got to Scotland and his family circle he became his balanced self again. Nevertheless it is disappointing to find that it was months before he saw Kirk or Rae when one would think it the obvious duty of a leader to gather his companions to share in such welcome as he got himself. Not even the most biased biographer, such as Dr Blaikie, can present Livingstone as a good or even a normal leader. He did not seek fame, it is true, but it never seems to have occurred to him to share what was thrust upon him with those comrades who had stood by him.

In his one big public speech, an address to the British Association at Bath, there was a chance to remedy this omission but instead he pursued the very doubtful policy of incensing the Portuguese still further against him. In fact he had quite broken with the Portuguese, and one can hardly wonder at it in a man whose last two journeys up the Shire had exposed the sham of Portugal-in-Europe pretending to control Portugal-in-East-Africa. It was gallant but it was hardly wise.

In late September he went, at the kind invitation of his old friend of Kolobeng days, Mr William Webb, to stay with the Webb family at their noble house of Newstead Abbey, eleven miles north of Nottingham. The invitation included his eldest daughter Agnes, and this stay in 'endless English comfort, by county folk caressed', was the very best thing that could have happened to him. He was there for nearly eight months and it enabled him not only to write his *Narrative* but to collect himself in health and in balance of mind for his next venture. They were certainly the happiest months he ever had in England, and the great house, with its ample grounds and ruined Abbey as annexe, was in itself a source of interest. His letters show a revival of spirits and even something approaching frolic which it is hard to associate with the dour and silent leader of Zambezi days. Yet he and his companions could not forget the scenes of devastation along the Shire and their memory tinged much of the book he now began to work at.

He was, Waller told Stewart, 'in bad odour at the Foreign Office' and we must explain why, for it was not merely because his expedition had spent a few more thousand pounds than was contemplated originally.

As Coupland explains in his *Kirk on the Zambesi* the Foreign Office was greatly embarrassed at this time by the action that France had taken over slavery. She had recently humiliated Portugal by insistence, supported by naval threats in the Tagus, on the return of a French barque which had been captured by the Portuguese, carrying so-called willing emigrants to the island of Bourbon who were manifestly purchased slaves. This was one reason why the British Government could not bully Portugal about the slave trade.

There was another and perhaps more potent reason. The Prince Consort was a cousin of the two successive kings of Portugal at this period, King Pedro and King Luiz. He had made it clear when the Expedition started that he thought it an intrusion upon Portuguese rights and he refused to be patron of the Universities' Mission. During the period of the expedition, when fulminating dispatches were coming back from Livingstone, there were several interchanges of courtesy between the courts of St James and of Lisbon over deaths and weddings. Coupland sums it up neatly by saying 'it was difficult to thrust the gaunt realities of far-off Africa on to that glittering picture, difficult to present His Most Faithful Majesty with the Garter on one day and to box his ears on the next for the sake of Livingstone and the Slave Trade'.

These explanations were probably quite clear to Livingstone

himself, but he took it as his business and his moral duty to expose the nefarious ways of most of the Portuguese officials in East Africa who disregarded or dodged the edicts of their home government.

It is interesting to note the reactions of the three Englishmen who had seen the slave trade in action most closely on the Shire.

David Livingstone, as we have seen, had declared from the first that edicts and protocols would never terminate the trade, it must be undermined and made unprofitable by legitimate trade, and he clung to his purpose of finding an entry for business and Christianity into Africa.

John Kirk agreed with him but felt that the exploration of routes was only too likely to pioneer new avenues for slavery to follow. There is that brief but profound sentence in his diary after they had visited the Shire Highlands the second time—'We had been the means of opening a slave-hunting country.' Stout-hearted Horace Waller was all for direct action though he knew it was impossible. In a letter to Stewart after they had both returned he lets himself go on the subject: 'I believe that till the Portuguese are interfered with, little or no good can be done . . . our lives would have been well and gloriously sacrificed if it had led to Tette, Senna and Quillimane being bundled into the rivers: but all this seems changed now. We tacitly allow the slave trade to go on and, what's more, don't intend to interfere with it, I think. Give me a seat in a man-of-war's boat to go up and burn Tette and I would leave England without (waiting to put) a hat on my head, and if I got shot at I should consider I had begun at the right end of the stick. It makes my blood boil when I think of the fiendish misery this handful of rascals creates on the Eastern side of Africa and of our own miserable policy, which can upset China, force open Japan, crush down those before us in New Zealand—for worldly ends—and yet, for humanity, say "Hush!" alone when this poor wretched country's case is pleaded for.'

The Portuguese case, too, was not an easy one for the court at Lisbon. They deplored, no doubt quite genuinely, that regrettable things were being done in their territory, but they insisted that they must deal with it themselves and wanted no more interference from explorers and missionaries whose ulterior motive was, thinly disguised, occupation of part of the country at least.

They had given in to the military threat of France, on behalf of slavery, and they were not going to give in to the pleadings of a timid diplomacy from London on behalf of freedom.

Meanwhile, by the early months of 1865, the three Englishmen were variously occupied, Waller becoming a fully qualified priest, Kirk rather at a loss as to what to do next and Livingstone writing his book and steadfast in his determination to go back to Africa and, this time, to by-pass the Portuguese.

Kirk was rather nursing the grievance of having spent six years unprofitably from the point of view of a career and of having had more kicks than ha'pence out of it. He was somewhat out of touch with Livingstone and perhaps did not realise that the 'Doctor' was exerting himself to have a good job found for him.

He allows himself plain speech about Charles Livingstone in a letter to Waller at this time after seeing his former leader and hearing something of his plans: 'Livingstone goes out again, but by the Rovuma; he is to have his son Bob home from America and to take him with him. I always thought he had tried the effects of relatives on Expeditions enough; it seems he is game for another. Well, an out-and-out wild devil is more hopeful than a sneaking mischief-maker, a plotting low scoundrel. But to a clergyman, as you *now* are, I have used too many bad words. Livingstone's mission, I think, is purely exploratory.' *

But that was just what Livingstone did not want to do, make a purely geographical expedition. Already, in January, Sir Roderick Murchison had sounded him on the matter, proposing that he should undertake a journey to settle the problem of the sources of the Nile, Congo and Zambezi. In fact he had outlined very closely what Livingstone did, in the end, attempt to do, but he made use of the expression that Livingstone should do it 'unshackled by other avocations than those of the geographical explorer'.

* The eldest son, Robert, had led an unsettled life and was at that time fighting in the Civil War in America, where he was wounded and died in hospital.

This was precisely what Livingstone did not want to be, and the fat was very nearly in the fire over the plan that was ultimately agreed upon. Livingstone wrote back very bluntly saying that he 'could only feel in the way of duty by working as a missionary.' He stated his intentions more clearly in a letter to his old friend and supporter, Mr James Young ('Paraffin' Young as he called him, as he had made his money out of that fuel) at the same time: 'I would not consent to go simply as a geographer, but as a missionary, and do geography by the way, because I feel I am in the way of duty when trying either to enlighten these poor people, or open their land to lawful commerce.'

Having shown his prickly side to Sir Roderick he now did the same to the Foreign Office but with more excuse. On a visit to a senior official he was acquainted with a proposal that he should go out again as a sort of consul-at-large to the heart of Africa, the office to carry no salary or pension. Whether the letter confirming the proposal was written by an underling or by Lord Russell himself, that 'cold' gentleman continued to be ungracious about any emolument.

Sir Harry Johnston in his book on Livingstone written in 1891 takes up the cudgels on his behalf on the financial aspect of his journeys and shows two things very conclusively, (i) that Livingstone had neither the desire nor the business acumen to make money by his journeys, and (ii) that this offer of status-without-pay from the Foreign Office looked like very shabby treatment to all who knew about it at the time.

The substance of Johnston's calculations is that in his total of thirty years of service in Africa, Livingstone acquired about £21,000, of which £12,000 came from the sale of his two books, and £6,000 from grants, awards and subscriptions. By simple subtraction, therefore, we arrive at the average rate of pay he received for all those years was but little over £100 a year.

He started his last journey with two equal grants of £500, from the Government and from the Royal Geographical Society, and a donation of £1000 from Mr James Young of Glasgow to assist in the maintenance of his family while he was away.

It is only fair to add that in all its one hundred and thirty years of existence the Royal Geographical Society has had to apportion such surplus funds as it had amongst all the continents and its contribution of £500 was reasonably handsome by comparison with its grants to other explorers. Its business has always been to promote rather than to finance exploration.

We can only account for the niggardly attitude of the Foreign Office by suggesting that they found Livingstone's recent work a great embarrassment and probably were in full expectation of more to come when he again got loose in Central Africa. Nevertheless, 'shabby' is the only word to describe its treatment of him, and it is significant to note that a single lecture in Bombay later induced subscriptions from local people far in excess of the Government grant.

He had finished his book by mid-April and went to London with Agnes where he attended a dinner at the Royal Academy, at which most of Her Majesty's Ministers were present and to his great alarm he was called upon to speak. He was not reported and we only have second-hand evidence that it included earnest references to the Slave Trade. He was well received by most of the Ministers including Lord Clarendon who patted him on the back and asked when he was going out to Africa.

No doubt these personal contacts with important people helped him to accept a compromise with the government, accepting a grant of £500 and acceding to their proposal that he should, for the present at least, receive no pay for the consular status, which would at least give him influence with the coastal Arabs.

John Kirk and Horace Waller went to Folkestone to see him off on his last journey on August 18th and, having left Agnes in Paris, where she was to attend a finishing school, he travelled as fast as he could to Bombay, which he reached on September 11th.

There he sold the *Lady Nyassa* for one-third of what he had personally spent on her, and that he lost by investing it in a local Indian bank which failed a little later. He was very much in official society during the three months he spent there and we know from a friend of his that he was 'much stouter, better, and healthier looking' than he was the year before.

The same authority, a reverend, also remarks that at an official gathering Livingstone 'was dressed very unlike a minister—more like a post captain or an admiral. He wore a blue dress-coat, trimmed with lace and bearing a Government gilt button. In his hand he carried a cocked hat'.

We can take our choice on whether this mode of dress was due to conceit, which is most unlikely, or whether he felt that as Consul-at-large he ought to dress the part.

While there, he was sowing seeds of trouble for himself by deciding to take with him twelve sepoys under a 'havildar' or senior N.C.O. He also took Indian buffaloes, hoping to introduce that moderately docile animal to Africa. He personally selected eight 'Nassick boys' as he always called them, they being boys captured from slavers by the British Navy and sent to a mission school near Bombay. Volunteers included Chuma and Wikitani, the two boys he had brought over himself, who were Yaos.

The Governor, Sir Bartle Frere, was most helpful in every way, and he not only promised that Kirk should become medical officer to the Consulate at Zanzibar, but arranged that Livingstone himself should present a steamer, the *Thule*, on behalf of the Bombay Government to the Sultan of Zanzibar. This meant that he and his retinue had cheap passage there in the *Thule*, though not a quick one, three weeks of ceaseless rolling according to his journal.

There was much to do at Zanzibar, which was to be his future headquarters, but more than enough time to do it in as he had to wait two months before he could get transport down to the Rovuma with the help of H.M.S. *Penguin*. The delay was definitely bad for the morale of his sepoys and Nassickers and he lost more than half of his Indian buffaloes in that period. He had added to his party by engaging ten 'Johanna men', that is, men from that island. One of them at least, Musa, had been a sailor in the *Lady Nyassa* and Livingstone should have known better than to take him, as he already had a bad reputation.

In his last minute arrangements there was an air of 'let's get off somehow, whether we've got the best men or not'. In sober fact it was probably less the character of his men than his way of handling them that was the occasion for the insubordination that began at once on landing. Livingstone never did have much idea of discipline, being liable to connect it with harshness rather than with efficiency.

The declared object of this new one-white-man expedition was a compromise between what he wanted to do himself and what Murchison had proposed he should do. He was to attempt once more to 'open Africa to civilising influences' especially by encouraging lawful trade and Christian missions, the two aims he had striven for already. He was also to enquire into the problems of the watersheds in that part of Africa.

The promoters rather expected it to occupy only two years or less, but it seems certain that Livingstone himself intended it to last much longer than that. He arranged, perhaps without due care, to have supplies sent to Ujiji on Lake Tanganyika by one of the Banyans or Indian store keepers of Zanzibar via one of the frequent Arab caravans. We shall hear more of Thani bin Salem, the Arab at Ujiji to whom these goods were entrusted.

So it was a very odd collection of men and animals which disembarked at the harbour of Mikindani, recommended to him by the master of a dhow, on March 24th, 1866.

There were six camels, three Indian buffaloes and a calf, two mules and four donkeys. All these were experimental, that is to say, he wished to find out which would best withstand the bite of the tsetse fly. In fact he knew that some were bound to fail in the test but considered it was money well spent to have the knowledge once and for all. What he had not allowed for was the carelessness and inhumanity of his men with regard to animals.

The party consisted of thirteen sepoys, ten Johanna men, nine Nassick boys, two Shupanga men, Susi and Amoda, and the two Yaos (which he now spelled Wayaus), Wikitani and Chuma.

While the animals were recovering from the knocking about they had suffered in the five days they had spent on the dhow the men were engaged in making saddles for some of them out of the local hard wood called *ntibwe*, which is the same as the *mohonunu* of Bechuanaland but here grows into large trees, very handsome with their silvery tufts of leaves.

The details of the next seven years' doings have, of necessity, to come from the journals of the principal actor in them, except for the few months that H. M. Stanley was with him. There is, of course, no doubt whatever as to their veracity: what is in doubt is their completeness, as we have already seen how liable he was to understatement or even omission of incidents which readers would regard as of interest and importance.

This review of the journey from the geographical standpoint can do no more than fill in gaps aided by deduction and helped, in a few places only, by some knowledge of the country he was passing through.

As before, he kept a note of the days doings and measurements in small pocket books, of which many are in the possession of the Livingstone Memorial Museum at Blantyre, and from these entries he wrote up his more deliberate journal, a larger book, from time to time.

The book published after his death (*Livingstone's Last Journals*) is largely a transcript of these journals with occasional excerpts from the smaller note-books. It was edited by Horace Waller whose care over it is obvious, but his interests were naturally in the man rather than in the geography.

We can judge of the satisfaction in Livingstone's mind at being once more on African soil by the very first entries in his journal after landing: 'The mere animal pleasure of travelling in a wild unexplored country is very great. When on lands of a couple of thousand feet elevation, brisk exercise imparts elasticity to the muscles, fresh and healthy blood circulates through the brain, the mind works well, the eye is clear, the step is firm, and a day's exertion always makes the evening's repose thoroughly enjoyable.'

There is a sigh of relief in that sentence, relief from having to conform to the conventions and niceties of conduct in England, relief from the close contact with his fellows of equal standards, from the trammels of having to fit his plans to those of his companions.

The lonely man was once more alone, from that point of view, alone with his Purpose clearly before him, with Freedom to pursue his aim and Faith within him that it was God's purpose and he was His chosen agent. He felt once more that he was captain of his destiny, free to shape that destiny under Providence and ruler absolute in his queer circle of sepoys and ex-slaves and camels and donkeys. So he bursts out with the pleasure, the animal pleasure of it all as many another traveller has done, ready to forget that African fevers can alter it swiftly, and sluggish blood, confused mind, and wavering step hinder the traveller.

Nor is it enough to be ruler absolute unless one rules and this is where one sees a changed Livingstone, and where the rift in the perfect lute appears that is to spoil much of the triumphant song which might have ended this journey.

An entry of but a fortnight later shows that he had lost his grip, that he was ready to submit where before he would have commanded: '. . . the Havildar assured me that two buffaloes were amply sufficient to carry all the sepoys' luggage. I now find that they have more than full loads for two buffaloes, two mules and two donkeys. When these animals fall down under them, they assure me with so much positiveness that they are not overloaded, that I have to be silent or only express the opinion that they will kill these animals.'

That ominous phrase 'I have to be silent' appears so frequently in one form or another in days to come, that one begins to feel that it is the servants who are running the expedition, not the white man.

The physical difficulties he could still cope with, hiring villagers to cut the branches which hindered the tall camels, being wise about the route, etc. but the human element in the problem seemed to catch him by surprise and bewilder him.

In a modified form it was the same fault as with the white men in the Zambezi expedition, to think it was enough to give general orders for their work and leave them to get on with it in their own time and fashion. If that was a poor way of treating a pleasant but young and inexperienced man like Thornton it was quite fatal with such sly people as the Havildar and Musa.

His journal at once settles down to its earlier accustomed form, full of observations, human, animal and vegetable, with occasional shrewd remarks about the run of the rivers or the shape of the land forms, yet these become more and more interlarded with sentences, such as:

'. . . we could not march more than a few miles owing to the slowness of the sepoys, they are a heavy drag on us and of no possible use.

'. . . they sit down and smoke and eat, leaving the animals loaded in the sun.

'. . . if I remain behind to keep the sepoys on the move, it deprives me of all the pleasure of travelling.

'. . . I went on ahead with the Johanna men and twenty four carriers, for it was a pleasure to get away from the sepoys and Nassick boys; the two combined to overload the animals.

'. . . It was such continual vexation to contend with their sneaking spirit, that I gave up annoying myself by seeing these matters, though I felt certain all the animals would be killed.'

What he needed, of course, was a stern man of the N.C.O. type in the rear to attend to these things—perhaps he expected the Havildar or Musa to fulfil that office, if so, his judgment of men was once more sadly at fault.

Notwithstanding these delays, difficulty in buying food because of famine and a certain amount of illness amongst his men, progress was fairly steady and he passed the point he had reached in 1862 before the end of his first month's travel, and reached the junction of the Rovuma and the Loendi by six weeks' travel, both rivers being too full to be crossed on foot. Livingstone was, of course, taking latitudes regularly and lunars when the moon served that purpose. Here he had to halt while the sepoys and Nassick boys came up, and it is possible that some of their 'idleness' was due to illness, for one of the latter died at this time. The sepoys were severely lectured and for a few days they improved.

They were now on the upper Rovuma on the regular slave-trade route, and passed numbers of dead bodies on the pathway, some still with the *goree* or slave stick round their necks and wounds showing they had been killed because they could not keep up with the slavegang. They were also approaching the region of the Mazitu, a branch of the Angoni who had come round the north end of the lake, so Livingstone left the river and turned southwards to avoid them when he was within eighty miles of Lake Nyasa. He was amongst the northern section of the Yao tribe so Chuma and Wikitani were helpful with the dialect.

On the southward route there was still famine and he had to push on with the stronger ones so as to send food back to the weak or lazy, of whom the sepoys seem to have been the worst.

Slave-stick or Goree

When they reached the town of Chief Mataka, with over one thousand huts, their food troubles were at an end, but they had taken nearly three months to do three hundred and fifty miles.

The old chief was gracious to them and the sick men recovered in the fortnight they stayed there, while Livingstone used the time in writing a long geological description of the journey up to that point. From here he sent the sepoys back to the coast under the care of one of the Arab traders, but kept the Havildar on at his own request.

When they resumed the journey they were avoided by at least two large Arab slave parties, and learned that from three hundred to eight hundred was the usual number in one gang. The marches went better and they reached the Lake in a total of four months and for a moment Livingstone is exuberant: 'It was as if I had come back to an old home I never expected again to see; and pleasant to bathe in the delicious waters again, hear the roar of the sea and dash in the rollers.'

He had thus, at his third attempt, pioneered a way to the lake by a route not under the control of the Portuguese, but he could not claim that it was a good route and, in fact, he never says much in its favour. It was used by the Universities Missions later, under Bishop Steere, but could never be more than a walking route as compared to a freight route.

The projected railway from the new port of Mtwara close to Mikindani may reach the lake on a line to the north of Livingstone's route, but only because of a promising coalfield at Songea near the lake.

Here he had to change his route a second time, the first being when the presence of the Mazitu prevented him from approaching Lake Tanganyika via the north end of Lake Nyasa. The alternative was to get a passage across the middle of Lake Nyasa by one of the dhows which he knew the Arabs had. But his attitude to slavery was much too well known and the dhow masters quickly sailed to the far side of the lake. So there was nothing for it but to march round the southern end of the lake, where he at least would know some of the chiefs, and could, for a certain distance, use his own map.

His passion for geography is expressed in his choice of route southwards, for instead of heading back to the divide which would be easy travelling he took the path alongside the lake with its ceaseless climbing up and down and crossing of rivers, each of them mapped with care over that eighty miles.

He was to do the same with Lake Tanganyika on his very last journey, but then it was a two hundred mile journey and he was a very sick man. No topographical difficulty ever put him off mapping new features, and anyone who looks at the steep mountains where he passed on either lake will sympathise with his carriers whom he dragged up and down athwart those steep valleys facing the lakes.

He was learning a great deal about the Arab slave trade and made a special visit farther south than necessary to call on a Yao chief, who was one of the chief actors in the raids on the Manganja, to discuss the slave trade.

The boldness with which Livingstone would go and tell a paramount chief that he ought to stop raiding says a great deal for his courage, but it also says something for African courtesy to travellers. A chief was traditionally host to any peaceful traveller even when his guest had come to lecture him on his conduct. In fact we may liken the whole of the next seven years, without too much exaggeration, to a man wandering unarmed into all the haunts of gangsters in Chicago telling them they were a bad lot.

This particular chief, Mukate, the fore-runner of the notorious Zarafi, who gave Sir Harry Johnston such trouble thirty years later, tried to laugh it off but he gave guides to assist them in hiring canoes with which to cross Lake Malombe a few miles below them. With charming inconsequence the journal passes abruptly at this point from the horrors of slaving to the incidence of earthquakes here, the occurrence of hot springs and the rift-like character of the valley he was crossing once more.

He went to see Chief Mponda, who was to become, later, another thorn in the side of Johnston at his village close to the present Fort Johnston—'a blustering sort of person but immensely interested in everything European.' Livingstone went to inspect a slave camp there: 'The majority were boys of about 8 or 10 years of age, nearly all were in the taming stick. The owners said that after feeding them and accounting for the losses on the way to the coast, they made little by the trip.' In fact it was an exact parallel to a visit I made once to a drove of cattle in Ngamiland, when the Damara drovers, thinking I was an inspector, carefully showed me their best beasts and tried to hide the sickly ones, and told me how well they treated them, but how little profit there would be at the end of the three hundred mile journey. Livingstone, however, ends with 'I told them it was a bad business altogether. They presented fowls to me in the evening'.

It was here that Livingstone parted, in characteristic fashion, with his Yao boy, Wikitani, who had been Bishop Mackenzie's favourite boy at Magomero. He found brothers and sisters near by, but it is clear that he also found a girl-friend.

In Livingstone's words: 'The father who sold him into slavery is dead and he wishes to stop with his relatives. . . . I did not attempt to dissuade him; his excessive levity will perhaps be cooled by marriage.'

When Lieutenant Young, R.N. came here nine years later bringing the Scottish Mission in the *Ilala*, he met both Wikitani and Mponda and in his breezy fashion described them.

He was very pleased to see Wikitani again and says of him that he was 'well born, smart of dress and now a youngster of some importance'. He was very useful to him as an interpreter. Mponda remembered Livingstone very well and he still wanted to go to England, but he was even more of a beer drinker and Young describes how he got one of his wives to massage him whilst drinking 'in order to make better stowage of his potations. In this way a good deal can be coaxed into corners and it is a pity Falstaff and Mponda never met, for there would have been high "jinks" between them.'

Livingstone's party walked across the base of the triangular peninsula of Cape Maclear to Marenga's large village at the end of that shallow gulf. Here an Arab trader told Musa that the country ahead was full of Mazitu and he and all his Johanna men refused to go any farther. Livingstone felt it was good riddance as they had stolen so much of his goods by the way, but it reduced his party to nine. Musa and his men got back to Zanzibar and concocted the story that they had met the Mazitu and Livingstone had been killed. Doubts were cast on the story when it reached England, particularly by Lieutenant Young, who knew Musa as a liar. A small expedition under Young went out, took up a steel boat in sections to the lake and disproved the story. This was a brilliant little expedition all done within eight months.

Young reached Shupanga on August 2nd, 1867 when Livingstone himself was to the south and west of Lake Tanganyika. The place was deserted, the Landeens having driven the Portuguese away but Mrs Livingstone's grave, with tombstone of bricks and mortar and a wooden cross, had been respected.

At Chibisa's the party had a great welcome, and help in particular from one of the Doctor's Makololo, Masiko, who supervised the carriers taking the sectional steel boat past the cataracts. Things must have gone like clockwork as they had put together and launched this boat, the *Search*, by August 30th.

Time altered their opinion of the Makololo, whom they found spoilt and lazy but they pressed on to the lake, greatly assisted by the hunting prowess of Faulkner, the second-in-command.

They first went some distance up the east side of the lake and met men who described Livingstone as passing through their villages, taking observations with his sextant and so on. They then crossed to the west coast and made their way round to Marenga's village near which Musa's desertion with his Johanna men had taken place. On the few occasions when the chief was found sober they got ample evidence of the falsity of Musa's story. Tried at Zanzibar, Musa got the comparatively light sentence of twelve months imprisonment.

Meanwhile more reports of Mazitu raids in the Kasungu district caused Livingstone to take a more southerly route than he had intended. By October 9th when the lowlands were becoming unpleasantly warm they had got up to a height of four thousand feet above sea level in the Mount Dedza district. Livingstone was impressed by the patches of cultivation which were 'so large and often squarish in form that but little imagination is requisite to transform the whole into the cultivated fields of England'.

He had, in fact, discovered a second highland, as suitable for European residence as that where he had taken the first missionaries, and it would now be just as closely occupied by settlers as the Shire Highlands, were there land available. It was country never before visited by white men as the route of the Portuguese, Dr Lacerda and others, to Cazembe, was far to the westward.

To illustrate this part of his last journey, we reproduce a manuscript map from his field note book. From Marenga's village he crossed the shallow bay by canoe and it was soon after landing that Musa and his companions deserted. His zig-zag course is explained by the quotation 'we had to go in the direction of the villages which were on friendly terms with our guides'. The map illustrates not only his skill as a mapper of what he saw but also the value of his interpretation of what he gathered from his ceaseless questioning. One sharp turn, however, was due to a Mazitu raiding party in the neighbourhood but it passed to the south of them, in which direction they saw the smoke of burning villages.

It is interesting to note that twenty odd years later those same Mazitu or Angoni were being very difficult neighbours to the

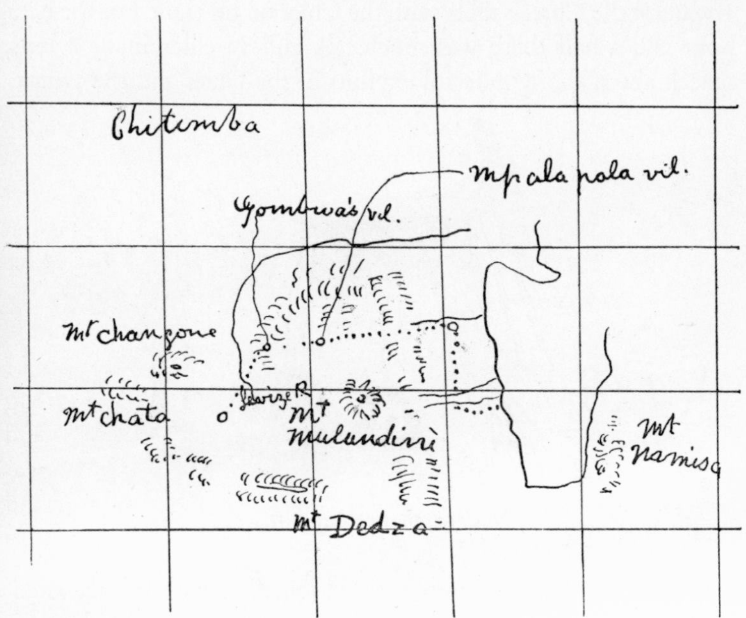

Tracing from Livingstone's field notes of the south end of Lake Nyasa

great Dr Laws and his second-in-command, Dr Elmslie, who ultimately established the Livingstonia Mission. At that time, under their redoubtable chief Mombera every man had an assegai without which he hardly took a step.

Another twenty-five years later and Dr Wilson, grandson of Livingstone, was helping the same Dr Elmslie among the Angoni and assegais were becoming slightly outmoded.

Yet another twenty-five years later the writer was given a ceremonial welcome by Mbelwa, successor to Mombera. An extract from a description by my wife of the occasion will give a notion of how times have changed.

A messenger was sent along to the imposing white house of the Chief, and presently a procession appeared issuing from it. In the middle was the Chief—the only portly man to be seen—around him the elders walking and singing and before him a leopard-man dancing. Then there were polite bowings and handshakings and the party settled down in front of the hundreds of Angoni, the Bwana at the Chief's table with the Chief on his right. For the next hour and a half there was much talk and an elder made a long speech about the wonderful exploits of the Chief and the visitor,

Native iron-smelting furnace

at the end of which the whole crowd joined in with full-throated cries of the Zulu "Bayete! Bayete!" Leopard-men executed many lively pirouettes, jumps and lunges with an assegai and flourishing of shield.

Unfortunately there was only one assegai and shield so these had to be handed over to each man who felt the urge to thus do honour to his chief and guest, including the son of the Chief who had to do these prancings clad in a zoot-suit and gaudy tie.

A sort of Greek chorus went on all the time of women shuffling round and round amongst the dancers, lu-lu-looing with rapid vibrations of the tongue, bobbing their heads like chickens and sometimes ducking to avoid the wild lunges of the one assegai. The proceedings ended by the Bwana taking a photograph of the imposing Chief, whose portly figure displayed to advantage a picture of the British Lion printed on his robe, worn unfortunately upside down.

O Tempora! O Mores! Only one assegai and the British Lion upside down!

Livingstone's party was now passing through hoe-manufacturing country on the divide, many villages of iron-founders and smiths—the two occupations always being combined. The

'Keep watch for each other and match Beauty with the Beast'

countryside was denuded of trees cut down for charcoal, just as was Sussex in the eighteenth century when it was an iron producing county.

In fact, Livingstone said that one could not go a quarter of a mile without meeting pieces of slag, calcined pipes and fragments of furnaces.

He now had only nine men with him and could not reduce his loads to less than twelve, so they had to relay whenever chiefs refused to provide carriers. Nevertheless, they travelled fairly quickly down a large tributary of the Luangwa, and there they picked up two derelict slaves, Yaos, to join as carriers, and made a very bad bargain indeed. The rains began in earnest when they descended into the valley of the Luangwa and attacks of fever began for all the party. They were here in *Mopane* country with heavy clay soil and slippery paths.

As there was famine in the land, Livingstone was forced to shoot game, for which the Luangwa valley is noted, and in spite of his maimed arm he managed to get all the difficult animals, like rhino, sable, kudu and even those boon companions of the open plains, zebra and wildebeeste, which so carefully keep watch for each other, and match beauty with the beast.

He disliked the business, but he does measure the animals' height, horns, etc. in the approved big-game-hunter fashion, though he never gives details of the actual hunt as they do.

The dearth of food became more general as they climbed up the western slopes of the Rift Valley, in which the Luangwa flows, the Machinga mountains of which he had heard so often from the Portuguese. The name was little guide as to where or what they were as it simply means Mountains of rocks.

He was pioneering a route up the Nyamadzi River which was to be used by most of the administrators in later years whose names are famous in the annals of Northern Rhodesia, Robert Codrington, Hector Croad, 'Bobo' Young, 'Chirapula' Stephenson, Sir Stewart Gore-Browne and others, of whom the two last are still with us.

Such of the memoirs of these men as are being collected by the active Northern Rhodesia Society are a valuable link over the gap of twenty years between Livingstone and the early administrators.

On the slopes of the Machinga Escarpment Livingstone was among the Babisa tribe who were great travellers and traders, but no match for the Angoni to the east of them or the Awemba to the north at fighting.

In spite of the hunger and the veiled hostility of the headmen, he writes of this time: 'I shall make this beautiful land better known, which is an essential part of the process by which it will become the "pleasant haunts of men".' To make it better known he is as busy with his latitudes and longitudes as ever, and plotting his route whenever he has time on a large sheet of paper ruled with a geographical network, or projection.

They were on the rim of the escarpment by New Year's Day of 1867, all very hungry and with the rainy season starting in earnest.

He records at this time that the boy who was carrying the chronometers had two falls on a path slippery with rain, which altered their rates. His longitudes for the next few months were twenty miles to the eastward in error, perhaps in consequence of these falls. This happened where he crossed the line of the present Great North Road from Mpika to Chinsali and Isoka, which was to be a vital artery for transport in the 1939–45 war. Going steadily northward he came to a very beautiful little lake, though he describes it in more matter of fact terms as 'about 5 miles long and one and a half broad. It had hippopotami and the poku (an antelope) fed on its banks.'

This has been given different names. On the official maps it is called Lake Young (after the 'Bobo' Young aforementioned) but it is also called by the native name of Shiwangandu or Lake of the Crocodiles, and close to it is the present baronial residence of Colonel Sir Stewart Gore-Browne who has been a prominent settler and friend of the Africans for forty years. Livingstone's men called it Chitane's Water because of a sad little accident that befell them there.

Livingstone had with him what he called a 'little poodle-dog' called Chitane, to which he had become much attached and it had served him well as a guard at night.

The party had to cross the upper shallow end of the lake which involved waist-deep wading in peaty stuff with deep holes in it, for a whole mile. They were 'all too much engaged with preserving their balance to think of the spirited little dog and he must have swam till he sunk'.

They were now on the Mansya stream, which he calls the Limansha, running into the Chambezi River, which is really the most remote source of the Congo. It is curious to reflect that he was to be in the basin of the Congo for the whole of the next six years, except for a short journey to the eastward but he was never sure whether it was truly the Congo basin or that of the Nile.

At Chitane's Water in fact he crossed the threshold of his final search and began the quest which terminated only with his life.

He must have taken his star observations quite near the future site chosen by Gore-Browne. As usual it is correct in latitude but his longitude is twenty miles too easterly. They are reduced to

The giant mushroom of Africa

after a photograph by J. E. Hughes

famine diet, including leaves and mushrooms, and of the latter he mentions the giant type, as 'large as a man's hat and is very good roasted'. The writer found them somewhat tough and tasteless but no doubt he lacked the sauce of hunger when he tried it.

They were on the way down to the Chambezi, which Livingstone always spelt 'Chambeze', when there fell upon him the great disaster of the loss of all his medicines. The two Yao ex-slaves deserted taking with them the box of mecidines, all the dishes, a box of powder, the tools and two guns. They tried to follow the robbers but heavy rain came on so that they could not track them. He writes in his journal: 'I felt as if I had now received the sentence of death, like poor Bishop Mackenzie: this loss of the medicine box gnaws at the heart terribly.' And yet the worst thing he has to say about these false knaves is 'they gave way to the temptation which their good conduct had led us to put in their way'.

Crossing the Chambezi at a junction which we can recognise from the name, his error in longitude has almost disappeared, and he was now in the domain of the Babemba tribe, a more warlike and more manly people than the Babisa he had just left. It was now the end of January when the second onset of heavy rain is usually due and the entry 'Northward through almost trackless dripping forests and across oozing bogs' is graphic enough.

The paramount chief, Chitapangwa, received him with some pomp of drummers and retinue of wives and servants, but the main point of interest at this stockade was that he met there a small party of coastal Arabs—'black Arabs' as he calls them—on their way to Zanzibar by whom he sent hurried letters which actually reached England, but only after Young had gone out with his little expedition to check the false story of Musa. The chief proved a shrewd and wily bargainer and Livingstone had to give in to some of his demands since his party was starving, and they were forced to stay for a whole fortnight listening to the importunities of this trading chief, and he became ill with rheumatic fever, 'the first attack of it I ever had—and no medicine!'

He got 'lunars' for his longitude and the result is again twenty miles to the eastward, which accounts for the sharp turn to the east of the route as marked in his map.

It is necessary to note at this stage the errors of longitude as we shall find in the last chapter that they have a very important bearing on his choice of route.

He intended to pass by the next chief Mwamba, who was Chitapangwa's brother, but his timid men prevailed on him not to give offence by so doing and therefore met the chief and doubtless his more notorious successor of the same name who gave some trouble to the early administrators. Moamba, as Livingstone spells his name, was 'a big, stout, public-house-looking person, with a slight cast in his left eye, but intelligent and hearty.'

His village was then a little to the north of the site of the present Kasama, one of the earliest bomas to be established in the area and now capital of the Province.

It is here that Livingstone made a mistake, very rare with him, about which way rivers were running, as he puts the Luombe river running east and then north to Tanganyika whereas it runs west and south into the long and semi-navigable Lukulu. The mistake will be readily understood by anyone who knows these rivers near their sources in the height of the rainy season, when each stream is in a flooded dambo and it is difficult to say which direction the water is finally taking.

He had now reached the point at which his route coincided with the one he was to take, in the opposite direction, five years later, and amongst the Ba-lungu who lived round the southern end of the great lake he was approaching. The village of Chibwe is just over the watershed of the Chambezi but Livingstone did not suspect that river to rise so far north, so turns the streams round to run into the Lofu (modern Lufubu) and thence into the lake. A possible reason for his confusion over the drainage pattern is that the long threatened fever from exposure to rain had come upon him and 'ill disposes me to enjoy the beautiful landscape. We are evidently on the ridge, but people have not a clear conception of where the rivers run.'

He foresaw a severe attack of fever developing and hurried on to get to the lake before it overtook him. On the 1st of April the party clambered down the two thousand foot slope to the broad bay with the large island of Kumbula at its eastern end. He did not realise that he had nearly doubled the length of the lake first discovered by Burton and Speke nine years before. Indeed he was incapable at first of taking much interest in his discovery as he was utterly prostrated by the fever, and had at least one period of being unconscious for some hours. It took a month of rest at a small village near the lakeside before he could make a move to continue his exploration, by which he intended 'to see whether this Lake narrows or not'.

There was news of a war to the westward between Arab traders and an important chief, Nsama, and Livingstone hoped to avoid that by travelling up the west side of the lake. But they had only gone fifty miles, to the mouth of the Lofubu, when he was warned to go no further as Nsama's son was ahead of him 'killing all who came that way'.

So they turned back to find the Arabs, mostly black Swahili, that is, half Arabs from the coast, and to present the letter of recommendation from the Sultan of Zanzibar.

This letter, supplemented, we may be sure, by Livingstone's tact in dealing with all black people, quickly put him in favour with the Arabs of whom the chief, Hamees, seemed to make himself responsible for the safety of the white man.

They were able to give him some account of the country to the west and south and Livingstone saw his chance of getting to Lake Moeru (Mweru as we spell it to-day) by passing to the south of the area disturbed by war, though Hamees was anxious to send him up the east side of Tanganyika to Ujiji. Possibly it was an embarrassment to these Arabs, who traded in slaves as well as ivory, to have an anti-slavery fanatic, however friendly, amongst them, especially as he had credentials from their own Sultan. Livingstone notes the difference between the Zanzibar Arabs, like Hamees, and the hybrid slavers he met at the south end of Lake Nyasa, whose coarse living and general brutishness disgusted him.

He had to stay over three months in the village while negotiations with the enemy were going on, and he always hated staying in one place though he employed his time 'in reading *Smith's Bible Dictionary*' (his one reading book), 'and calculating different positions which have stood over in travelling.' He was expecting trouble over his longitudes and there is a note 'Chronometer A stopped to-day without any apparent cause except the earthquake'

The party got away at the end of August and travelled for a while with an Arab named Tipo Tipo or Hamidi bin Mohamad whom we shall hear more about. Also in the vicinity was Syde bin Habib, his acquaintance of twelve years earlier.

Livingstone's party descended into the valley of the Lufubu and crossed it to climb up the divide to the watershed of the large streams running into the swampy area of Mweru Wantipa. Here he met the chief Nsama who had resisted the Arabs and found him to be 'a very old man with a good head and face and a large abdomen. He was the Napoleon of these countries; no one could stand before him, hence the defeat of the invincible Nsama has caused a great panic'.

Hamees here married the daughter of Nsama, partly to cement the uneasy treaty they had made, partly no doubt because she was 'a nice modest, good-looking young woman'.

As a result of these peaceful protestations Livingstone was able to set off towards Lake Mweru with an Arab party, and they took a route due north crossing the swampy Chisera with some difficulty. The enormous number of game in this valley is remarked upon by Livingstone, and indeed it is still there. He was now travelling with Syde bin Hamid, whom he often calls Hamidi, but there are many delays, time being of little consequence to the Arabs. When they do go they find empty villages, the owners having fled for fear of attack. They were now marching round to the north of Nsama's country and his notes on the water courses, the vegetation and the animals are profuse. The long line of slaves and carriers and women camp followers, four hundred and fifty in number, comes in for graphic description.

They reached Lake Mweru early in November, just as the rains were beginning and as usual he is very calm at attaining his objective, writing only a line or two in description.

Livingstone was now indeed at the heart of Africa and in the region he had longed to reach for years past. Though he badly needed the goods, and especially the medicines, that should be waiting for him at Ujiji, he easily abandoned that wise plan and turned south again for further exploration.

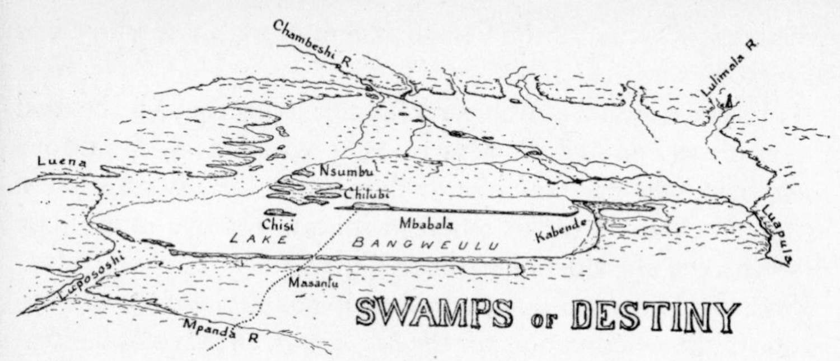

SWAMPS OF DESTINY

CHAPTER NINE

On the left hand there was a very dangerous quag into which, if even a good man falls, he finds no bottom for his foot to stand on.

JOHN BUNYAN

Two days before he reached the actual shores of Lake Mweru there is the entry in his notes: 'As Syde and Tipo Tipo were sending men to Casembe for ivory, I resolved to go thither first, instead of shaping my course for Ujiji.' As it turned out it was to be another year and a half of alternate journeys and delays before he did get there.

Casembe was one of a long line of chiefs of the Lunda people, which still has considerable influence in Northern Rhodesia, and it was a predecessor of his whom Dr Lacerda, the Portuguese traveller, had visited seventy years earlier. Lacerda died within ten days of his arrival there, but this men stayed on there for eight months and one or two later Portuguese who had reached the same place had also spoken of Casembe's as an important centre.

At long last Livingstone had solved the problem of the rivers in this area, namely that the Chambezi entered Lake Bemba or Bangweolo and came out of it as the Luapula which then turned through more than 90° and entered Lake Mweru from which it flowed out again as the Lualaba in a north-westerly direction, but

* The headpiece is a bird's eye view of the Bangweulu Swamps as seen from the west.

whether it was part of the Congo system or not Livingstone was never to be sure.

For some reason the Arab party did not accompany him beyond the northern end of Lake Mweru so he was alone with his nine men again, who had now been with him for nearly two years and as some of them were to remain with him for five more, they deserve some introduction to the reader.

Susi, the Shupanga man, who had joined Livingstone in 1859 as one of the wood-cutters for the *Ma-Robert*, already stood out as leader and we shall hear more of him, and of Chuma, the much younger Yao boy, who at this stage was laughter-loving and irresponsible, yet very loyal. The third man who stood by his master to the end, Gardner, was a Nassick boy but we rarely hear him of him except that he served constantly and faithfully.

The other six stood by the Doctor until the evil days that came to them in the next chapter when they fell away, but some came back to his service for the last journey. Amoda, also a Shupanga wood-cutter, was one of these, most valuable perhaps for his wife, Halima, whom he picked up later on and who became Livingstone's cook.

Abram was the chief interpreter while passing through the Lake Nyasa region as he came from there and had learned fair English in Bombay, but he was of the timid kind, and so was Simon. Both were apt to alter Livingstone's words to a chief or feign ignorance: 'When Abraham does not like to say what I state, he says to me, "I don't know the proper word"; but when I speak without him, he soon finds them. He and Simon thought that a cringing manner was the way to win a chief over. It is difficult to get these lads to say what one wants uttered; either with enormous self-conceit, they give different, and, as they think, better statements, suppress them altogether, or return false answers.' Nevertheless it was Simon who at least twice on hungry marches gave up his meal to Livingstone and went without himself.

It was Baraka who was trusted to carry the precious medicine-box 'because he was so careful', but he evidently had lapses, for it was he who exchanged his load with the Yao ex-slave for a lighter one, when the thieves stole it and other things. He attempted to desert a month or so later and so did James, who was never very satisfactory and was killed in the Manyuema country in 1871. James used to carry the chronometers but he at least left them on the ground when he ran away with Baraka. The last of the nine was Mabruki who appears to have been a willing worker but easily persuaded into bad company.

Livingstone was now entering a region which was to become very familiar to him in later journeys but we must note that his longitudes were in error in an unlucky direction, due probably to the chronometers, of which he had three, having had a fall and also being affected by the earthquake, which stopped one and altered the rates of the others.

Besides these chronometers he had a watch, which he calls a hack-watch, that is to say, one which could be carried on the person and used for observations provided it was checked against the chronometers before or after use. He probably wore this himself, putting it under his armpit in very wet weather or when wading deep streams.

We have noted that on his way up to Lake Tanganyika the error was about 20′ or 20 geographical miles too far to the east—quite a reasonable error for such a journey.

But when he reached Lake Mweru the easterly error had changed into a westerly one of the same amount and it became worse as he went south. His detailed mapping, however, becomes more careful than ever, with little sketches of the streams he crosses and always a note as to how deep and how wide they are. He finds where Dr Lacerda died and hears accounts of the quarrels between his Portuguese and some 'Ujijians' who were there at the same time. The name Casembe means 'a general' and he records the names of the seven previous ones. The town or large village had been moved with every change in the succession and in Livingstone's day it was near the eastern bank of the large lagoon of Mofwe, about five miles from the Luapula itself.

Casembe received him reasonably well but he was not exactly a likeable character. 'He has a heavy uninteresting countenance, without beard or whiskers, and somewhat of the Chinese type, and his eyes have an outward squint. He smiled but once during the day.' He had a habit of cropping the ears and lopping off the hands of those who displeased him. It takes a saint to endure a sinner and certainly Livingstone got on well with this callous potentate and stayed there for a whole month. He was possibly more the guest of an Arab, Mohammad bin Saleh, than of Casembe, and this was the man who had been detained at the court for at least ten years, under no less than four Casembes.

Livingstone saw the chief and his retinue frequently and his brief descriptions excite interest to hear more of the curious characters by whom this sullen ruler was surrounded. For instance there was the court jester or dwarf, one Zofu, who was less than four feet high and was present at all public ceremonies, to make antics or utter pleasantries before his chief. Near him would be the executioner, with a broad sword and large scissors hanging to his neck for cropping ears off. The principal wife was 'a fine tall, good featured lady, with two spears in her hand, and a carrier bearing before her two enormous pipes ready charged for smoking'.

The most interesting character of all must have been old Pérémbé, reputed by the Arabs to be one hundred and fifty years old, and a 'sensible old man'. He was credited with having children when Pereira visited Casembe in 1796, and when Lacerda came in 1799 he had forty of them. He must have been a hundred years old yet Livingstone was perhaps expecting a little too much when he complains that he could not induce Pérémbé 'to tell anything of times previous to his own'.

When Livingstone left to return northward en route to Ujiji he was accompanied by Mohammad bin Saleh, the Arab who had been virtually a prisoner, and it seems that Livingstone's letter of recommendation from the Sultan of Zanzibar had a good deal to do with his release.

One reason for going north is contained in a sentence from a letter written at Casembe's to Lord Clarendon: 'I am so tired of exploration without a word from home or anywhere else for two years that I must go to Ujiji on Tanganyika for letters before doing anything else.' But when he rejoins his Arab friends at the northern end of Lake Mweru he finds they are unwilling to travel to Ujiji in the rainy season and he has another long wait before him, and the usual remark follows: 'I am ill with fever, as I always am when stationary.' Meanwhile he collected a great deal of doubtful information about the geography of all central Africa from these much-travelled but very ungeographical Arabs. He is cautious over these conversations and writes: '. . . the most enlightened of these informants leave the impression on the mind of groping in the dark.'

Yet it was these gropings of enlightened informants which were to sow the seeds of an obsession in Livingstone's mind which was to influence all his subsequent journeys.

He must have given the statements of the Arabs far more credence than he admits and since they affected his future plans we must give an outline of the discoveries concerning the sources of the Nile, discoveries which he was liable to interpret to fit the assurances of the Arabs.

In 1858 Burton and Speke had discovered Lake Tanganyika at Ujiji, but had examined very little of it and could not say where was its outlet. Speke, on a separate journey, discovered the Victoria Nyanza, which Livingstone styles 'Speke's Lake'. Speke, with Grant, went out again in 1860 to confirm this discovery, and walked round it to the outlet at Ripon Falls. He returned, down the Nile, meeting Baker on the way and Baker, accompanied by his wife, discovered Lake Albert, which he called the second source of the Nile.

Livingstone knew of these discoveries before he left England in 1866, but he may not have heard in detail of the level of Baker's Lake Albert. The levels of all three are important and, as given by the men concerned, they are; Victoria, about 3700 feet above sea-level, Tanganyika, 2500, and Albert about 2000.

An entry made by Livingstone in his journal of April 2nd, 1868, foreshadows his belief that the final sources of the Nile had not yet been discovered: 'If I am not deceived by the information I have received from various reliable sources, the springs of the Nile rise between 9° and 10° south latitude, or at least 400 or 500 miles south of the south end of Speke's Lake, which he considered to be the source of the Nile.' The reason for this belief follows: 'Tanganyika is declared to send its water through north into Baker's Lake; if this does not prove false then Tanganyika is an expansion of the Nile.'

We have seen from the levels that Tanganyika is five hundred feet higher than Baker's Lake Albert and therefore the Arabs were not 'declaring' an impossibility. The strange thing is that probably this did happen at one time, before the Mufumbiro volcanoes erupted and reversed the drainage back into Lake Tanganyika whence it had to find an exit to the west into the Congo system.

Something of the new theory must have influenced him in a very sudden decision he made a few days later. He had been forced to wait for the rains to finish before starting for Ujiji, but now, when they were all but over, he decided to go south again to find Lake Bemba or Bangweolo. He must have been badly upset by all this waste of time and impatient to do something, for on April 11th he argued with his friend Mohammad who was strongly opposed to the Bemba plan and Livingstone ends his journal for that day with 'I fear I must give up this Lake for the present'. But the journal for the very next day begins with 'I think of starting tomorrow for Bangweolo'.

This raised a storm of protests, and particularly from his own nine men, protests which made Livingstone dig his heels in and become obstinate, especially as Mohammad had clearly suggested to his own men that they should refuse to go.

So he started with only five of his men and that night one of them, Amoda, ran away, back to the Arab encampment. Livingstone writes of the deserters: 'I did not blame them very severely in my mind for absconding: they were tired of tramping and so verily am I.'

He had some difficulty in making his way a second time to Casembe as the village headmen suspected treachery, as of the Arabs, but the paramount received him kindly, wondering at the strange desire of the white man to go and see Lake Bemba 'which is only water—the same as Luapula, Mofue and Moero; nothing to be seen'. During this visit he made as certain as he could of his longitude: 'I have taken lunars several times, measuring both sides of the moon about 190 times, but a silly map-maker may alter the whole for the most idiotic of reasons.' This is a hit at Mr Cooley who had several times thrown doubts upon Livingstone's accuracy, in notes to the Royal Geographical Society.

They were delayed for three weeks at Casembe's but started again, in company with some Arabs, on May 30th, the floods having subsided somewhat and the cool weather coming on.

For this journey we are fortunate in having Livingstone's field book, from which in due course he wrote up the journal which went back to England with Stanley. It is a small black Lett's 'metallic note book' of some hundred and forty pages, of which no less than sixty-six are taken up with astronomical observations. It is in the possession of the Rhodes-Livingstone Museum by whom it was lent to the author. The little wooden pencil is still in its sheath though it has lost its lead, which was obviously fine pointed as much of the writing is microscopic. He was already coming to the end of his stationery and the pages are covered completely with notes on everything he saw, interspersed with star sights, tiny sketch maps and even an occasional attempt at a portrait, which he probably smiled at just as much as will our readers. One end of the book is almost entirely taken up with 'lunars'. These are not worked out but were later sent to Sir Thomas Maclear, who made himself responsible for them, as applied to the map finally published in the *Last Journals*. It is possible and even probable that there were work sheets, not now available, on which he computed a few of his longitudes so that he could make the usual preliminary plotting on a ruled network, his invariable custom.

He made sketch maps of his route, adding to them every day, entering distances marched in hours, barometer and thermometer readings and giving geological details. At any halt he seems to have entered up the time marched and the nightly camp is marked with a cross with the total hours underlined twice. These route maps show the whole journey, occupying four or five pages, only one of which is reproduced here, below, on which the route and the rivers are traced but the notes are re-lettered as they had to be read with a magnifying glass.

The Arabs had a slave gang with them and by this time Livingstone had evidently accepted such company as the only means by which he could travel. Two notes at the

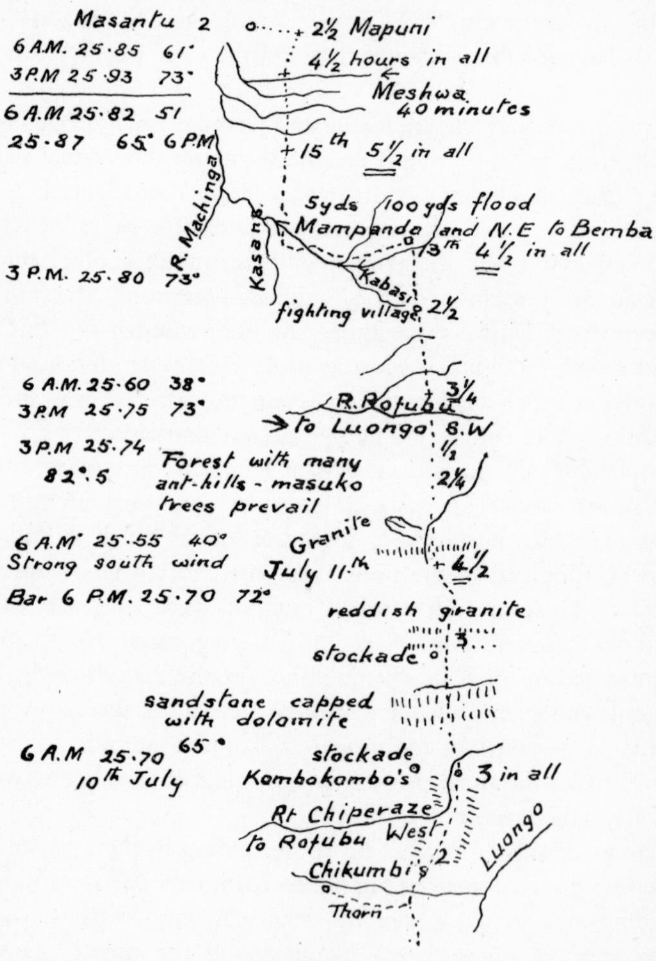

Page from Livingstone's fieldbook, detail traced but manuscript re-lettered

beginning of the journey on these slaves are damning in their very brevity:

'15th June. A slave tried to break out of his slave stick last night and actually broke half-inch iron with his fingers, but the broken part stuck in the hole.

'17th June. A slave in the slave-stick burst out into a loud cry last night, sobbing bitterly—could not say why—a few switches from his master quieted him instantly.'

It took them a fortnight to reach a brother of Casembe, Moenempanda (Moene meaning Chief), who gave Livingstone 'a public reception, which was like that of Casembe, but better managed', with drums, musical instruments, etc., but no court jester is mentioned. Thence they crossed the Luongo river and went down its left bank to reach another leading chief, Chikumbi, whom he asked for a guide to take him to the lake.

Not far from Chikumbi's village was the stockade of a coast Arab whose native nickname was Kombokombo and here his Arabs stayed while he went on. The likenesses of the three chiefs mentioned at least show a difference in head-dress but little else, and the grecian nose of Kombokombo can only be taken as meaning that it was less negroid than those of the local chiefs.

In this wet district the white ants build roofs to their ant hills and Livingstone's outline of them is really not much less informative than the one on p. 253 done by the author with every facility at hand.

We may now drop the name Bemba that he has hitherto used for the lake, as he was told that 'Bemba is not a lake but a country, it is therefore better to use the name Bangweolo, which is applied to the great mass of the water, though I fear that our English folks will bogle at it or call it Bungyhollow'. The modern spelling is Bangweulu and it is not difficult to pronounce if one remembers that in Bantu language every vowel is given its full value.

He now went on alone with his four men and a guide, a dangerously small party for moving about an unsettled country side. In one case at least he was in imminent peril from a large armed party who were in a quarrelsome mood from having

Sketches by David Livingstone in notebook

drunk largely of the native beer (pombe): the journal records that he 'could not feel the inebriates to be enemies, but in that state they are the worst one can encounter, for they have no fear as they have when sober.'

In fact, in Bunyan's words—'He held his peace and set a good face on it, and so went by, and catcht no hurt.'

His mapping on this journey was less accurate than usual because he had not his usual helpers to see that he had peace for his sketching and his sextant work.

In one place he writes: 'Observed stars again because I had only a fire to read off by,' which must be interpreted as meaning he observed stars for latitude only, needing to read the sextant only once for each, whereas 'lunars' for longitude require frequent readings and quick observing. For one reason or another his longitude error increased until it was about fifty miles too far westerly. Some day an expert working out his sights again with the appropriate tables and nautical almanac may discover the cause of this error, which was to mislead him so seriously five years later.

It is clear from the map compiled for the *Last Journals* that the draughtsman accepted the longitudes as correct and ignored the sketch map (reproduced here on p. 248) whereas we know now that he would have done better to stand by the sketch.

It will be realised that since his mapping of his route up from Lake Nyasa was 20′ too much to the east at Chitane's Water and that of the western shore of Lake Bangweulu was 50′ too far to the west he now had seventy miles more of space on his map than was in fact there, and this affected most seriously his very last journey.

A portion of the map which shows the route of this his first discovery of Lake Bangweulu is reproduced facing p. 297 and is taken from the large map published in 1874 to accompany *Livingstone's Last Journals*. It was compiled by Mr John Bolton, attached to the staff of the map-maker, Mr Stanford, from such material as came home after Livingstone's death.

He had to do the best he could to fit the description in Livingstone's journal with the longitudes from the field note-books.

We shall have to return to this map but for the moment we will call the reader's attention to the river Mampanda which he crossed about fifteen miles from the lake and also to the river Mpanda running into the Lipososhi river some sixty miles further east, which he reached, but did not cross, on his last journey.

They are, in fact, the same river, but Mr Bolton, of course, did not know that, and it is doubtful whether Livingstone himself did, the unfortunate gap in the longitudes having deceived them both.

Now that the country is mapped it is possible to work out very closely the route he followed from Casembe. It was indeed roughly that of the present-day dirt-road from Kawambwa to Fort Rosebery for the very good reason that they both follow the divides in order to avoid difficult river crossings.

He must have passed close to the pleasant spot where Mafupa Mission now stands. Near this point was the village of Kizinga, the scene of a recent raid in which the Babemba attackers were beaten off by the help of gunfire from Kombokombo's people who had built a stockade there as a centre for their trading for ivory and copper. From here he crossed the Lufubu River, which he writes 'Rofubu'. This is a common name in this region, occurring three times at least within fifty miles. It was the next day that the incident occurred of the villagers 'running about poising their spears at us, taking aim with their bows and arrows, and making as if to strike with their axes'. He adds, 'There is usually one good soul in such rabbles,' and it was due to this man that they got away without bloodshed.

It is what he calls the 'fighting village' in his sketch map and presumably the chief's name was Kabasi. He had here crossed into the watershed of the lake itself and we must follow his notes and his sketch map rather carefully for the next few miles if we are to understand fully the mischief which his error in longitude was brewing for him.

On June 13th he stopped the night at a village on the Mato rivulet, a name not in use now but his latitude taken there shows that it is the upper Mampanda. From here his guide evidently took him along the side of that river which the sketch map shows as having been crossed twice, the second time a little above a rivulet he marks as the Kasans or Kasais, the name being almost illegible. This may be the Kasie and beyond it is the Machinga, both shown in Bolton's compilation as flowing into the river which is repeated fifty miles apart, but from different directions.

He had some trouble here with some drunken villagers and with his own boy Simon who said there was no water in front. Livingstone went on alone heading south-eastward and his men followed

'Umbrella' or 'Pagoda' ant-hills, one overturned and re-capped

later rather ashamed of themselves. Though it was three months after the end of the rainy season the 'oozes' were still full of water and all are carefully recorded as to depth and breadth. The village he reached at the edge of the lake, Masantu, is easily recognised from the warm spring there, and his first entry there is a curious one: 'Went over and saw the Chambeze coming from the East and entering into Bangweolo or Bemba.'

At this point he was opposite the opening between two long sandspits which fringe some thirty miles of the western shore of the lake. Livingstone was very calm on reaching the goal of his desires, merely saying that he walked a little way out of the village and 'saw the shores of the lake for the first time, thankful that I had come safely hither'. With his usual care he noted down the natural features, temperatures, weather, etc. He is rather struck by the broad fringe of what he calls 'strong rushes' a hundred yards wide at the edge of the lake. This rush is the curious *machinga*, which is tough but light, each stem consisting of a green spike some two or three feet long, quite hollow, inside which the seeds are borne and which has no flower of any kind. He rightly concludes that the lake is shallow, though regretting that his sounding-line had been lost when his own men had deserted weeks before. The deepest part of the lake, we now know, is little more than thirty feet in depth.

At Masantu he was on the shore of the long Chifunauli Lagoon, and it is just possible that he was misled into thinking it was a river the first time he viewed it.

Negotiations over hire of canoes delayed him a few days and as he was determined to get a good longitude sight there are six pages of observations for lunar distance.

He succeeded in hiring a canoe with five paddlers, but as the canoe had been stolen by the canoe-men from the island of Chisi the party had to avoid that interesting island and head for Mbabala instead. Livingstone gives the dimensions of the canoe—45 feet long, 4 feet deep and 4 feet broad. Very few of such a size could now be found, but the Chisi islanders always make the best ones because they live out in the lake and can use only seaworthy craft.*

At the north end of Mbabala the paddlers would stay only two nights, because of their fear of retribution, but the Doctor walked across the island and took bearings of what he could see. The large island of Chilubi was quite close, and he probably saw also the island beyond and nearly attached to it, called Nsumbu, where four years later he met Chief Matipa.

There is one curious entry in his diary of what he saw from this viewpoint. As the modern map shows, he was within ten miles of the junction of the Swamp with the lake, and he says that he 'could see the tops of the trees on Kasango, a small uninhabited islet about 30 miles distant'. He goes on to say that 'this uninhabited islet would have been our second stage had we been allowed to cross the lake, as it is of the people themselves. It is as far beyond it to the mainland, called Manda, as from Masantu's

* Livingstone's spelling of native names is different from modern usage, and he writes Chiribe and Kisi and Mpabala for these islands.

to Mpabala'. The mention of these names, told him by the natives, is interesting, as we can identify them without much difficulty. To the south-east there is a Kansenga, for instance, which means 'a sandy place' and is part of the large Lunga Bank. It now has no trees but it could have had them at that date. It is about twenty miles from where Livingstone was standing. Manda, however, is not the mainland but an area at the southern edge of the same Lunga sandbank, and is only about half-way across the Swamps from Chilubi Island to the southern edge of the swamp. This natural mistake, derived from hearsay, is partly responsible for his map, for he made the lake area a long east-west oval, whereas really it is as broad as it is long.

A most interesting sentence in this entry is: 'The mainland to the south of Mbabala is called Kabendé.' He may have been able to see it from his central position since it is marked by the forty-foot terrace at Mpanta Point. Four years later, when he was only twelve miles to the east of Mbabala, but without knowing it, he discussed with Chief Matipa going to this Kabende by canoe but rejected that sound plan for reasons that we shall be trying to discover in the last chapter.

The information Livingstone got on this first visit was extraordinarily accurate in some respects. For instance, he writes: 'The Luapula is an arm of the lake for some 20 miles, and beyond that is never narrower than from 180 to 200 yards, generally much broader, and may be compared with the Thames at London Bridge.'

In his map, however, he puts this Luapula 'arm' to the west of Mbabala instead of to the south, and the island itself is made small and round whereas it is really about twenty miles long. He should have been able to see its whole length from the high point at its northern end; that he does not remark on it may possibly be due to a high level of the lake at the time, in which case the low part of the island to the south might well have looked like swamp or even shallow reed-covered lake. His misunderstanding of the name Manda as representing the southern side of the Swamps is responsible for a further misinterpretation of what he was told. He writes: 'The river of Manda, called Matanga, is only a departing and re-entering branch of the lake.' This is precisely how the local inhabitants would describe the major channel of the Chambezi passing through the south-eastern section of the Swamp past the populated island of Matongo. He marks the latter as a river running into the lake westward of the Lulimala, the river near which he died.

It was most unfortunate for Livingstone that his paddlers were using a stolen canoe and would take him no farther than Mbabala island, for it stopped him just short of a point at which he would have solved the riddle of the lake.

From the top of his island, only forty feet above the lake you can see Chilubi Island very clearly with its curious promontories and bays, but you cannot, at eight miles distance, see the long line of the edge of the swamps, sweeping southwards to the exit of all the lake water in the district of the Kabende he entered on his map.

Seeing an open flat horizon to the southeast of his view point he naturally concluded the far side of the lake was very distant indeed. In fact he calculated that his discovery must be 150 miles across in an east-west direction whereas the lake proper is only 25 miles across, and 50 miles of that calculation was due to his error in longitude.

Had they but taken him two hours farther he would have recognised that most of his 'lake' was a vast swamp of reeds and papyrus, never more than a few feet deep, seamed with native channels for their small dug out canoes but no place to attempt to cross in a direct line as he wanted to do. Had he been taken that short extra distance he would soon have got into the shallow water near the swamp edge and at that time of year would have observed that his paddlers disturbed the black mud at the bottom sending up myriads of bubbles of marsh gas, the product of its slow decomposition.

He would have recognised it for what it was and refrained from testing it as did a party in a steel canoe eighty years later. When told that it was inflammable, an unbelieving white man immediately threw a lighted match overboard causing a pillar of fire at our stern. There was no way of putting it out except by steering for deeper water which took us an hour or so, during which all the paint was burnt off the stern of the canoe, with our paddlers loudly complaining that these wretched white men were trying to burn up their lake and their livelihood.

It was the guilty conscience of Livingstone's paddlers which caused them to land after dark and creep away before dawn two days later so that Livingstone never saw that his island was a long strip of low sand for twenty miles south of the small elevated bit

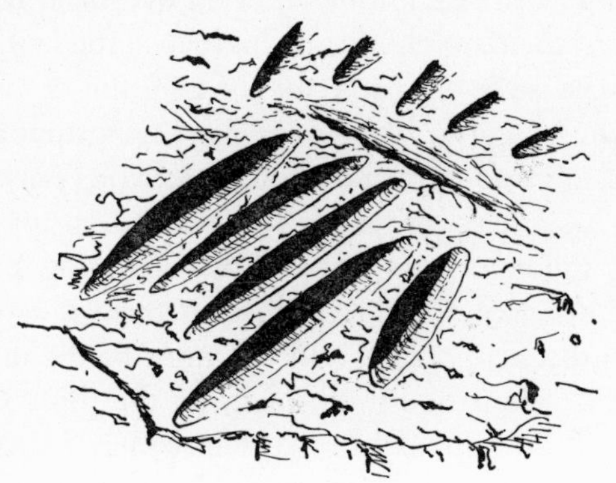

The footprints of God
(from a photograph)

of it he had walked over. Most of it is so low that at two miles distance it looks like reeds in shallow water. Livingstone logged it as a small island and Chisi as a large one, whereas the case is just the opposite.

We have dwelt on these apparently minor accidents of fortune, which happen on all expeditions, because they acquired a major importance on his last journey to the swamps four years later.

For some reason he did not set down his findings in a sketch map in his note-book. There is one page where he seems to have begun such a rough sketch but it is scribbled over with magnetic bearings taken from one or two points and odd information he gathered from his paddlers. The most important note reads: 'Land of Rovumbu or Matipa is S.E. of Masantu.' This is the first mention of Matipa, the old chief whose territory included the northern shore of the lake, the island of Chilubi which Livingstone had almost reached, and the vast forest on the mainland beyond that island which is now spelt Luwumbu.

There is another isolated note here which can be explained in the light of our present knowledge, but to which Livingstone attached undue importance at the time. His ceaseless questions of the headmen on the western shore of the Lake produced this statement: 'There are underground store-houses at Kibya and the marks of the feet of Mungu or Reza on the island Moezia.' Mr Bolton entered these storehouses on his map in the *Last Journals*.

Now Moezia is the old name for the long spit of sand running south from the Lifungwe Island on which Livingstone had landed. It is not an island, and some miles south of it you come to Samfya, which now has a harbour, and a research station for the fishing industry. I cannot identify Kibya but everything points to its being the same place. To the north of it there is a well-known cave, of no great proportions and this must be the underground storehouse. A little to the south of it, on the shore of the lake, there are the footprints of Mungu, which may mean either the First Man or a Supreme Being. In the hardened sandstone here, there are a number of deep grooves, shaped like canoes, which are actually the grinding places in which early man sharpened his stone axes, a cult which died out with the invention of iron-smelting, and their origin long since forgotten. In the sketch of one of these grinding sites there is a vague similarity to the mighty scratching of a super foot. There is now a plaque set into the rock by the Ancient Monuments Commission to record this ancient grinding site or factory for stone axes.

Before we accompany Livingstone back to the north we may pause to assess what he had done in this bold dash with four men to the Lake Bemba or Bangweolo he had so often heard about.

With such slender resources (he had traded his last 'cloth' for the hire of the canoe) he could not explore his discovery at leisure and was forced to accept what he was told of the surrounding features from which to construct some kind of a map. Another few miles over the lake or a few more days on its western shore would have cleared up some of the puzzles in his mind. The fact that his longitudes were too far to the west would not have mattered at all if he had not come to the lake region again on a slightly different route, still believing they were not seriously wrong. As it turned out the error was to become vital to his decisions on his last journey.

We cannot give full details of his return northwards from the lake, but it proved to be far more adventurous than the outward journey. The fact is the country people had been thoroughly roused by the masterful treatment of the coastal Arabs and there was an added complication from attacks by the warlike Babemba, from far to the eastward. At Kizinga he joined up with the Arabs, who would not hear of him returning by the way he had come from Casembe's with his very small party, so he had to wait six weeks until the Arabs were ready to retreat—it was truly a retreat—to the northward. There were nearly five hundred in the caravan, but they had to build a stockade every night for defence till they reached the Kalungwisi (spelled Kalungosi by Livingstone) and marched along it to a ford where it was only his presence with the Arabs that prevented Nsama's men disputing the crossing. As the journal remarks, 'confusion prevailed all over the country.' They arrived at the main headquarters of all the Arab traders north of Lake Mweru at the end of October, so his dash to Bangweulu had taken nearly five months.

There he found that the whole country had risen against the Arabs whose ruthless methods had ruined their own trade and his former acquaintance, Syde ben Habib, had joined them from the west, where he had been buying copper from the native Katanga copper mines.

His daily entries in journal or field notes entirely ceased for much of this return journey, but while detained at Kizinga he wrote what is practically a geographical treatise on the whole region in which he deals with all its outstanding features. It is far too long to quote, but we must record that his account of the many 'dambos', or 'sponges' as he calls the valley swamps is a masterpiece and could hardly be improved upon even now when we know them well. One quotation must suffice: 'These sponges are a serious matter in travelling. They had many deep holes in the paths and when one plumps therein every muscle in the frame receives a painful jerk. When past the stream, and apparently on partially dry ground, one may jog in a foot or more and receive a squirt of black mud up the thighs; it is only when you reach the trees and are off the sour land that you feel secure from mud and leeches.' This time he was traversing the dambos in the midst of the dry season, next time he was to wallow in them in the middle of the rains, when they become really dangerous.

While waiting once more for the Arabs to go with him to Ujiji he returns to the subject of the sources of the Nile in his journal in a long digression, interlarded with day-to-day notes. He seems to have quite persuaded himself that Speke and Baker were much too far north with their Nile sources as he ends the remarks with 'Old Nile played the theorists a pretty prank by having his springs 500 miles south of them all'.

Tired of waiting for the dilatory Arabs he was on the point of starting north with his own small party early in November and it is a pity that he did not for on November 22nd the whole encampment was attacked by the Babemba forces, allied with the local tribes. For the next three days the attack was renewed with spirit, much to the surprise of the Swahili Arabs who 'expected them to flee as soon as they heard a gun fired in anger, but instead of this we were very nearly being cut off'.

Consequently the final move-off on December 11th was nothing less than a retreat by 'a motley group, composed of Mohammad and his friends, a gang of Unyamwesi hangers-on, and strings of wretched slaves yoked together in their heavy slave sticks. They were travelling in the beginning of the rainy season but for three weeks Livingstone kept his health fairly well, in fact until they were half way to Lake Tanganyika.

Then, as he said, he got a wetting once too often and developed pneumonia in the right lung. His friend Mohammad bin Saleh had him carried in a *kitanda*, a frame like a cot on poles and they did not arrive at the Lake until mid-February. Here he persuaded, with some difficulty, his former friend, Syde ben Habib, to convey him in one of his canoes to Ujiji. The voyage on that stormy lake took nearly three weeks of dashes from one bay to another and waiting for calm intervals, so that it was a very tired and sick man who got ashore at Ujiji on March 14th, 1869, having taken nearly three years from his leaving Zanzibar in March 1866.

Rendering of photograph of David Livingstone

CHAPTER TEN

I saw a man clothed with rags standing in a certain place, with his face from his own house, a book in his hand, and a great burden upon his back.

JOHN BUNYAN

We come now to a period in the life and travels of Livingstone which is difficult to explain and painful to read. Yet we must attempt to do so even though this is not a psychological study. We are primarily concerned with him as a geographer and our faith in him as such has not dimmed, since his field-work continues to the last as actively as ever. But there is no doubt that his judgment on geographical problems has become warped, and a strange hallucination has taken hold of a mind, to which there was none to minister or raze out the the written troubles of the brain.

He had arrived at Ujiji, a pilgrim who had just passed through the Valley of the Shadow of Death. There he found that most of his goods had been stolen by those to whom they were entrusted; he was, comparatively speaking, penniless.

There were few letters for him and none from his family after three years' wandering in his lonely wilderness. He was all but cut off from communicating with them for he was clearly warned that his own letters would not be allowed to reach the coast. He found himself in a veritable city of Vanity Fair where were to be seen 'thefts, murders, adulteries, false swearers and that of a blood red colour' or, in his own words, rather than those of John Bunyan—'this is a den of the worst kind of slave-traders: it is not a trade, but a system of consecutive murders: they go to plunder and kidnap and every trading trip is nothing but a foray.'

What, in the name of all reason and common sense, should a man do in such circumstance? Everything pointed to his going out to Zanzibar himself, to repair his health,—and particularly his teeth—to re-equip his party, and to contact his friends. It was a seven hundred mile journey, perhaps taking four months, but there were parties going and coming on a known road.

But what did our pilgrim do? He stood with his face from his own house and a great burden upon his back. There is never a word in his journal of such an idea as going to Zanzibar, it hardly seems to have occurred to him. Instead, his first words as to plans, after he had recovered some strength, were of finding 'a boat and crew to go down Tanganyika', plans to go north or south or west, but never to the east. It was magnificent in its way, but it was not exploration or common sense and it requires some explanation. One's mind inevitably runs to Shakespeare, but we cannot accept it as a case of an enterprise of great pith and moment sicklied o'er, and turned awry; there must have been something more than fantasy in such a course, nor does it show a heart unfortified, a mind impatient.

Neither Shakespeare nor Bunyan are really any help and we must seek some other justification for what he did, something less lofty, something more mundane and capable of analogy.

There is, or was—for report has come of his recent death,—a man living far out in the west of the Kalahari who shunned all Europeans, an intelligent man, once an officer in the Merchant Service, who spent his time devising inventions to improve the efficiency of the British Navy. A strange character, and one who was difficult of approach since he kept a German sabre with which to keep off visitors, unkempt but not uncouth, and not in the least wild-eyed and fanatic. He was living in a single-roomed hut next to a native store and the only European he willingly saw was the District Commissioner who paid a visit to this outpost of administration, Lehututu, once or twice a year. He had not 'gone native', to use that apt but derogatory phrase which carries an imputation of immoral conduct, for he had no truck with native women nor did he ever touch alcohol. In a long talk with him the writer saw no sign of fanaticism except when we got on to the subject of their Lordships of the Admiralty, who paid scant attention to his letters to them. He was essentially a shy man but not a wild man, even though he was credited with going to almost any length of violence to preserve his utter seclusion from fellow Europeans. One could hardly become friendly with such a man but one could dimly understand his shyness and his eccentric twist, due to his conviction that he could invent improvements for the Navy, combining to turn him into a recluse, and far from an unhappy one.

It may come as a great disappointment to the millions of devoted admirers of David Livingstone to have him compared, even remotely, with a queer character from the Kalahari, yet if we are to make anything of Livingstone's decisions and doings at this time we must find some parallels of human conduct. I would rather do that than listen for an instant to the criticisms of him that have already appeared accusing him of callous desertion of his family, of a guilty conscience and other still more ignoble imputations, such as that he sought martyrdom, that he was mentally deranged and so on.

I would rather believe that his actions were more or less a natural result of his African experience, working upon a mind which was inclined to mysticism, and a temperament which was essentially shy and retiring. That horrid word, escapism, comes to mind, and is rejected because of its usual connotations. After all, most human decisions are prompted by some degree of escaping from the distasteful, the irksome, the unfamiliar. The ordinary social conventions had all become a strain and an embarrassment to one who had spent some twenty years away from civilisation, more or less alone with his thoughts and his visions and his ideals, never having to explain or to excuse his conduct to his followers. When we add to that the fact that he was a true Christian, conscious of a purpose with divine support, and that he was also a scientific geographer with very advanced notions on rivers, we can, I submit, reach some understanding of why he turned his back on home, family, comfort and fame.

It explains, however inadequately, why, with the cause of anti-slavery imprinted on his heart, he could yet travel for years with slave traders. It gives some clue, however partial, to the way in which he persuaded himself that he was about to solve the age-old problem of the Nile.

For that is the burden of his tale in these succeeding journeyings, they are a search for the sources of the Nile, which had now become an obsession, a quest, a sacred duty.

Nevertheless, we believe we have chosen a fitting headline for this chapter, for the next two years were full of frustration for him, a struggle he thought well-nigh hopeless against the evils of slavery, which he was to meet more closely than ever before, and, for his quest, a series of rebuffs and repulses to his great plan of sailing down the great Lualaba hoping to find it part of the Nile. When we include the persistent attacks of fevers and the frequent risks of assassination, and more galling than all, the disloyalty of all his 'attendants' except a faithful trio, we may well regard it as the Slough of Despond, which he was 'left to tremble in alone: but still he endeavoured to struggle to that side of the slough that was further from his own house'. The one thing that Livingstone could never do was to turn back when he ought to do so, thus falling short of Thomas Middleton's Elizabethan wisdom, 'that he travels best that knows when to return.'

It is a melancholy task to review these years and we propose to cut it as short as will serve to give some picture of what he went through and to show how in the midst of trials he remained a geographer to the end.

He was now fifty-seven years of age but his constitution must still have been robust for with scant medicines he recovered from his chest trouble within a very few weeks. His first task was to write letters and he sent off no less than forty-two in the first month, none of which ever reached Zanzibar. He hardly expected them to, for he now found his early acquaintance Syde ben Habib becoming his enemy—'he refused to allow his men to carry my letters to the coast; as he expected I would write about his doings in Rua', that is to say, the Katanga region.

Livingstone was now truly suffering from the defect of that grand quality of his of speaking his mind about slavery to the culprits. Here he was in their midst and they must have been sorely puzzled as to what to do with him. They must have hoped he would not go to the coast himself, they certainly stopped him from writing to the coast, but how to keep an eye on his activities without letting him see too much of their iniquitous methods sorely exercised their minds.

His wretched agent, Thani bin Suellim, was dishonest and worse than useless, in fact he was openly boasting of Livingstone's helplessness, in spite of the original letter of recommendation from the Sultan at Zanzibar, now three years out of date.

It is remarkable that though Ujiji is only one hundred and twenty miles from the north end of the lake, few of the Arabs had been to that end and none of them had any clear idea whether the river there was an outlet of, or a tributary to, the lake, in fact that journey was his first plan since 'all the Ujiji Arabs who have any opinion on the subject assert that Tanganyika, Usigé water and Loanda are one and the same piece of river'. Since Usige is the district at the north end and Loanda is Ruanda—further north still, they were correct in a sense, but the river Lusize runs into and not out of that end of the lake.

After long discussion he decided not to go with an Arab party to the north end which had already been once raided and 'that it will be better for me to go to Manyuema and, if possible, trace down the western arm of the Nile to the north—if this arm is indeed that of the Nile and not of the Congo.' He added, 'I feel exhilarated at the thought of getting among people not spoiled by contact with Arab traders,' but alas, the Arab trader Mohamad Bogharib* came with him, and in a sense Livingstone was once more to be the unwilling means of opening up new country for slavery. This would have happened in any case as the Arabs had spoiled the country to the north and south and only the west

* From this point Livingstone always calls Mohammad bin Saleh by his other name, Bogharib.

remained. His health and energy had returned in full when he started in early July for, in crossing the lake, he was busy sounding (326 fathoms), and he records 'Lunars on 20th. Lunars again on 22nd'. His chronometers must all have run down while he was so ill in coming to Ujiji, but the longitude of that place being known he obviously started them again for the new journey.

By an unlucky accident he and Bogharib started westward from the lake only fifteen or twenty miles to the north of the real outlet to the lake, the Lukuga river, where the great Belgian lake-port of Albertville now stands. It was one of those pieces of ill luck which dogged Livingstone's footsteps in the same way as the one section of the Zambezi he had missed in travelling down it was the one which nearly wrecked the plans of his second Expedition.

In fact he had passed the true outlet of Tanganyika when lying sick in the canoe coming up to Ujiji a few months earlier, though even had he been well he might have missed the Lukuga since it is usually clogged with swamp plants. On the other hand, had he chanced to camp within the bay leading to it he would almost certainly have heard of it and investigated.

Five years later Commander Lovett Cameron had some difficulty in discovering it and passing down some five miles of a channel frequently blocked with 'sudds' or floating islands of papyrus and reeds.

Had Livingstone had the least idea of an outlet being there he would certainly have persevered and gone down its valley to the Lualaba instead of taking the route only a few miles to the north which led, at first, along a stream which obviously flowed into the lake.

The caravan or *safari* travelled fairly quickly for an Arab one and as the way led over high mountains Livingstone suffered a good deal from shortness of breath, a legacy from the pneumonia of four months earlier. They reached the large village, Bambarre, of the ruling chief of the Manyuema people, and the first thing the Arabs did was to perform the ceremony of 'mixing blood' in token of peaceful intentions, since they intended to use the place as a headquarters whence to send parties out to buy ivory. The country folk were not long in discovering their real intentions, for within a fortnight one of these foraging parties under an unpleasant Arab, Dugumbé, of whom we shall hear more, returned with ten goats and ten slaves they had seized, 'though great kindness had been shown: this is genuine Suaheli or Nigger-Moslem tactics.'

Rather unwisely Livingstone made his first attempt to reach the Lualaba river by following the route this raiding party had used. He had only about eighty miles to go but he met with increasing hostility, being taken for a colleague of the slave-raiders, as was only natural. Finally they were turned back by threats of attack and returned to Bambarré, where he found that 'a large horde of Ujijians had arrived, all eager to reach the cheap ivory, of which a rumour had spread far and wide'.

He was now getting occasional bouts of fever and had no medicines whatever, but after Christmas he started with Bogharib, the most moderate of the Arabs, to reach the Lualaba by first going north and then west.

The people were civil but very excited at seeing strangers and as there were constant feuds between villages it was difficult to persuade each new headman that their intentions were peaceable.

The rains were in full swing and Livingstone was constantly wet through, with consequent attacks of fever and dysentery. This is the first time in all his books that he mentions taking the precaution of boiling all water for drinking and it arrested what he called the 'choleraic purging'.

He was more or less brought to a standstill at a centre called Mamohela for nearly five months, during which there are very few entries in his journal and these refer mainly to reports by his Arab companions of their parties getting ivory and slaves, or demanding tribute for leaving villages alone.

The 'long rains' as they are called in the equatorial belt, had continued until June, fifty-eight inches in less than six months, and when they ceased he had trouble with his own men, only Susi, Chuma and Gardner staying with him, and starting off with him for the Lualaba. They did not get far before they had to give up and turn back, partly because of the difficult travelling but also because 'for the first time in his life', as he says, his feet failed him, irritable ulcers forming which resisted treatment, so by late July he had 'limped back to Bambarré'.

He was growing disgusted with the cruelty of the people he was associated with, even Bogharib taking to 'punishing' head-men for resistance, and this with his bad feet produced fits of depression which are dimly indicated in the very occasional entries in the journal.

The long delays between actual journeys, the lack of any intellectual conversation and no doubt, his bad health, were all combining to give him gloomy thoughts relieved only by an occasional departure into realms of fancy or mysticism. A long entry on August 18th, 1870, shows the direction in which these fancies or theories based on rumour were leading him.

At least a year earlier he had met two 'black Arabs' who had been to the region of the Katanga copper mines and they had given him a somewhat confused account of the rivers which rise there.

The gist of their account was that there were four separate sources, or 'fountains' as Livingstone calls them, two of which flowed north as the Lufira and Lualaba rivers and two south as the Liambai (that is the Zambezi) and the Lunga (which runs into the Kafue). There is, in fact, a place on the present border between Northern Rhodesia and the Belgian Congo, some twenty miles west of the railway, where such a description is approximately correct, that is to say, you can find springs close to each other which run respectively into three of these rivers, and not far to the west one of the sources of the Kabompo or upper Zambezi.

These four upper rivers do therefore divide themselves as described by the Arabs, two running to the south and two to the north, into the watersheds of the Zambezi and the Congo respectively. No doubt the Arabs spoke with absolute certainty of what they had seen which led Livingstone to believe them. There was no harm in that belief, but he immediately fitted the description to that given by Herodotus for the sources of the Nile.

Quoting from his journal he says of the 'mound' or range of hills described by the Arabs: 'This possibly gave occasion to the story told to Herodotus by the Secretary of Minerva in the City of Sais, about two hills with conical tops, Crophi and Mophi. "Midway between them", said he, "are the fountains of the Nile, fountains which it is impossible to fathom: half the water runs northward into Egypt, half to the south towards Ethiopia." '

Doubtless he had often pored over this quotation from Herodotus about the Nile and his mystic faculty revelled in such similarity as he could find in the tale of the Arabs, so he jumped to the conclusion once more that the Lualaba, and hence the Luapula, Bangweulu and Chambezi were all parts of the Nile. Strangely enough he rejects the part of the story which might be based on fact, as he continues, 'the conical tops to the mound look like invention, as also do the names,' but accepts the 'four fountains impossible to fathom'.

He goes on to say: 'I am thankful to old Nile for so hiding his head that all "theoretical discoverers" are left out in the cold. With all real explorers I have a hearty sympathy and I have some regret at being obliged, in a manner, compelled, to speak somewhat disparagingly of the opinions formed by my predecessors . . . it seems necessary to explain, not offensively I hope, wherein their mistake lay. My opinions may yet be shown to be mistaken too, but at present I cannot conceive how.'

This was perfectly fair and proper language for his private journal but a year earlier, just after he had reached Bambarré, he had written in very positive terms on the same subject to his son Thomas and to his astronomer friend at the Cape, Sir Thomas Maclear. These letters were injudicious because he had, even then, so persuaded himself that his theory was correct that he stated it as almost proven.

To his son he wrote: 'I gradually gained more light on the country and slowly and surely saw the problem of the fountains of the Nile developing before my eyes. The vast volume of water draining away to the north made me conjecture that I had been working at the sources of the Congo too. My present trip to Manyuema proves that all goes to the river of Egypt. In fact, the headwaters of the Nile are gathered into two or three arms, very much as was depicted by Ptolemy in the second century of our era.'

To Maclear he is a little more careful of his words, giving

reasons for his theory and stating his plan for settling it once for all, by going down the Lualaba 'to see where the two arms unite—the lost city of Meroe ought to be there' and then to 'finish up by going round outside and south of all the sources, so that I may be sure no one will cut me out and say he found other sources south of mine'.

So sure was he of the existence of these four fountains that he named them on his map after four of his supporters, Palmerston, Frere, Webb and Young.

He also made many references to Moses having been in that part of Africa and hoped to find evidence of it.

There is a very important letter from Livingstone to Lord Stanley, begun in November 1870, but not sent home for some reason, so it was not received at the Foreign Office until April 7, 1874, a year after the death of the writer.

We must quote at some length from it because it shows two very interesting aspects of his mind, namely the philosophical and even whimsical attitude he had to the trials of African travel, and, on the other hand, the stubbornness, almost amounting to folly, with which he proclaimed his theory about the Nile sources.

Describing the difficulty of travel through the elephant grass of the region he says: 'The leaves of this megatherium grass are armed with minute spikes which, as we worm our way along elephant walks, rub disagreeably on the side of the face where the gun is held, and the hand is made sore by fending it off the other side for hours. . . . The stalks fall and block up all passage save for a path made and mixed up by the feet of elephants and buffaloes. The slough therein is groan-compelling . . . in some cases the subsoil has given way beneath the elephant's enormous weight; the hole is filled with mud and one, taking it all to be about calf-deep, steps in to the top of the thigh, and flaps on to a seat soft enough but not luxurious: a merry laugh relaxes the facial muscles, and I conjecture that this gruesome fun will be all I shall ever get for the exploration.'

Later in the letter he describes his theory of the four fountains almost as though he had visited them already and justifies the personal names he allots to them.

But the real depth of the obsession is shown most strikingly, and indeed painfully, in a couple of despatches prepared by him for the actual occasion of his discovery. They were probably written when he was entangled in the swamps of Bangweulu, hoping to get clear and march straight to the mound and the fountains.

The brief one runs: 'I have the pleasure of reporting to your Lordship that on the I succeeded at last in reaching your remarkable fountains, each of which, at no great distance off, becomes a large river. They rise at the base of a swell of land or earthen mound, which can scarcely be called a hill, for it seems only about feet above the general level. . . .'

In the longer paper he says: 'I venture, from the dim recollections of reading the ancient historian in boyhood, to conjecture that possibly these four gushing fountains may be the very same that were mentioned to Herodotus. . . .

'The geographical position of the mound, or low earthen hill, may for the present be taken as latitude , and longitude . The altitude above the level of the sea , and geographers will all sympathise with me in naming it, as a memorial of a very dear departed friend, "Murchison's Mound". I loved him with very great affection, and I believe that the affection was mutual. Not to meet him till in the spirit land takes away much of the pleasure of re-discovery.'

Yet here again his common sense occasionally breaks the spell of his obsession for there is a postscript: 'P.S. I should not be making a clean breast of it if I did not add that there still remains a blush of suspicion that, like others, I may be mistaken, and find this to be the Congo instead of the Nile.'

The enforced idleness at Bambarré for three months while his foot ulcers were healing got thoroughly on his nerves and it appears in some of his letters at this time. Thus he boils over concerning the instructions written out for him by some members of the Royal Geographical Society. He had the greatest admiration for the President, Sir Roderick Murchison, but he gives his blunt opinion of those who told him he was 'to furnish a survey on successive pages of his journal, take latitudes every night, pay attention to the hydrography of Central Africa'. 'For mere board,' he complains, 'and no lodging I was to work for years and hand over the results to them.' At this time too there are various 'digs' at Burton, Speke and Baker, which it is unfair to quote since he was sick and frustrated and lying for weeks in a hut when he wanted to be up and doing: 'I am grievously tired of living here. Mohamad is as kind as he can be, but to sit idle or give up before I finish my work are both intolerable. I cannot bear either, yet I am forced to remain by want of people.'

The 'deserters' as he called them were still hanging about trying to join the Arabs or be taken on again by Livingstone, but he was adamant and would have nothing to do with them. Of them he only mentions Simon and Ibram (Abraham his former interpreter) but Amoda and James must have been among them. We cannot be critical since we are ignorant of the facts, yet we cannot but remember how he was always apt to put on the screw of discipline too late and too hard. Even the noblest of men, wallowing in the Slough of Despond, must be 'grievously bedaubed with dirt', even though he reads the Bible through four times, as he did during the Manyuema years.

His powerless situation and his loneliness get the better of him in letters to his closest friends, and in one to Maclear he says: 'My chronometers are all dead; I hope my old watch has been sent to Zanzibar, but I have got no letters for years, save some, three years old, at Ujiji. I have an intense and sore longing to finish and retire.'

The case is not much better when, in February 1871, some of the men sent in with goods to Ujiji by Dr Kirk arrive, for they turn out to be 'slaves of the Banians', that is of the Indian merchants who supplied the goods, and they would not go farther with him unless their rate of pay was doubled.

However, Livingstone started off once more with them towards the Lualaba, accompanied at first by Mohamad to whom he paid a large sum for assistance, and after a six-weeks' journey they reached Nyangwe on that river. He found the Arab traders had already made it a centre from which to send out trading or raiding parties, he was too late to find the Manyuema people in their unspoiled state.

Almost his first care on reaching the river was to make measurements of it, sounding it and finding it 'a mighty river truly'. His boiling point apparatus made it about two thousand feet above sea level, but he evidently distrusted this figure which is lower than the altitude Baker had found for Lake Albert, where Livingstone hoped it was bound for, and where Stanley in his map published two years later makes it flow, even though he gives the height of the lake as 2750 feet.

Livingstone would not have been so blind to hydraulics as that and if he believed in his own figures at all he would have postulated the course of the Lualaba as some roundabout route by which it could flow into the White Nile which is at a low enough altitude to make it possible, though highly improbable.

He had some difficulty in fixing the position of Nyangwe owing to his 'dead' chronometers but he did it, most successfully, as it turned out, by a somewhat unorthodox method: 'I tried to secure a longitude by fixing a weight on the key of the watch, and so helping it on: taking successive altitudes of the sun and distances of the moon. Possibly the first and last altitudes may give the rate of going, and the frequent distances may give approximate longitude.'

Without going into technical details it may be stated that these figures, when sent later to Sir Thomas Maclear, could be worked out to give as he says an 'approximate' longitude, which in fact is only a few miles in error.

Again he found outward protestations of help from the Arabs, but inward suspicion of his attitude to their doings, it was the same old impossible situation for both sides, which Livingstone's detestation of the slave trade never allowed him to see in full perspective.

He found that Dugumbe was the principal Arab here 'with 500 guns', and that he intended to settle there for several years with all his family. And so he did, for when Cameron arrived four years later he found him there and describes him faithfully: 'Dugumbi, finding himself a far greater personage here than he could ever be in his native place, devoted his attention to establishing a harem. He had collected around him over three hundred slave women and the ill effects of this arrangement and his indulgence in bhang and pombe were plainly noticeable in his rapid decline into idiotcy.'

It was to this kind of man that Livingstone appealed, with a promise of £400, for ten men 'to replace the Banian slaves' and got no firm answer. His great need was canoes but he was foiled

Manyuema marketwoman

in every attempt to buy them, as was Cameron when he sought the same means of travelling from Nyangwe. The argument of the Arabs presumably was that an Englishman with a land party was bad enough, but could at least be followed, but Englishmen in canoes would be quite beyond their control.

While negotiations for canoes and men were going on Livingstone settled into a house built by his men and became fascinated by the huge market, or 'chitoka' that was held two or three times a week. On this scale it was a new experience to him, sometimes over three thousand people attending and most of the bartering being done by the women. He goes regularly to the market to watch the amusing scene and hear the gossip and is much struck by the truce that ruled the market, for villages more or less at war with each other would attend it without arms and in perfect safety. Yet it was this peaceable market which was the scene of the blasting of all his hopes and plans.

On July 15th, 1871, there was burning and raiding of villages across the river but fifteen hundred people came to the market. Livingstone was surprised to see Arabs there with their guns but thought they must be ignorant of the tradition that no arms were permitted there. He had only just left the market when a wholesale massacre began, the Arabs shooting into the defenceless crowd. Many of them dashed down to the canoes left in the little creek which passes between the two sections of the town and there were shot or drowned by overcrowding the canoes. Livingstone's account of it is factual yet dreadfully dramatic. His first intention was 'to pistol the murderers' but Dugumbe restrained him and all he could do was to gather some of the fugitives under his protection.

The massacre went on for hours, 'as I write I hear the loud wails on the left bank (of the river) over those who are slain. Oh, let Thy Kingdom come! It made me sick at heart, it gave me the impression of being in Hell.' The Arabs themselves assessed the number killed at four hundred.

There could no longer be any thought of travelling with such men as the Arab slavers, there was nothing for it but to return to Ujiji. ' "Don't go away," say the Manyuema chiefs to me; but I cannot stay here in agony.'

They started five days after the massacre but it was now a very risky journey with a small party. Though some of the traders' people joined him it proved no help for they were ambushed in thick bush a few days later, and a spear grazed his back and another passed a foot in front of him. The assailants took him for an Arab, especially as he was wearing a type of red jacket favoured by the Arabs.

For five hours they had to run the gauntlet, and he makes the interesting observation: 'I became weary with the constant strain of danger, and—as, I suppose, happens with soldiers on the field of battle—not courageous, but perfectly indifferent whether I were killed or not. By the time he reached Bambarré he was seriously ill with his old trouble of haemorrhage and had to stay there for ten days. It took the party another seven weeks to reach Ujiji.

There, he had just found out that he was destitute of goods, which had been stolen by the man sent in charge of them from Zanzibar when, a few days later, the caravan of H. M. Stanley arrived and there occurred the oft-quoted greeting of 'Dr Livingstone, I presume,' as given by Stanley in his dramatic account.

There are no exclamation marks of any kind in Livingstone's journal, but in a later entry he says: 'I am not of a demonstrative turn, but this disinterested kindness of Mr Bennett, so nobly carried into effect by Mr Stanley, was simply overwhelming.'

To a man sick and destitute as he was just then it certainly was overwhelming, and made all the difference in the world to his plans. That the kindness of the press magnate was not entirely disinterested, and that nobility was not a marked characteristic of Stanley's character did not affect the result which was a renewal of health and vigour for a weary disappointed man. The very next sentence in his journal shows that he took Stanley's story of his journey inland at Stanley's valuation, for he says 'his helpmates turned out depraved blackguards, who, by their excesses at Zanzibar and elsewhere, had ruined their constitutions and prepared their systems to be fit provender for the grave'.

Even Stanley did not put the fate of Farquhar and Shaw in quite that light, for they were merchant service officers chosen by himself and they succumbed to African fevers, assisted by the high pressure put upon their powers by Stanley.

The meeting of Stanley and Livingstone is one of the strangest episodes in the story of exploration and not the least curious aspect of it is the way in which two men, utterly dissimilar in temperament, each swayed the other. Livingstone most certainly toned down Stanley's harsh realism and Stanley, for the moment, led Livingstone to write with a touch of journalese. The wonder is that they managed to get on well together for a whole four months, as they certainly did, though Livingstone's journal is very brief and includes very little about Stanley.

I think that if Livingstone had been made to state his opinion of Stanley he might have quoted *Pilgrim's Progress* and said: 'He was a man that had the Root of the Matter in him, but he was one of the most troublesome Pilgrims that I ever met with in all my days.'

Sir Reginald Coupland, in his book *Livingstone's Last Journey*, has put the whole matter in its true perspective, which was very necessary since no white man ever saw Livingstone again and except for his letters sent back by Stanley the only account of their association is in the latter's book *How I found Livingstone*, which would have horrified Livingstone had he ever seen it.

It is a most self-revealing book that Stanley wrote after he returned while he was being alternately congratulated and scorned by people in England, and it is open to the reader to class it either as a *riposte* to the doubts cast upon his story or as skilful journalism making the most of publicity, and egging on the opposite sides.

It is not a pleasant book but it is very readable, even if one marvels at the long conversations in it, suspects embroidery to many of the stories and regrets the public washing of soiled linen which so disfigures it.

The real blot on it and the whole expedition is one of which Stanley himself is sublimely unconscious, namely the care he took to hoodwink everybody as to his real purpose, sounding Dr Kirk as to where Livingstone might be but giving out that he himself was going to explore quite another part of East Africa. This is aggravated by taunts at Kirk for not guessing his duplicity and fears lest Livingstone should hear of his approach and refuse to be 'found'.

The expedition was in fact planned as a journalistic 'scoop' and from that point of view was a huge success but it involved saying one thing and doing quite another and the world does not always appreciate being fooled. Stanley himself could not understand that attitude any more than Amundsen did when in 1910 he told the world he was going to the North Pole, and only his brother knew that he was going to race Captain Scott in getting first to the South Pole.

In both cases magnificent journeys were made and enormous publicity was achieved but both leaders were very much surprised to find that a section of the public did not like things done in that way, and were soured at the reception such people gave to their feats, calling it 'not cricket'. Their reply was, in brief, that 'scoops', publicity, etc. do not know the phrase, and that indeed was the trouble, the leaders did not recognise such an old fashioned game as cricket.

We are not here concerned with these dead-and-gone bickerings and accusations in themselves but only with their effect upon Livingstone as a geographer.

Perhaps, as Coupland points out, the worst result was that he was persuaded by Stanley's undoubted animosity to Kirk that his sufferings of the last two years, his losses by robbery and mutiny were due to Kirk's sending him 'Banian slaves', in fact neglecting his interests. In his book Stanley accuses Kirk of doing so deliberately, and he encouraged Livingstone to believe that not only Kirk but his own Government and the Royal Geographical Society were indifferent to his fate.

One of the few subjects on which there is complete unity in the accounts of both men is that Stanley (in Livingstone's words) 'used some very strong arguments in favour of my going home, getting some artificial teeth and then returning to finish my task'.

At the beginning of this chapter we have suggested one reason why he did not fall in with such an eminently sensible plan but I think there is another one at this point. Had Stanley told him there was a gallant Kirk at Zanzibar doing his best to send him supplies, wondering where he had got to; that Murchison and his other geographical friends were puzzled and worried at his silence due to his letters being destroyed; that his Government would help if they but knew how and where to send it, then I believe Livingstone would have returned, at least as far as Zanzibar. But when he had a picture of an almost hostile Kirk, an indifferent Government and an unappreciative Geographical Society Livingstone may well have set his teeth in his customary way and resolved to stay in Africa, alone, and either complete his task or be 'cut off' in the attempt.

He knew well enough by now that only with a white man in charge of a caravan would supplies be likely to get through to him, that he was fit for travelling as he had just done three hundred miles from Ujiji to Unyanyembe, and completed it in better shape than Stanley himself, and that he could do little but wait there for some months for the supplies and men to be sent by Stanley.

In fact his own assertion, that he must stay in Africa and complete his task was the very best reason for his going to Zanzibar with Stanley and securing his supplies and men himself.

What else but a desire to be alone coupled with disappointment at Kirk's alleged treatment could have deterred him from doing what common sense advised?

His own letter to Kirk almost suggests that he could trust no one but himself to obtain what he needed, when he says 'I feel inclined to relinquish the hope of ever getting help from Zanzibar to finish the little work I have to do. I may wait twenty years while your slaves feast and fail'. Apart from the veiled accusation surely such words mean that he would have to come and get the help himself.

Stanley arrived for the dramatic meeting on November 10th, whereas Livingstone logged it as October 28th, the loss of thirteen days in his reckoning being due to his various illnesses. The meeting was a veritable tonic, both physical and mental, to the tired man and we can well believe what Stanley reported at their first talk of his repeating, 'You have brought new life!' This is only one instance of the anecdotes with which Stanley brightens his narrative, details such as Livingstone hardly ever put in his journal but without which it is difficult to picture the scenes around him. For example, this is the first time we hear of Halima, the wife of Amoda and Livingstone's female cook, who was in a state of delightful excitement at seeing the Doctor eat largely with the white stranger when she had tempted him in vain before to eat. She had evidently been some time with Livingstone, for Stanley writes, 'While we listened to the noise of her furious gossip, the Doctor related her faithful services,' but added that she never knew the difference between tea and coffee. She alone of several women who accompanied Livingstone on his last journey was mentioned by name when she told him of a theft by one of his men and his further comment is 'This was so far faithful in her, but she has an outrageous tongue'. Her shrewish tongue was not always in evidence for, in another place, Livingstone says 'She has been extremely good, I never had to reprove her once. She is always very attentive and clever and never stole, nor would she allow her husband to steal: she is the best spoke in the wheel'. Halima was one of the party which carried her master's remains to Zanzibar.

The frequent vignettes given in *How I found Livingstone* enlighten us more on Livingstone's reaction to Stanley's coming than the very few comments in his own journal. Thus, on the morning after arrival, Stanley is soliloquising to himself on what to do next, and wondering whether he can persuade the Doctor to give him news for his newspaper, and he says: 'I think from what I have seen of him last night, that he is not such a niggard and misanthrope as I was told he was by a man who said he knew him. (This must be one of Stanley's constant hits at Kirk.) He exhibited considerable emotion, despite the mono-syllabic greeting when he shook my hand. Neither did he run away, as I was told he would, though that perhaps was because he had no time. Neither does he mind my nationality.'

And then there escapes the news that a white man's approach was not such a surprise after all, as Livingstone had heard one was approaching with 'boats, plenty of men and stores' and had expected him to be a Frenchman. At breakfast that morning Livingstone confessed to not knowing why Stanley had come, taking him for some 'luxurious and rich man, when he saw my great bath-tub carried by one of my men and when my knives and forks and cups, saucers, silver spoons and silver tea-pot were brought forth shining and bright, spread on a rich Persian carpet'.

The contrast between their equipment must indeed have been staggering for, as Stanley says, 'What could he do, with five men and fifteen or twenty cloths.'

We must be grateful too for the picture given of Livingstone at this time: 'He is about sixty years old, though after he was restored to health he appeared more like a man who had not passed his fiftieth year. His hair has a brownish colour yet, but is here and there streaked with grey lines above the temples, his beard and moustache are very grey. His eyes which are hazel, are remarkably bright; he has a sight keen as a hawk's. His teeth alone indicate the weakness of age. When walking he has a firm but heavy tread, like that of an over-worked or fatigued man.'

Then he spoils this pleasant description by accusing Kirk of misleading him as to Livingstone's character and industry, by diatribes against 'easy-chair geographers' and by raising 'cock-shies' of various kinds in order to demolish them, such as that Livingstone had become garrulous, demented, took no notes or observations and even that he had been married to an African princess.

Stanley did not pretend to be a geographer so we are not surprised that he was inclined to accept Livingstone's view that the Lualaba was the Nile. He has hard work, it must be admitted, in convincing himself that with the levels of the Lualaba and the White Nile being so little different they could be the same river but gets over the difficulty by assuming a long, level lake some four hundred miles in length. Neither he nor Livingstone realised that it was the latter's original theory of Africa being a long elevated trough that was really behind this idea of an enormously long Nile.

There was one aspect of the theory that could be tested quite quickly with Stanley's resources and that was whether there was an outlet at the north end of Lake Tanganyika leading towards Baker's Lake Albert, and that, in a very few days, they decided to do. Stanley says that it was at his suggestion and that was probably so since he alone had the means of hiring canoes and providing men. So 'in a week or so' after his arrival Stanley provided the means for Livingstone to go to this key point which Speke had tried to visit but failed on account of local hostility.

In a large canoe with sixteen paddlers and some camp-followers they set off to the north on a trip which lasted a month. It occupies only four pages in Livingstone's journal but thirty-five pages in Stanley's book, for which we must be truly grateful, especially as it gives an eye-witness account of Livingstone at work as a geographer. Almost at once there is an important note on Livingstone's liability to diarrhoea—'it is his only weak point, he says, and, as I afterwards found is a frequent complaint with him. Whatever disturbed his mind or any irregularity in eating, was sure to end in diarrhoea.'.

The astronomical work was done by Livingstone but Stanley assisted with compass bearings, The result was that there are two maps, one labelled 'Stanley's Survey', in his book, and one in Livingstone's own hand, a part of which is reproduced in facsimile opposite page 320. The difference between them is that Stanley's has more detail of bays and promontories, while Livingstone's is far more correct in its latitudes and longitudes. There is a good deal of discrepancy between them right at the northern end. It shows how indefinite are the ideas of Africans on such geographical matters as the flow of rivers, that headmen to within a few miles of the end of the lake differed as to whether the Rusizi River ran into the lake or out of it. They settled the matter for themselves by taking the canoe a mile or so up the delta channels and finding a current of two knots against them. An intelligent chief here gave them additional and sound information about Lake Kivu and the mountains beyond. It was clear to the explorers that Sir Samuel Baker had stretched his lake unduly far south as the chief was quite sure there was no lake other than the small Kivu within one hundred miles of where they were.

So ended one of the chances that Lake Tanganyika could be 'an expansion of the Nile' as Livingstone had suggested on the authority of Arabs and perhaps on the analogy of Lake Nyasa which has such a large and unmistakable outlet at one end, which is where one would expect it to be in a long lake,

Stanley was rather surprised that 'the Doctor still adheres to the conviction that there must be an outlet to the Tanganyika somewhere'—and apparently would have been content without one himself, in spite of its fresh water.

There were one or two incidents on the way when Livingstone by patience and firmness avoided clashes with the lake-shore people, to the great admiration of Stanley who would apparently have resorted to arms. There can be no doubt that these two men

Dr Livingstone at work on his Journal

from *How I Found Livingstone*, by H. M. Stanley (Sampson Low, 1872)

of very different temper and attitude towards the black man, learned something from each other. Stanley confesses it but although Livingstone, as usual, is silent he must have been envious of the discipline which Stanley had established in his followers.

Concerning Livingstone's few men Stanley expresses a curiously qualified admiration of Susi, 'the gallant servant, who would have been worth his weight in silver if he had not been an incorrigible thief.'

Livingstone persisted in calling the trip a 'picnic' which seems to have perturbed Stanley, who clearly considered it had been a dangerous one. In fact Stanley had never met anyone like David Livingstone, and he came firmly under his spell in the weeks during which they travelled together, without any real differences of opinion. It says a very great deal for Livingstone that this should be so, for Stanley almost boasted of being a rough diamond, a man-of-the-world, a realist, and he might easily have thought Livingstone weak and pious and rather helpless, and shown it. Possibly this very diversity of outlook was the reason for their friendship, had they been more similar in temperament they might well have seen motes in each other's eyes when they could ignore the beams so clearly visible.

The sketch he made of Livingstone writing his diary on their verandah at Ujiji, when improved by an artist in England, seems to have caught the far-away, almost wrapt look in his eyes that is to be seen in several of his photographs and is reproduced here to give an idea of his personal appearance at this time, only eighteen months before his death.

On their return to Ujiji Livingstone had decided to meet Stanley's common sense suggestions so far as to go with him to Unyanyembe to get the supplies which had been lying there for months. He would wait there for men and goods to be sent in from Zanzibar by Stanley. Stanley was determined to make the journey an easy one for Livingstone and his men, and took a delight in arranging all the details and planning a new route which should avoid some at least of the hostile tribes he had passed through on the way up from the coast. At this kind of work he was always supreme, his energy, command of detail and his practical common sense combining to make him the first class explorer he eventually became.

He bought the only riding donkey in Ujiji for Livingstone to ride, and this donkey, with other animals, was taken down the coast by a land party. Two large canoes were hired to take the main party to the point, Urimba, whence they thought they could go eastward in reasonable safety.

It is most interesting to read the journals of the two men on this their first land journey together and to compare their attitude to the incidents of caravan travel. It must be admitted that the journalist makes his account far more interesting than the geographer, though we must allow for the fact that Stanley's was written up later.

A typical entry of Livingstone's is 'Pass Viga Point—red sandstone—cross the bay of River Lugufu and Nkala village—transport people and goats—sleep'. Stanley, on the other hand, describes how one canoe is laden with goats, the difficulty in binding and stowing safely 'the fractious and ill-natured donkeys', the threat of hippos and crocodiles and so on, in relaying both parties past the flooded river.

The rainy season had begun and once on the march with daily wettings for both men it was Stanley who went down with fever, and had to use the 'riding donkey while the Doctor though he owned a donkey had walked on foot' most of the way. On the other hand, it was Stanley who kept the party supplied with meat by his shooting and it was he who steered the party by Livingstone's compass when the guide was lost. Their roundabout route to the southward of the usual one proved a peaceable though a hungry one at times, since there were few villages and the game was dispersed owing to the rains.

Stanley expresses tremendous admiration for his companion as a traveller. '. . . his knowledge is great about everything concerning Africa—the rocks, the trees, the fruits and their virtues are known to him.' It was at Livingstone's suggestion that they had milch-goats with them and again that Stanley should melt down his zinc canisters to harden his bullets when the lead ones failed to kill buffalo and giraffe.

Livingstone's toughness is illustrated by the story of the only attack they suffered—from a swarm of bees. Stanley galloped off on his donkey and had only four stings on his face, but Livingstone's account of the experience was as follows: 'In going a swarm of bees attacked a donkey Mr Stanley bought for me, and instead of galloping off, as did the other, the fool of a beast rolled down and over and over. I did the same, then ran, dashed into a bush like an ostrich pursued. They gave me a sore head and face, the donkey was completely knocked up by the stings and died in two days in consequence. We slept at Misonghi.'

Stanley tells the whole truth, not only a part of it, at the end of the day: 'As this was an unusually long march, I doubted if the Doctor could march it, his feet were so sore, so I sent four men back with the *kitanda*; but the stout old hero refused to be carried and walked all the way to camp, a march of eighteen miles. He had been stung dreadfully in the head and face, the bees had settled in handfuls in his hair; but, after partaking of a cup of warm tea and some food, he was as cheerful as if he had never travelled a mile.'

Very soon the *kitanda* had to be used for Stanley himself, carrying him during the worst of his fever attacks. The following is a characteristic entry in the Doctor's diary near the end of the journey: 'Wade across open flat with much standing water. They plant rice on the wet land round the villages. Our path lies through an open forest, where many trees are killed for the sake of the bark, which is used as cloth, and for roofing and beds. Mr Stanley has severe fever.'

On the fifty-fourth day from Ujiji they reached Stanley's former encampment at Kwihara (a little to the south of Unyanyembe and the modern Tabora), with flags flying and guns firing, after a journey which both looked back upon as a pleasant one on account of their companionship.

When the boxes left there for Livingstone a year earlier were examined the ravages of the agents in charge of them and the white ants, were apparent, there was little of any value left and even Stanley's store-room had been broken into. Here was ample evidence of how impossible it was to send goods intact to the interior unless they were in the charge of a white man. Even the courtly Arab governors were liable to stoop to robbery, and with effrontery ascribe empty bottles of brandy with corks replaced with corn cobs to the wiles of the white ants.

Yet Livingstone, influenced by Stanley, was still inclined to blame Kirk for carelessness in choosing the agents, and to write most regrettable letters to his old friend and companion. It was another friend of his, Horace Waller, who replied to these accusations in a long letter to Livingstone which fortunately he never received, so plain was the language he used.

Coupland explains Stanley's animosity to Kirk by his friendship with a Scotch adventurer in Zanzibar who had been indicted by Kirk for clandestine slave buying, but whatever the reason there was no doubt it was vindictive, a blot upon Stanley's character and largely responsible for the very mixed reception he had when he returned to England.

As we have suggested, this estrangement from Kirk may have had something to do with the decision to stay at Unyanyembe instead of doing the two month's journey with Stanley to Zanzibar, the most obvious thing to do especially after their recent success as fellow travellers. There is literally nothing in Livingstone's diary to explain it, in fact rather the reverse as there are many references to 'waiting wearily' for the men to be sent by Stanley.

The latter's account of their parting is highly emotional whereas Livingstone's journal merely says: 'Mr Stanley leaves. I commit to his care my journal, sealed with five seals. Positively not to be opened.'

This contrast does not mean that Stanley is untruthful, I think it highly probable that they did have 'a sad breakfast together', that the Doctor accompanied him a little way, that Stanley wrung his hand and said, 'Goodbye Doctor—dear friend' and that 'Susi and Chumah and Hamoydah—the Doctor's faithful fellows—must all shake and kiss my hands before I could quite turn away'.

That Stanley broke down and had to hide his emotion, by shouting harshly at his own men to march, is a little less credible, but we can accept it, as long as we are not asked to believe that Livingstone broke down too. At their first meeting the emotion was nearly all on one side, but Livingstone's gratitude was unmistakable.

With great generosity Stanley had given him all his surplus stores and some that he might have needed on his journey back to Zanzibar, including the famous bath, a medicine chest and paper. The donor makes a little bit too much of this generosity in his book and says it equipped Livingstone for four years, but we may take it that, provided he could get men to carry it, he was more fully equipped than he had ever been before. The list of things Stanley was to send back to him from Zanzibar contains the Nautical Almanacs for 1872 and 1873, a chronometer and 'a chain for refractory people'. So parted these two great personalities of African exploration, the one about to end his career, the other just beginning it, the one who had walked across Africa with a Bible in his hand and friendship for the Africans in his heart, the other who was to do the same with a rifle in his hand and discipline as his chief security. Their undoubted friendship was all the more strange because of their extreme diversity of purpose in making Africa their life's work.

Livingstone now spent much of his time writing up his journal and reading books and papers left by Stanley. He is plain spoken about the certainty in Speke's and Baker's language concerning their discovery of the two Nile sources and writes: 'I wish I had some of the assurance possessed by others, but I am oppressed with the apprehension, that after all it may turn out that I have been following the Congo.' He worked hard at preparing his maps and observations for sending to Sir Thomas Maclear at the Cape, but in general he was finding it hard to support inactivity for the five months he had to wait.

He had two letters from his son Oswell, who was down at the coast with the expedition which had set out from England in February and arrived in Zanzibar on the day that Stanley left him. His journal contains nothing about this expedition which so contradicted the suggestions made by Stanley that British geographers were indifferent to his fate. It is usually forgotten that the expedition, raised by private contributions when it became known that Ujiji was more or less cut off by local wars, was sent out with great despatch and urgency to Zanzibar to reach Livingstone. Stanley had hidden the real purpose of his journey and made successfully the scoop that his newspaper manager had planned a year earlier, leaving the expedition nothing to do. It was only too easy to make news capital out of such a situation, playing up the foresight of Stanley in getting there first and playing down the secrecy with which he did it.

It was a queer turn of fortune that by such incongruous means our pilgrim was not only pulled out of the mire of Despond but taken to the House Beautiful. Yet he still had his burden upon his back and his face still more steadfastly turned from his home and family.

David Livingstone, from a photograph

CHAPTER ELEVEN

Here he in great measure lost his senses, so that he could neither remember nor orderly talk of any of those sweet refreshments that he had met with in the way of his pilgrimage.

JOHN BUNYAN

If we are to understand this strange lonely man we must do so now, before he begins his last and fatal journey, because his frailties become more obvious, his illusions more painfully dominant and his impatience more ill-advised with every onward step.

After the busy four months of companionship with Stanley he had now seven months of time for reflection though, to tell truth, he was more given to planning for the future than to reviewing the past. He had time in which to use 'that inward eye which is the bliss of solitude', but which can also feed delusion and betray the balanced mind.

His great dream of helping 'to heal this open sore of the world' —to use his own phrase—was still with him, but has taken a different turn, a more indirect route.

His intense desire to make a great discovery on the problem of the Nile sources turned itself into a service in the cause of anti-slavery, on the basis that the prestige which would follow such a feat would focus public opinion upon the curse of Africa.

Such roundabout reasoning, though probably correct, was not

his custom and seems to hide his real feelings about what he had already done in this his sacred cause. What those feelings really were we do not know, for he never confided them even to the privacy of his journal, but there is no doubt that those dreadful two years in Manyuema haunted him: 'The sights I have seen are so nauseous that I always strive to drive them from memory,' yet 'the slaving scenes come back unbidden, and make me start up at dead of night horrified by their vividness'.

I believe therefore that in the back of his mind he was harassed by a sense of failure and that it coloured all his thoughts and plans. He had penetrated that darkest Africa hoping to shape a paradise, and it had not been attained. He might have echoed Milton and confessed that 'rather darkness visible served only to discover sights of woe, regions of sorrow, doleful shades where peace and rest can never dwell'.

He was an intensely disappointed man and it would be only natural if a touch of remorse came into his thoughts of wherein he had failed. If this were so then we have a still further reason for his utter rejection of the sensible suggestion from Stanley that he should go home and recuperate,

As relief from thinking of the past he spends most of his time devising plans for the coming journey, and in these the geographer is almost completely in the ascendant; yet it is often a bemused geographer, whose wishful thinking outweighs the doubts in his mind on whether he has 'not been following down what may after all be the Congo'.

With no one to challenge his theories or recall awkward facts in opposition to them, it was fatally easy to lose his sense of proportion, and to lull his own suspicions, almost to the extent of salving a conscience and seeking ease of mind. So, as the journey proceeds we find that he has less and less doubt that his quest will be successful in the end and he finds, without knowing it, that

'Vain wisdom all and false philosophy, yet with a pleasing sorcery could charm pain for a while, or anguish, and excite fallacious hope.'

So in this last chapter we shall find we need sympathy and understanding so that we may excuse the foibles and frailties of a mind still noble, but befogged by vain dreams and fevered fantasy.

It was as early as February 1872, while Stanley was still with him, that he announced his plan in his journal, the one from which he never diverged. He wrote then: 'It is all but certain that four full-grown fountains rise on the watershed eight days south of Katanga, each of which at no great distance off becomes a large river; and two rivers thus formed flow north to Egypt, the other two south. . . . I propose to go round south of Lake Bangweolo and due west to the ancient fountains. . . . This route will serve to certify that no other sources of the Nile can come from the south without being seen by me.' These were the four fountains on the map which he sent back to England with Stanley, naming them after four friends and supporters.

It is easy for us now, sitting in our armchairs with complete maps of Africa before us, to see the fallacies, the sheer question-begging, in this plan, but we can defend some part of it. He knew well enough that his first plan, of following down the Lualaba to see where it went, was the only way of proving it to be indeed the Nile. That way was now utterly blocked. The alternative therefore was to make for some part of the gap between his farthest at Nyangwe and Baker's Lake Albert or even further west. Yet this way too was blocked by the war between the Arabs and that stout-hearted chief Mirambo, a war that had diverted all recent caravans going from the coast to Ujiji. We have an uneasy feeling that he did not give enough thought to some way of bypassing that troubled district, and a still more uneasy suspicion that he did not do so because he hated going where other white men had gone. He never mentions such a plan, but it must have occurred to him as the sole remaining chance of proving his theory. Instead, he made the grand assumption that the Lualaba *was* the Nile and preferred to make sure of the sources, of which he already had discovered one in the Chambezi.

In a letter to his brother he refers again to the indirect value of successful discovery as a kind of excuse for his plan: 'The Nile sources are valuable only as a means of enabling me to open my mouth with power among men. It is this power I hope to apply to remedy an enormous evil. Men may think I covet fame, but I make it a rule never to read aught written in my praise.'

We must admit that such a specious argument for seeking fame was not worthy of the earlier Livingstone we knew, especially if we note the expression used to Sir Thomas Maclear in a letter written only a few weeks before his death, though it is but a repetition of what he had written before, that he was 'going round outside this lake (Bangweulu) and all the sources so that no one may come afterwards and cut me out.' The obsession that he alone held the secret of the Nile was now lending itself to urgency that he must get to the sources before any one else could 'cut him out'.

By mid-August the strong party of fifty-seven men sent back by Stanley had arrived and Livingstone was probably better equipped for exploration than he had ever been before. To this party carefully selected by Stanley and including many of his own proved men he could add his faithful five, of whom Susi was head, Chuma who had now married (at Livingstone's urging), Amoda with his Halima, Mabruki and Gardner. We never hear just how many women and children were with him as camp followers, but the whole party could not have been less than eighty. They included some more 'Nassick boys' brought across from Bombay for the Dawson relief expedition, but most of these were rather young and had to be given half-loads. Prominent amongst them was Jacob Wainwright, who was well educated and therefore became the chief spokesman of Susi's party when they returned to Zanzibar with Livingstone's remains. He was lacking in character, however, and could not withstand the fame which his education had brought upon him.

There was a second and more famous Mabruki with him, whom he always calls Mabruki Speke to distinguish him. He had achieved notoriety when with Speke and Burton, and the latter described him as 'low browed, pig-eyed and pug-nosed'. Stanley took him on in spite of a maimed arm and calls him 'Bull headed Mabruki, stupid but faithful, ugly and vain, but no coward'. He had been set upon by some of the Sultan of Zanzibar's soldiers over some private feud, who tied him to a tree by the wrists and left him for two days when he was accidentally discovered. Dr

Kirk did his best for him and managed to save one hand, and he went with Stanley and again with Livingstone, who records that his famous donkey, resisting being tied down in a canoe, 'bit Mabruki Speke's lame hand.' Another valuable addition to the party was Chowpereh, 'a sturdy short man of thirty, good natured and humourous,' described by his first master in his curious journalese as 'the strongest, healthiest, amicablest and faithfulest, embodiment of a good follower'.

Livingstone was fully conscious of how much he was indebted to his friend for sending back such a good lot of men, many of whom must have been trained in the discipline which was so much the secret of Stanley's success, and, perhaps in the same tradition, they carried a drum.

They started with ten head of cattle besides goats and two donkeys, one of whom was to rival the fame of Sinbad, the ox on his journey to Loanda, but unfortunately his name, if he had one, is never given. The donkey survived his owner but unfortunately was killed by a lion near the Luapula river.

So all was set fair for a good and rapid journey, first retracing their steps towards Lake Tanganyika along the successful route pioneered by them at the beginning of the year.

In spite of an attack of his old dysenteric trouble which delayed them for nearly a week, they reached the lake in six weeks, where they were rather prostrated by the heat which always precedes the rains. It will be noted that the route he chose took him along two sides of a triangle, and that must have been because of his passion for mapping and his desire to complete the survey of the east side of the lake.

As they traversed the many valleys leading down to the lake the travelling became more and more difficult, food harder to purchase for his large party and he himself had more frequent attacks of illness.

Nevertheless, he was in good spirits at this time and in a long unfinished letter to his friend Horace Waller he is hopeful of finishing his task in a few months, even asking Waller to 'speak to a dentist about a speedy fitting of artificial teeth and to look for some decent lodgings for him near Regent's Park'.

As they neared the southern end of the lake these valleys became such obstacles that they turned inland. For this reason they crossed the Kalambo river some 1500 feet above the lake and some miles upstream of the falls. It seems a needless shaft of ill fortune that caused him to miss so narrowly the discovery of the highest falls in Africa, having already discovered the broadest.

They crossed the Lucheche stream close to the site of the present Abercorn and a few days later, when the rains came on in earnest, they reached the path he had followed five years earlier when coming up from Lake Nyasa. He renewed acquaintance with the new chief, Kampamba, the son of the Kasonso who had befriended him then but had since died.

They were detained here for three days by set-in rain at the end of November and it would obviously have been a very suitable base at which to stay, at least until the early rains were over. But Livingstone was in no mood for delay and off they went again southward on their old track. One of the donkeys had succumbed to tsetse fly some weeks earlier but they still had some of the cattle, and, except for an earlier desertion by two porters, the party seems to have been complete and healthy, and well furnished with cloth and beads for purchasing food. But December and January is the lean time of the year when villagers are living on stored grain and waiting for the new crops to ripen, so the feeding of his very large party was bound to be difficult.

Livingstone had proved over and over again that one can travel in the rainy season, but just as often he had said that travelling in wet clothes was sure to bring on sickness. In fact he had told Stanley when they were going to Unyanyembe in the last rainy season that he 'never travelled' in the rainy season, a remark which Stanley probably interpreted as 'Do as I say, not as I do', for he knew well enough that Livingstone paid little regard to the season.

So we soon come to sentences in the journal such as, 'No food to be got, the people themselves are living on grubs, roots and fruits.' 'Send off men to a distance for food, here there is none for love or money.' In fact his party was reduced to seeking giant mushrooms just as they had had to do when he was in this region before.

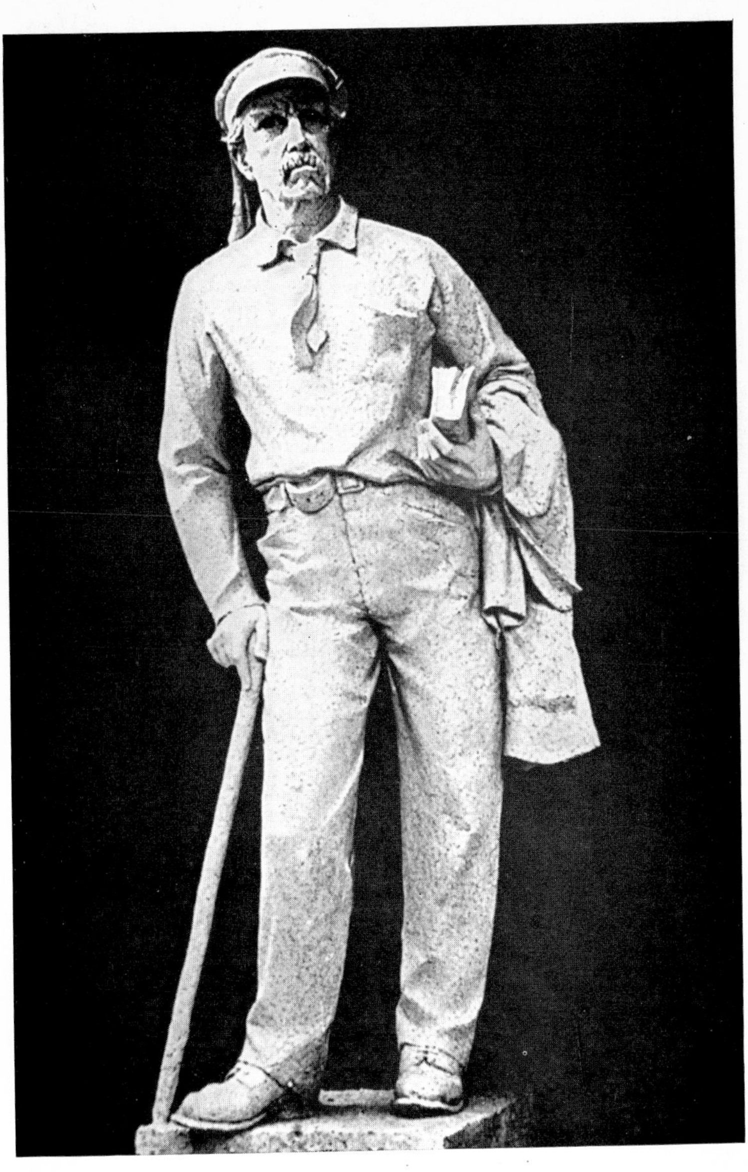

The Statue at the Royal Geographical Society
Scupltor: T. B. Huxley-Jones

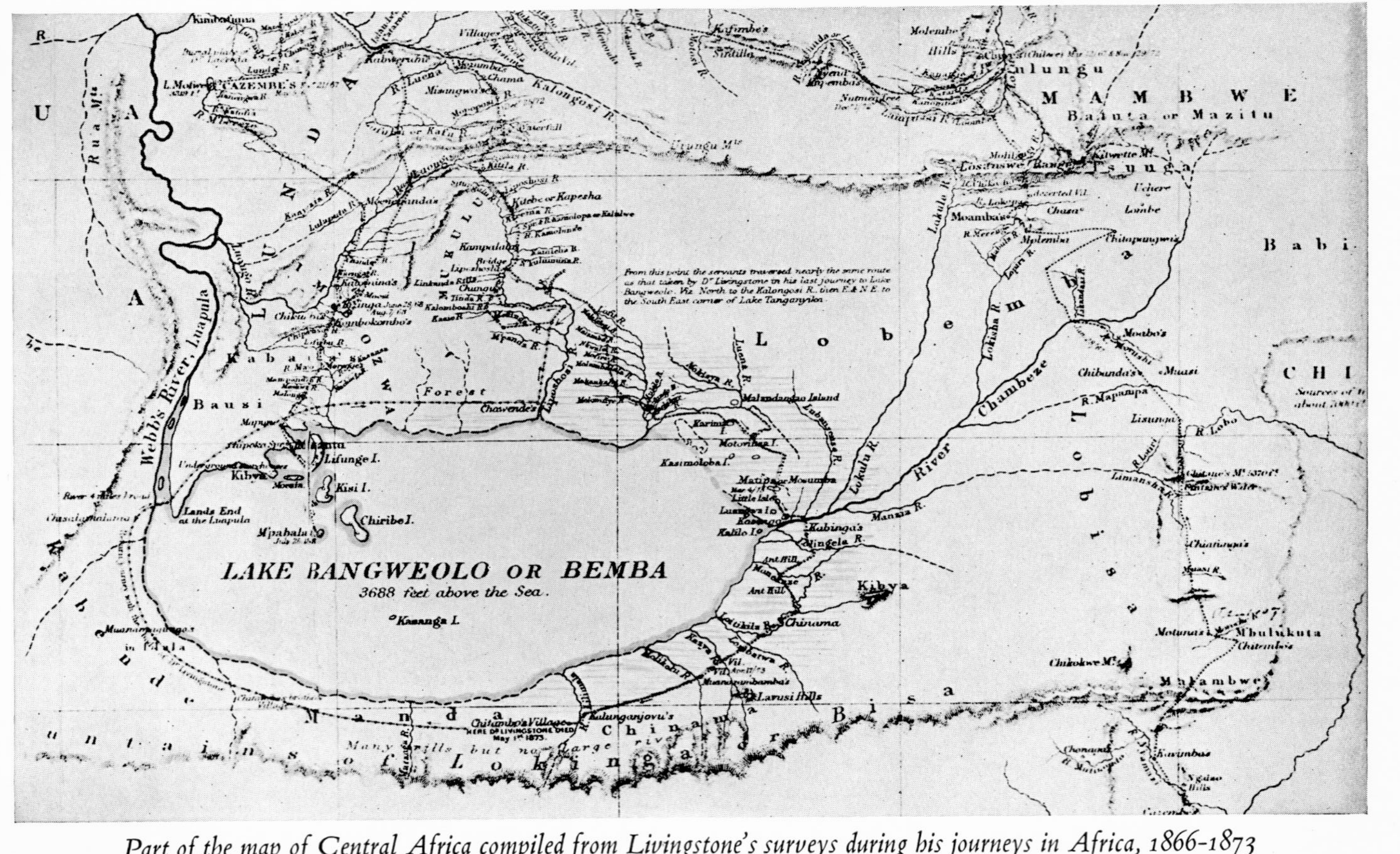

Part of the map of Central Africa compiled from Livingstone's surveys during his journeys in Africa, 1866–1873
from *The Last Journals of Livingstone*, ed. H. Waller (John Murray, 1874)

It was probably the food shortage which caused him to abandon his original plan of continuing southwards until he had crossed the Chambezi and passing round to the south of Lake Bangweolo. The only entry which seems to refer to this change is on December 3rd when they were a few miles north of the present Kasama: 'A stupid or perverse guide took us away N.W. The guide had us at his mercy for he said, "If you go S.W. you will be five days without food or people".' And a little later: 'Here our guide disappeared and so did the path.'

With our modern knowledge we have to agree with the guide because a S.W. course would have taken them across the Chimpili divide into the area between the Lukulu and Luansenshi rivers which even now is sparsely populated and rather densely forested. It was at this point that they heard the Arabs had killed Casembe with the help of some rebels in his own village, and that 'his pretty wife escaped over Mofwe and the slaves of the Arabs ran riot everywhere'.

Up to this stage Livingstone had been taking few sights for position probably because he had been on or near his former route, which we must remember was here about twenty miles too far east in longitude but correct in latitude. In his last astronomical field book, now at the Royal Geographical Society in London, there are two latitude sights near the south end of Lake Tanganyika and then nothing until they reach the vicinity of Lake Bangweulu. It is therefore difficult to make out his exact route to the westward except that it was evidently between the valleys of the Luangwa (which he calls the Kisi) and the Kalungwisi which he spells Kalongosi.

Both of these rivers are large and difficult to cross. He crossed the Kalungwisi by his account 'about a mile above the confluences of the Luena', but to reach such a point he would have had to cross the Luangwa (Kisi), and as he does not mention doing so I am inclined to think that he made the single crossing about five miles above the Luena confluences. Mr Bolton, in trying to reconcile the journal, places the Kisi confluence below that of the Luena which is definitely wrong. Livingstone deplores the fact that it was 'so cloudy and wet that no observations can be taken for latitude and longitude at this real geographical point'. They made the crossing with some difficulty on December 19th and the party could now turn southwards in the direction of Lake Bangweulu. Their immediate difficulties were the heavy rain and the unfriendliness of the local chief, Chama, who endeavoured to send the visitors off in the wrong direction.

Livingstone coped with the distrust of the villagers by being firm but the swollen streams were rapidly becoming a major hindrance. He mentions a 'sedgy stream which we could barely cross. We hauled a cow across bodily'. From this point hardly a day passes without mention of these 'soaks', 'sponges' and 'oozes' as he variously styles them. He sometimes used the Swahili word Mbuga or Bouga, but never the local word Dambo. In this part of Northern Rhodesia they are so frequent that they take up nearly twenty-five per cent of the area. A typical dambo is marked by a sudden change from open forest to an apparent grassy plain. But the true grass soon gives way to coarse tussocky reeds with hundreds of the small grey ant hills known as *mafwesa*, and then to dense aquatic plants such as the strong matete reeds and even papyrus.

In the next few days, after turning southwards, he crossed first the 'Lopopussi' and then the 'Lofubu' and avoided the confusion that would have overtaken a lesser man when later he crossed the divide into the Bangweulu basin and immediately came upon two other rivers with precisely the same names.

On the last day of 1872 he crossed the Luongo, running westward to the Luapula, and recognised it as the river he had crossed lower down in going to and returning from Lake Bangweulu four years before. He did not know how far he was from that former crossing place for two reasons, firstly that his longitudes here on his first visit were some thirty or forty miles too much to the west, and secondly because the cloudy weather prevented him from taking any now. In fact, he could not get any for another six weeks, and the lack of longitudes caused him to get completely lost, as we shall see, and contributed towards his fatal decision later on to go the long and weary way round the swamps to his death.

We will endeavour not to tire readers with a multiplicity of native names and a confusion of maps, yet they must appear in some fashion if we are to follow the steps which led to his death before he had completed his task.

By the kindness of Livingstone's greatgranddaughter, Miss Diana Livingstone-Bruce, we are able to reproduce a tracing of the map in his handwriting which was the one used by Mr Bolton in compiling the one in the *Last Journals*, of which part is shown facing p. 304. This map was drawn by him when he was staying for three weeks at 'Matipa's islet' as we know from internal evidence. We note at once that the map is upside down as we would say, with south at the top, notwithstanding his mistake in writing N and S in the wrong places. E for east is correct as we can see from the latitudes written in. The meridians have no longitude numbers on them, not because he had not got some by that time but because he distrusted them. It is especially valuable as it relates to his wanderings when he was more or less lost, and we may note that it places Matipa's island close to the confluence of the Chambezi and the Lubansense, and it may have been added to when he had got to that confluence.

There is another map of this area, in the keeping of the Livingstone Memorial Museum at Blantyre which, at first sight, is very similar. Close inspection shows that it is not a single map but three or four preliminary plottings which have overlapped each other. This has been reproduced in facsimile as an end paper in Dr Macnair's excellent volume of *Livingstone's Travels*, published in 1954. This, which we will call the Macnair map, seems to represent day-to-day trial plottings which have been made to different scales and have run into each other. Nevertheless, one part of it is very valuable and more accurate than the Matipa's islet map.

The map on p. 300 represents the author's interpretation of the evidence given in the journal and in these two maps. He takes full responsibility for this interpretation of where Livingstone actually went, but he is indebted to Messrs Greenall and Waddington, members of the Administrative Service in the district, for assistance. He also found useful hints concerning the route in a paper by Mr Rawsthorne a former district commissioner. This help, added to a small amount of personal acquaintance with the area encourages the writer to consider the final product fairly close to the truth.

We will now follow his route with quotations from his journal in some detail, and the story thereby unfolded is a painfully dramatic one. We must remember that Livingstone planned to get to the south side of Lake Bangweulu and from there work

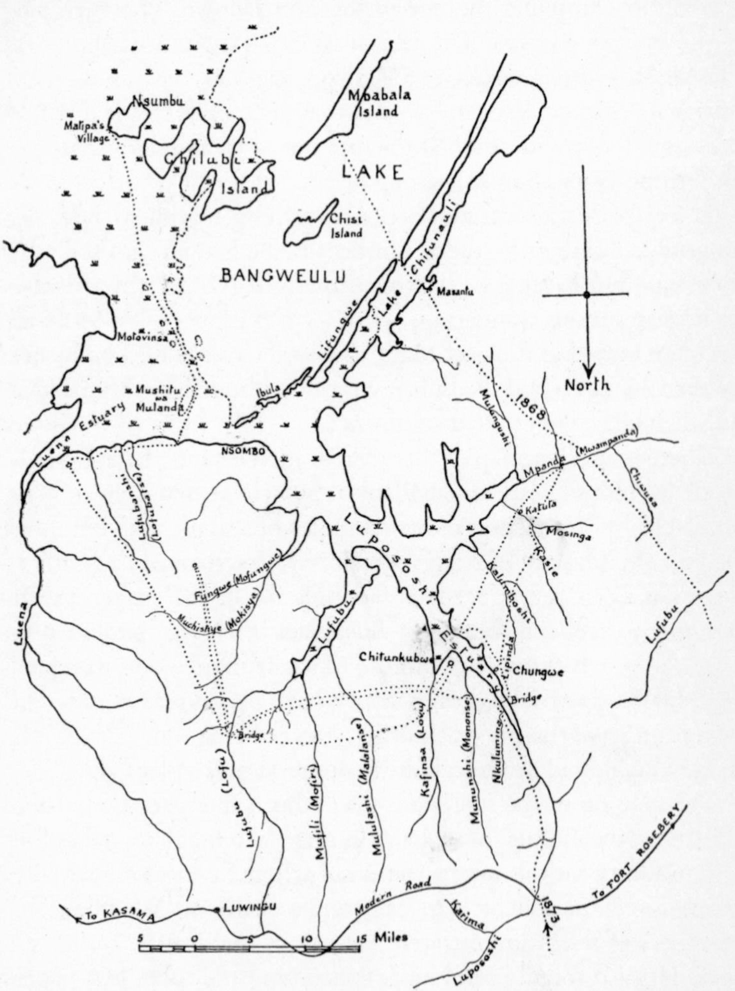

Author's interpretation of Livingstone's routes inserted on a modern map

westward towards the Katanga copper districts where he counted on finding his 'four fountains'. He was now approaching the northern side of the lake and, remembering his former visit, when, from an island in its midst, he saw and heard of Kabende, a district and village at its southern end, he had the sound idea of making for it either by land or canoe. We must remember, however, that his longitudes were forty miles to the westward on that journey and as yet he had got no longitudes at all but was trusting to his guides.

We join him on January 4th, 1873, when he crossed 'the Lopoposi stream of 25 or 30 feet, now breast deep and flowing fast southwards to join the Chambeze. Camped on the rivulet Kizima after very heavy rain'. Here the chief Ketebe or Kapesha was friendly and gave him three guides to take him on to his elder brother, Chungu, a more important chief.

Heavy and continuous rain kept him at the next village of Moenje, marked on the Macnair map, but on January 9th they 'crossed the rivulet and sponge of Nkulumina and after another hour the large rivulet of Lopopozi by a bridge which was 45 feet long and showed the deep water'. They then crossed the Linkanda rills and arrived at Chungu's village.

But the chief would not see them in person and 'excused his fears because guns had routed Casembe and his head was put on a pole'. Apparently he supplied guides, and a dry day enabled them to move forward to the sluggish Pinda and on to the next stream where they were 'Storm stayed by rain and cold on the rivulet Kalambosi, *near the Chambeze*'.

Illness and vexatious delays always brought his obsession about the Nile to the fore, so we find him writing at this time, 'Cold and rainy weather, never saw the like; but this is among the sponges of the Nile and *near the northern shores of Bangweolo*.' The italics in those quotations are ours and are used to focus attention on those curious phrases, for he was a long way from the Chambezi and near the western, not the northern shore of Lake Bangweulu.

Next day they crossed the Mozinga at its confluence with the Kasie and then there is the entry, 'After 4½ hours we were brought up by the deep rivulet Mpanda, to be crossed tomorrow in canoes.' With such a large party we can hardly expect a rate of more than one and a half miles an hour so we can fix the point where they reached the Mpanda at six miles from the above-mentioned confluence, and as shown on the modern map; it is only three or four miles distant from where he had crossed the same river nearly five years before. Had they gone that extra few miles it is probable that he would have recognised it, even though he had crossed it then in the dry season.

The entry for the next day, January 15th, is: 'Found that Chungu had let us go astray towards the lake and into an angle formed by the Mpandé and Lopopussi. Chisupa, a headman on the other side of the Mpanda, sent a present and denounced Chungu for heartlessness. . . . We were treated scurvily by Chungu. He knew that we were *near the Chambeze but hid the knowledge* and himself too. It is terror of guns.'

The only explanation for this confusion and tragic failure to recognise the Mpanda seems to be that Livingstone thought he was very much farther east than he was, and that suspicion grows as we read on. The similarity of the name Mpanda would not help him since river names are constantly repeated as we have already seen. Had he realised it was the same river he would presumably have kept on to the southward and reached the Kabende he was aiming for in a few days and then the Luapula and a route towards Katanga.

Instead, he turned round 'back to the River Lopopussi, which now looms larger and must be crossed in canoes'. But the short cut by water was denied them, as they could get no canoe large enough for the donkey and the river there was 'quite two miles wide and full of rushes, except in the main stream'. This was almost certainly at Kamfumu where there has always been some kind of a canoe ferry service. So they had to toil back to the bridge again, a seven mile trek which took them six hours. 'We lost a week by going to Chungu, a worthless terrified headman,' but we must admit that if Livingstone had asked for guides to take him to the south of the lake region, Chungu had been right in sending him down the west side of the lake. The error in his earlier longitudes and complete lack of observations now was causing great confusion both to him and to such guides as he obtained.

From the bridge they went on towards the East and crossed the Mononse or Mununshi which 'though only ten feet of deep stream flowing S, had some 400 yards of most fatiguing, plunging,

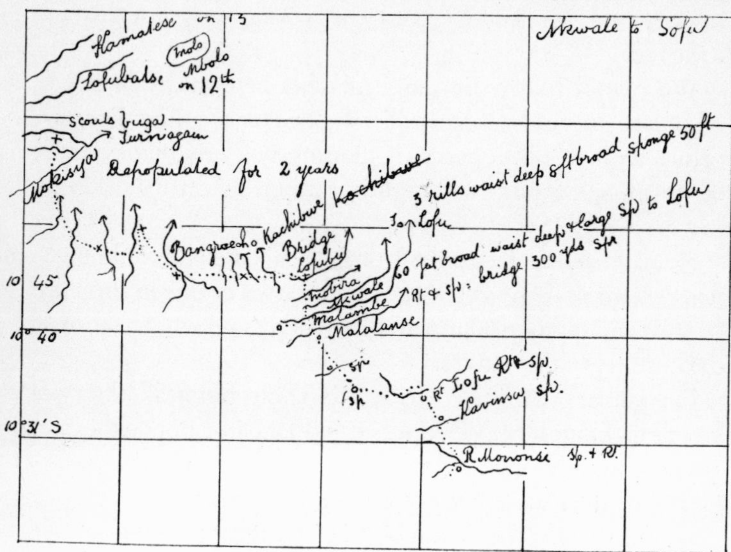

Tracing from the Macnair map: reduced

deep sponge, . . . then on to sponge Lovu . . . crossed it by a felled tree lying over it'.

Once more Livingstone was to be the victim of the repetition of native names, or possibly a faulty guide, for this Lovu was a tributary of the Kafinsa river, not the Lufubu which came later. He naturally tries in his map to fit the first Lovu to the second one. No wonder he writes a little later: '. . . the streams are so numerous that there has been a scarcity of names. Here we have Loou and Luena, we had two Loous before, and another Luena.'

The extract from the Macnair map is more accurate for in it the names are correct and he approaches the next few streams on their right banks. When thinking it all over and constructing the map at Matipa's, he seems to have been determined to make the two

Lovus the same river which causes him to approach its tributaries on their left banks, which was wrong.

That part of the Macnair map is therefore reproduced on p. 303, as the author is determined to show that Livingstone's first mapping was as sound as ever; it was only later when he began to compile a map from his preliminary plottings that he went wrong, and Mr Bolton used the wrong map for his reconstruction.

We cannot follow his daily marches here in detail, but those who care to read Chapter X of *Livingstone's Last Journals* together with this little piece of plotting will find that every detail of stream and sponge and nightly camp is reflected exactly in the map.

He had tried to get guides from a local chief Chitunkubwe and was refused so he was now steering his own course in this maze of streams and sponges, a prey to the weather and what he took to be the hostility of the natives.

On January 22nd he writes: 'No astronomical observations worth naming during December and January; impossible to take any, owing to clouds and rain. It is trying beyond measure to be baffled by the natives lying and misleading us wherever they can.'

It seems likely that some of this 'misleading' was due to misunderstanding, for if Livingstone was asking for guides to the south side of the lake they would take him south and west, which he rejected as he felt that would mean the longest way round. The next day he wrote: 'I don't know where we are and the people are deceitful in their statements. Rain, rain, rain as if it were never tired on this watershed. The showers show little in the gauge but keep everything and every place wet and sloppy.'

The last is a reminder that in spite of all these difficulties of travel he was recording the rainfall in a portable gauge, the amounts being recorded every day, with the temperature, in a corner of the daily notes. Was there ever such a persistent and conscientious scientific explorer?

His men were showing their quality nobly and sparing Livingstone exertion as much as they could, and the drawing from the *Last Journals*, reproduced here, shows how manfully they were doing it. It was after a graphic description of this crossing, probably of the Mofira river, that he writes: 'Our progress is distressingly slow. Wet, wet, wet, sloppy weather truly and no observations except that the land near the Lake being very level, the rivers spread out into broad friths and sponges.'

The author must here interject, in defence of this pleasant district, that in the dry season Livingstone would have revelled in

'The main stream came up to Susi's mouth'

from *Livingstone's Last Journals*

its sober beauties of tree and flower and abundant game. There is an embarrassment of dambos it is true and crossing them may be a damp process even in the dry season, but readers must realise once more that the face of Africa in the rains is only a partial portrait.

When he reached the real Lovu or Lufubu and built a bridge across it he calls it in his field notebook 'the Lovu or Lopu of Chambeze' which is further evidence that he thought he was far to the east of where he had been in 1868, whereas he was really on the same meridian as Mbabala Island.

His bridge was only a few miles below what is now a favourite picnic spot on the main road crossing the river, where in the dry season one leaps across the Lufubu with ease.

Here he mentions for the first time his desire to reach the chief Matipa. He had obviously heard of this chief as living on the island of Chilubi, which he had seen in the distance from another island in the Lake, and therefore he might be able to lend them canoes to cross the lake.

But Livingstone's illness was heavy upon him at this time—'I lost much blood, but it is a safety valve for me, and I have no fever or other ailments,' and now hunger was to be added to their difficulties.

On January 29th he wrote: 'Tramped to a broad sponge (the Mokisya or Muchishye). All was stream flowing through the rushes knee and thigh deep. On still with the same, repeated again and again till I resolved to send out scouts S, S.E., and S.W. The music of the singing birds and turtle doves and the screaming of the frankolin (partridges) proclaim man to be near.'

One of the scouts went 'about eight hours south and has seen the lake and two islets'. This would have been somewhat to the west of the present village of Nsombo from whence he would see the islets of Misangwa and Ibula. I take the name Mbolo for the islet on the Macnair map to be the scout's rendering of Ibula.

The scouts could not find people, the district having been depopulated by war for the last two years, and there was nothing for it but to turn back: 'Killed our last calf and turn back for four days hard travel to Chitunkubwes.' On the way he 'tried lunars in vain, either sun or moon in clouds' so he still had no longitude.

On this return journey there is proof of his iron constitution and disregard of pain for they accomplished the forty-one miles back in fifteen hours' marching, spread over four days. He would have been riding the donkey in between the sponges, of course, but the haemorrhage of the bowels was persistent.

Having arrived at Chitunkubwe's village, he found the chief much more kindly disposed than he expected, 'a fine jolly looking man, of a European cast of countenance and very sensible and friendly.' He told Livingstone that his men had been close to some villages belonging to Matipa: 'He showed me two of

Matipa's men who had heard us firing guns to attract one of our men who had strayed; these men followed us. It seems we had been close to human habitations, but did not know it. We have lost half a month by this wandering but it was all owing to the unfriendliness of some and the fears of all.'

Here we quote from an excellent paper by Mr C. H. G. Rawsthorne, written in 1936 when he was District Commissioner at Luwingu: 'There are several men living who remember Livingstone's arrival at Chitunkubwe's village. One was then a boy of about ten years' of age but he remembered "Engereze" well. He described his "cloths" to the writer, his large bales of goods and named the two guides whom Chitunkubwe detailed to guide the party. The then Chitunkubwe was a young man of about 20 "for he had only one child" and it was the same chief who died in 1928, 55 years afterwards, "a very old man".' It was during his four-day stay here that a great misfortune befell Livingstone, though he was never to realise its gravity.

In his diary for February 5th, he writes, 'I got lunars for a wonder' and he was able to get another set the next day. These were the first observations for longitude he had got for two months, in fact since he crossed the Kalungwisi where he knew his position to within a few miles. For all that time, during which he had travelled to and fro for over two hundred miles, he had had to rely on his compass bearings and dead reckoning for some idea of where he was, with the added complication that the route he had plotted in 1868 was up to forty miles too far west without his knowing it.

He was indeed desperately anxious to get longitude sights and now at last he had them. So he must have been aghast when he had worked them out for they were palpably wrong and placed him somewhere near where he had crossed the Chambezi years before, obviously a hundred miles and more in error.

He must have been sorely puzzled, though there is no mention of it in his diary; he knew well enough the results were wrong but the net result must have been that he considered the direction of the error was right; in other words, that though he was not so far east as 31°30′, he might be somewhere about 30°30′E. We make this supposition because it accounts for his placing of Matipa's island near the Chambezi in the map on p. 325 and also, with a more desperate result, for his decision when he was with that chief.

This, in fact, is the second catastrophe in these last few weeks of his life, the first being when he turned back on the Mpanda just before he reached a point he might have recognised.

Readers will wonder how such a skilled navigator as he was could have got over two degrees wrong in his longitude and the explanation is to be found in the astronomical note book, in two notes he added two months later below his calculations.

On the page for February 4th it reads: 'Note—something went wrong in the silvering of the large reflector of sextant and it was only at the confluence of Chambeze that I succeeded in correcting it.'

On February 6th: 'A large error crept in by a change in the silvering of the reflector—corrected only at Chambeze confluence. Two images appeared, one a long way horizontally from the other.'

To the layman it may be explained that of the two mirrors in a sextant one is enclosed and if moisture gets in behind the silvered surface damage may be done. These two notes were for the benefit of his friend Maclear when he came to rework the sights.*

After four days' stay in this friendly atmosphere Livingstone started off again, evidently refreshed, for he reached the repaired bridge on the Lufubu in a day and a half—a distance of some twenty-five miles. From this point the guides took him, apparently in a fairly straight line, in the direction of the estuary of the Luena River. Three days from the bridge he says that they came within sight of the Luena and the lake, but he found that the

* The author suggests that by the large reflector Livingstone means the index glass and that what had happened was that moisture had got into the metal tray behind the mirror and had lifted some of the silvering off the glass on to the tray, thus causing two images to show on the horizon glass. In that case one of the images would still be correct but if it were the fainter of the two the observer would tend to ignore it. Livingstone does not say *how* he corrected it two months later, but, short of resilvering it (which he could probably do), a clearing of the index glass silvered surface would get rid of the lifted silvering and leave a fainter but correct image.

guides were now 'more at a loss than we are, as they always go in canoes in the flat rivers and rivulets'.

So once more the party were more or less lost. There was reason to believe that the villagers usually in that vicinity had been dispersed by a recent raid from the fierce Ba-Bemba, and were either away or hiding in fear from any strangers. Livingstone sent on two men to find one of Matipa's villages in order to get canoes to navigate the lake or a guide 'to go east to the Chambeze, to go round on foot'. This wording in itself shows that at the time he thought that he was much nearer the eastern end than the western. Similarly, two days later, when he had still failed to contact Matipa's men, he says he is sending a message 'with a request to Matipa to convey us west if he has canoes but if not to tell us truly and we will go east and cross the Chambeze where it is small'.

His men appear to have been just as lost as the leader at this time, for the scouts whom he sent to find Matipa's people consistently failed to do so or got faint-hearted and returned. The sad fact is that he arrived somethere near the banks of the Luena Estuary on February 13th and it was not till March 1st that he finally embarked on the journey to Matipa. He was excessively ill with haemorrhages at this time, and his map suffers in consequence. In fact the original is of little use in showing where he actually was. The very 'uncomfortable spot' where he was on February 19th would appear to be well up the Luena Estuary, since from that camp he was 'carried three miles to a canoe and went westward, in branches of the Luena, very deep and flowing west, for three hours'. Three hours in a canoe, even without a regular channel, should take him between four and six miles: I would suggest therefore that his first camp was somewhere near the swampy mouth of the Lelangwa, as shown on the map.

Meanwhile he had sent men to communicate with Matipa, whom he thought would be on the Chirube Island he knew and on February 26th the trustworthy Susi returned: 'With good news from Matipa, who declares his willingness to carry us to Kabende for the five bundles of brass wire I offered. It is not on Chirube, but amid the swamps of the mainland on the Lake's north side.

He means that Matipa is not on Chirube, but on a distant island far from it. Kabende was marked on his map made on his first visit as an area to the south and west of the lake proper. It was really an important village at the south end of the lake opposite the terminus of the long Mbabala Island.

It was quite the best route to get to where he wished and Livingstone's judgment was again unerring in spite of his confusion as to where he was at the time.

There was a wait of two days for the canoes to arrive from Matipa and on March 1st they started, 'going three hours south east to Bangweolo.' There seems no doubt that the point of embarkation in Matipa's canoes was about five miles east of Nsombo, whence he would go down the well-used Matuku channel towards the lake. Livingstone uses the curious phrase that from this point of embarkation he could 'hear Bangweolo bellowing'. Perhaps we may take this to mean indications of various kinds that the lake was not far off, though in fact it must have been six miles away, and he never saw the open lake on this journey, though he may have been within a few hundred yards of it, hidden by the papyrus from his view.

The channel passes by the large, sandy, densely-wooded island called Mushitu Wa Mulanda, much frequented by the fisherman for the long stiff stems of the Chiwale palm which they use as punt-poles. This would appear to be what Livingstone calls on his map 'Malandangao Island'. His party did not land on it but went on to the small Kafinsa group, low sandy islands just inside the edge of the reeds, and therefore not on the lake itself. Here he found people drying fish over fires, just as they do to this day. Livingstone calls the islet 'Motovinza', and one cannot identify this absolutely, since there are no less than thirteen low sandy islets, each with its fishing-camp, along the route to Chilubi Island.

From this resting-place it took seven-and-a-half hours' punting to reach the chief Matipa, who was then living on Nsumbu Island. This is separated from the much larger Chilubi Island by deep water and permanent swamp known as the Molonga Channel, a name which appears in his map. Livingstone uses the term 'prairie' to describe this flooded area. His estimate of distance from his starting-point as thirty miles is not really very far out, for by the shortest route it would be at least twenty-five miles.

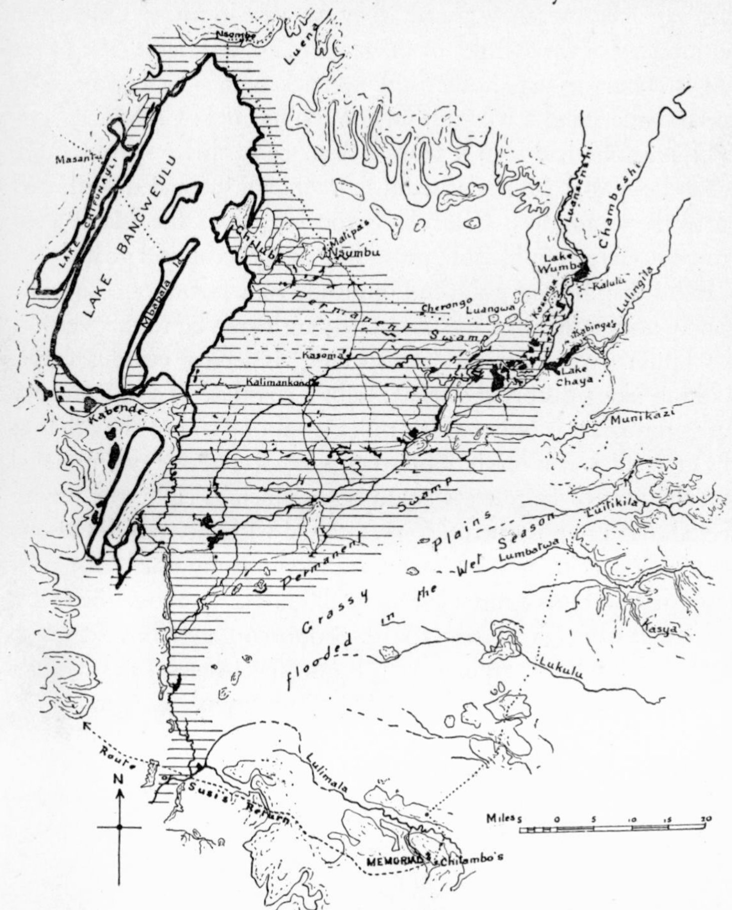

The Bangweulu Swamp

Matipa's canoe-men would have taken him at this time of flood, by one of the many channels over the 'prairie', well away from the deeper water near the lake because they prefer punting to paddling and shallow to deep water, since their canoes sink if capsized. It must also be remembered that the canoe channels of which there are hundreds in the Bangweulu are bordered for the most part by high reeds so that one very rarely has a view to a distance.

These facts have an extraordinary significance, a pitiful one in this case because they meant that on this journey, sometimes within two or three miles of the large island of Chilubi, he never saw it. This was yet another unkind trick of fate for Livingstone, and to understand it we must say something about Chilubi.

Livingstone had seen it from a distance of three or four miles when he was at Mbabala island in 1868, and he had described it correctly as follows: 'Chirubi is the largest of the islands and contains a large population, possessing many sheep and goats.'

In his map he had put it in Longitude 29° 5′E and, of course, he had no notion that that was about fifty miles too far to the west.

Chilubi (to use the modern spelling) is a most curious shape, looking like a distorted starfish, with a coastline of some seventy miles though it is only twelve miles from one end to the other as the crow flies. It is rarely more than forty feet above swamp level but the tops of large trees could be as much as eighty or ninety feet above. Livingstone must have passed within two miles of one such group of trees, a *mushitu* it is called, on the north east promontory, and it is a miracle that he did not see it above the reeds, because it serves as a landmark for people coming from the north by canoe, but it was raining at the time. Nevertheless I am ready to believe he did get a glimpse of it and either took it to be part of Matipa's island or else, asking what it was, was given the name of a neighbouring village, perhaps Kasimoloba, instead of the name of the whole island, Chilubi.

The map on p. 311 shows its situation and that its south side is only about twenty miles from the Kabende he wished to reach, travelling along the edge of the swamp. It was sheer bad luck to miss seeing the island he knew, or, seeing it, to be told the name of some minor feature on it. But much worse luck was to come on this very matter of where he was.

He reached Matipa's headquarters, which at this time of year was not on Chilubi but on the much smaller Nsumbu, and is just round the north-east corner of the island; in other words, just out of sight of Chilubi.

It was, and still is, a pleasant village, and there was plenty of food: the next day, March 3rd, he called upon the chief and there is a vital passage in his diary for that day which must be quoted in full: 'Matipa says that five sangoes or coils [of wire] will do to take us to Kabende, and I sincerely hope that they will. . . . I visited Matipa at noon. He is an old man, slow of tongue, and self possessed; he recommended our crossing to the south bank of the Lake to his brother, who has plenty of cattle and to go along that side where there are few rivers and plenty to eat. Kabende's land was lately overrun by Banyamwesi, who now inhabit that country, but as yet have no food to sell.'

Matipa's brother Kabinga lived far to the east across the swamps, and not on the 'south bank of the Lake', which is only Livingstone's interpretation of where it appeared to him to be. Matipa thus dissuades him from his former plan and it is hard to understand why he does so, unless it was in order to enable his brother to share in the cloths or coils of wire of the strange white man.

Then comes an illuminating sentence in the diary—'I am rather in a difficulty, as I fear I must give the five coils for a much shorter task.' The actual distances are much the same in mileage and the sentence is another indication that Dr Livingstone believed he was near the eastern end of the swamps.

Whether he knew that at Matipa's he was not many hours canoe-journey from the Kabende that had been his first choice will perhaps never be known for certain. Horace Waller, the editor of the *Last Journals*, after conversation with Susi and Chuma produced an interesting footnote on this point: 'The men say that the actual deep-water Lake lay away to their right (when coming from the north to Matipa's) . . . and, on being asked why Dr Livingstone did not make a short cut across to the southern shore, they explain that the canoes could not live for an hour on the lake but were merely suited for punting about over the flooded land.'

Livingstone himself knew that larger canoes could be had, as he had used such five years before, and in any case the course to Kabende is not in the open lake but along its swampy edge, so that reason by itself is not sufficient to explain the Doctor's change of plan.

As given in the diary, the wording of Matipa's advice is curious since his brother's village at the Chambezi mouth can hardly be said to be on the south bank of the lake though Kabende would be correctly so described. Similarly, the phrase 'where there are few rivers and plenty to eat' would fit Kabende well.

In fact, earlier commentators, such as Mr J. E. Hughes in his excellent book, *Eighteen Years on Lake Bangweulu*, have interpreted this passage to mean that it was Matipa who was urging the Kabende route and Livingstone who rejected it. In a spirited passage in his book Hughes says: 'This Kawendi is the Kabende mentioned by Livingstone in his diary, February 26th, 1873. The Chief Matipa of Chiruwi had offered to send him through to there on payment of five bundles of brass wire. Matipa was telling the truth for once; it would have been the very thing. Livingstone would then have had open water to Mbabala Island, a good footpath down that island, then after crossing a narrow channel, a firm, well wooded mainland, thus avoiding all the swamps in which he so soon met his fate.'

It is clear therefore that without a longitude he still did not know whereabouts he was with regard to the places he knew from his former visit and he proceeds to amend that lack.

On the night of his arrival at Nsumbu he gets a latitude by star which works out at 11°11′S which is correct. On the same page there is a 'lunar' for longitude, worked out to give 31°3′E, which is sixty miles too far east. Moreover, it is one hundred and twenty miles east of the position he gave 'Chiribe' Island on the map from his first visit. He must have had some doubt about this figure, for on March 5th there is the entry in his diary: 'The real name of this island is Masumbo, and the position may be probably long. 31°3′; lat. 10°11′S.' There is a mis-quoting here for the latitude, but the significant words are the cautious 'may be probably'.

He was clearly ill at ease over this figure and on March 5th he spends a solid two hours taking more 'lunars', three sets of them, and works them out. The results are more discomforting than ever, and are put down in his note-book:

	31	10
	32	3
	31	42
Mean	31°	38′

followed by the remark, 'Matipa's all wrong.'

This phrase could conceivably mean, 'Matipa, the chief, is all wrong,' which is rather meaningless unless he has been arguing with him about where he was. My own interpretation is that it was a note, written in later to guide Maclear, and means: (The above figure for) Matipa's (islet is) all wrong.

At the time he probably considered he still had a large error to the eastward, since the mean figure would put him somewhere near his route up from Nyasaland in 1867, and we may suppose that he thought he might be nearly in 31°E, which is where he places Matipa's islet on the only map (on p. 325) in which he put in the longitudes. If he considered Chilubi island at all he would have presumed it to be from fifty to one hundred miles to the west, whereas it was precisely *three* miles away from his camp, hidden from it only by trees.

The author has camped on the identical spot where he used the mosquito net shown in *Last Journals*, and it is dry, sandy, and well away from the very large *mushitu*, or clump of dense vegetation which still overpowers the village. A walk of about a mile north from his camp would have enabled him to see the large island of Chilubi just to the west, and his omission to mention that island seems to be proof that in his weak state he did not take that walk. He did in fact stay there for three weeks owing to delays in securing canoes but not once in his diary does the name 'Chiribe island' appear.

His longitudes having failed him, his one chance of knowing where he was would have been a question about where his 'Chiribe island' was, yet, supposing it to be more or less over the horizon to the west, he evidently never asked it.

To readers this must seem as incredible as it is to the author, that he never found out that he was next door to the island he knew of, yet there is no doubt it was a fact, as both his diary and his maps amply prove. Bolton's map, based on Livingstone's, show Matipa's islet as one hundred miles to the east of Chilubi. There is further proof on the map in his own hand that is printed on p. 325. This, which shows entries up to within four days of his death, is part only of a larger plotting in which Masantu is placed on the meridian of 28°E. Chiribe Island is not plotted but he knew it to be only about forty miles eastward of that little village he had stopped at in July 1868.

Here then is the third instance, more incredible than the other two, of circumstances cheating him of knowing where he was. Turning back from the river Mpanda was just ill luck, and the misfortune of a faulty sextant was perhaps a natural accident of travel, but we need a new word altogether to describe the frown of fortune which arranged that no one in his hearing for a whole three weeks mentioned that Chilubi island was literally just round the corner.

We know now that the result of this ignorance was nothing less than calamitous for had he known where he was he would have gone back to his first wise plan of taking canoes down to Kabende, instead of embarking on the dreary six weeks of floundering through the swamps which led to his death.

Surely we must reckon it a sorry trick of Fortune that first made an error in longitude the cause of disaster to the greatest geographer of Africa and then threw further slings and arrows to ward off from him the merest chance remark of villagers which would have told him that he was at the doorstep of Chilubi.

On March 21st, still at Nsumbu Island, he got another set of lunars, heading the page with 'Matipa islet—Mosumba' but the result was more mystifying than ever, giving a longitude of 29°12′E, which is fifty miles too far to the *west*. He had criss-crossed the page with pencil lines as though to show that he discarded the whole observation, and on the next day began another set but the figures tail off with the remark 'Clouds obscure all' and underneath it 'Sextant erroneous'.

On the last day before he left he tried again but the result was to put him farther east than ever and the workings conclude with the terse remark, 'Sextant in error'.

Acting on Matipa's strange recommendation that he should go eastward to his brother Kabinga and, suspecting that it was a shorter distance than to Kabende, Livingstone requests canoes from the chief. Matipa is the hereditary name for this chieftainship of the Ba-Bisa tribe, and it means 'mud', in this case an honorific title instead of the reverse, since it commemorates the strategy of the first chief of that name in leading his people away from destruction by the fierce Babemba, across the matipa or mud of the swamps to safety on the islands.

There was much delay over getting canoes and after a fortnight of it there is a note in the journal which gives a possible explanation of why Matipa wanted to send him eastwards. Livingstone writes: 'As I thought, Matipa told us today that it is reported he has some Arabs with him who will attack all the Lake people forthwith, and he is anxious that we shall go over to show them that we are peaceful.'

Meanwhile the slackening of the rainy season—they had nine days without rain—and the rest seemed to have benefited Dr Livingstone who says nothing of his state of health during his stay. But his diary is rather piecemeal at this time and he may have been ill and unable to write clearly except over minor matters such as the arrival of the donkey by canoe, the local fish or how his people made bread.

He accuses Matipa of 'acting the villain', presumably because he promised canoes which were not forthcoming, so he 'made a demonstration by taking quiet possession of the chief's village and house; fired a pistol through the roof; Matipa fled to another village.'

The effect was instantaneous for within an hour three canoes were produced and he got the valiant Susi off with a party of twenty men to the east to the 'Chambeze'.

Susi returned on the 23rd and the Doctor himself embarked the next day. And here we come to the most puzzling mistake in his map, namely, the very short distance it shows between the island he had just left and the Chambezi River. This is really about thirty miles, but in his map it is given as about ten. The party 'punted six hours to a miserably small islet without a tree'; and since this route is the normal one for crossing the northern end of the swamp they probably went at about three miles per hour, which is an average rate for punting in those waters. The 'little islet' was Cherongo, a patch of sand still used as a temporary halt, and it now does possess a tree, a small chiwale palm tree.

The route took him rather to the north of the two main centres of the swamp-dwelling Ba-unga people at Kasoma and Kalimankonde where he might have seen the two sacred pots which date back to beyond his time. The one with four spouts has magic

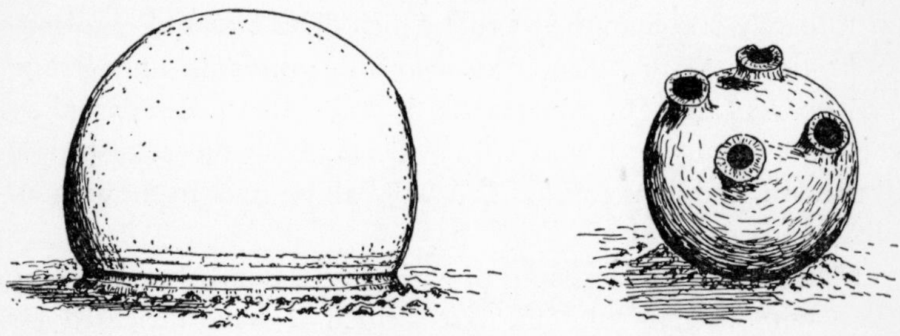

The sacred pots of the Bangweulu swamps

powers since it is able to transfer itself by night from one village to another, such a removal portending grave events to come. It accomplished such a journey during the author's last visit but the matter-of-fact District Commissioner divined its flight as a sign that the lucky village wanted to assert its seniority. The other pot has no such occult powers and can only be called an emblem of dynasty. The large one visible is the latest of no less than nine, of which eight are hidden under it. Some potentate of Kasoma decreed early in the last century that a small pot had a mystic connection with the dynasty and that another one must be fashioned over earlier ones at every change of chief. Lying as it does in the midst of a crowded village the wonder is that the pile is not broken by goats or piccanins, and to tell truth, that did happen on my last visit, so the chief's sister, the traditional potter, had to make a new and larger one which is that seen in the sketch.

Livingstone recognised that a good part of this journey was

over what he called 'prairie', that is, with grasses, showing that in the dry season it would be no longer swamp but pasture land for thousands of the lechwe antelope. The next day, 'after another six hours punting, over the same wearisome prairie or *bouga*, we heard the merry voices of children.' This was on the small island of Kansenga, where they slept, having passed the large island of Luangwa.

The next day they had some trouble, which is not fully explained, in crossing one of the ana-branches of the Chambezi. These branches run fairly fast, but not dangerously so. One presumes that the trouble was due to a leak in the canoe rather than to turbulent water. The tale of the loss was a slave-girl belonging to Amoda and the donkey's saddle; the ammunition also sank, but was fished up. From Livingstone's description of the crossing it is possible to recognise where it took place—namely, near the mouth of Lake Wumba, which is the real junction of the Luansenshi with the Chambezi. Livingstone was much impressed by the size of the two rivers. The camp seems to have been formed on the slightly higher land on or near the shores of Lake Chaya. That he does not mention the lake as such in the journal might be because at that flood time it would be difficult to recognise it as a lake, but he plots it in approximately the right shape and position on the map showing his later route.

He sends the canoes back again to Matipa for the remainder of the party, about twenty men, and the weather improves sufficiently for him to take more 'lunars' on April 2nd and 3rd. At the conclusion of the working out he writes 'sextant corrected' which presumably means that he had got rid of the double image he referred to earlier.

The mean of his four observations was 29°27′E which was reasonable compared to those of a month earlier, though about fifty miles west of the modern figure. It will be recalled that on his first visit to Lake Bangweulu his longitudes were thirty or forty miles too far west and the figure he had now got would at least harmonise with the map he was carrying.

This was three days after the heavy haemorrhages had started which culminated in his death a month later yet we can imagine that as he put away his sextant for the last time he felt relieved at having put it right and probably looked forward to clearing up the confusion of his earlier sights when he got home to England.

They had to wait at this camp for nine days for the large party, including the donkey, to be brought over from Matipa's in relays and while that is going on his haemorrhages take a more alarming turn. Five days after they had resumed their journey he writes: 'I am pale, bloodless and weak from bleeding profusely ever since the 31st of March, an artery gives off a copious stream, and takes away my strength.'

One would think that the most ordinary discretion now counselled a rest, at least until the rainy season had ceased, and I am told that, for the complaint that he was suffering from, the one chance of cure was complete rest and a milk diet, both of which were available at Kabinga's, who kept cattle and goats. But discretion was a word he hardly ever recognised in connection with his own health and he applied to this far more dangerous illness the same slogan as he used for a bout of fever—'when suffering from fever the best thing is to march.'

Whether he felt that he must hurry on while life lasted or whether his impatience was a consequence of his painful disease, he pushed on, sending his men by land while he went by hired canoes with guides and goods.

By this time his men had been floundering in the swamps half way round Bangweulu for the whole four months of the rainy season, yet there was never a hint of trouble with them. It had been a patriarchal progress with men, women and children in the party, but in the worst conditions, and we need some explanation of why it went so smoothly compared to his journey in Manyuema. The first and main reason is that the men were Stanley's selection, but a secondary one is that they were travelling independently and away from the influence of the Arabs and their slave-parties, who had always infected his lesser men with a spirit of insubordination.

But one cannot read the last chapter of Waller's *Last Journals*, reconstructing the march back to Zanzibar with their leader's body, without realising that a spirit of devotion to Livingstone had descended on his men. Not even the organising capacity of Susi, or the eagerness of Chuma could have controlled that group had they not been able to appeal to a deep-seated affection for this lonely white man who was so unselfish, who seemed to have some sacred mission of his own which drove him on regardless of obstacles, but who never forgot their needs.

It has not been possible hitherto to plot Livingstone's route from the Chambezi confluence to the place of his death with any accuracy because there was no map of this part of the Bangweulu

Susi

swamp. A map is now available, of which that on p. 311 is a simplification and on it we have marked his route as deduced from the last few pages of his note-book.

The zig-zag course up and across the first three rivers is due to the need of keeping in touch with the land party which had to go well upstream to get the donkey across at high flood. In his diary at the end of the first day Livingstone writes: 'It is quite impossible at present to tell where land ends and Lake begins; it is all water, water everywhere. It is the Nile apparently enacting its inundations, even at its sources. The amount of water spread out over the country constantly excites my wonder; it is prodigious. Pitiless pelting showers wetted everything.'

Here at the Lulingila the flood spreads out at this time of year to a depth of five feet above the dry season level and only the tops of large ant-hills can be seen, usually crowned with bushes and low palms. The canoe party camped on one the first night—'we watched by turns, lest thieves should come and haul away our

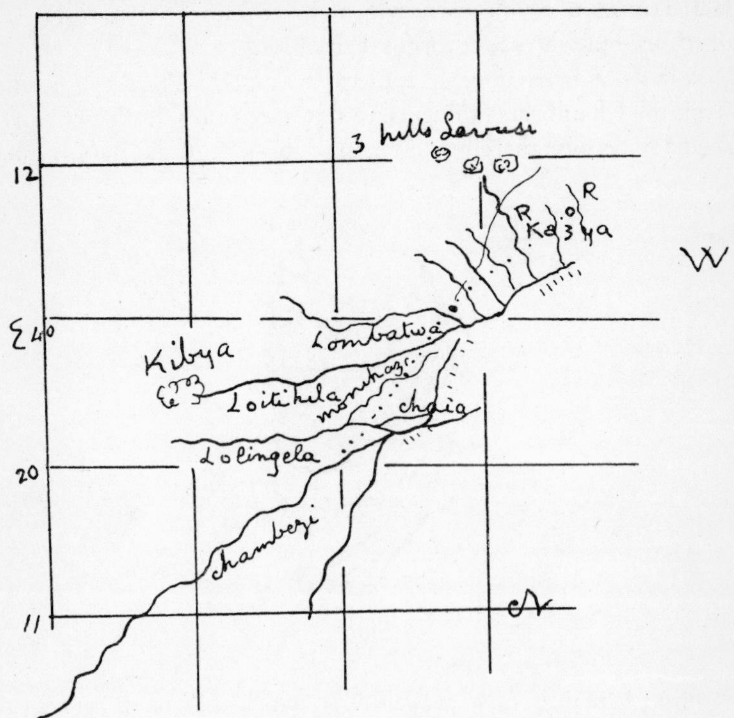

Facsimile tracing of the second last map drawn by Dr Livingstone. Last entry was made about 20th April

canoes and goods. Heavy rain. One canoe sank, wetting everything in her. The leaks had been stopped with clay and a man sleeping near the stern had displaced this frail caulking.'

The people of the swamps are most expert with their canoes and use them at every degree of leakiness. Stopping a hole with a wadge of peat or clay is the standard method of dealing with leaks but it has its disadvantages. The two accidents of this kind met with by the author had an amusing side and may relieve the gloom of this last chapter. In the first case our large canoe had such a temporary bung of peat and someone had loaded our boxes over the leak so that we did not see when the peat had been displaced. Our paddlers guessed and took us quickly to a shallow part where we sank gently in two feet of water as we climbed out on to some floating peat. This was all right as long as one kept moving, but if one stopped to talk the island began to sink beneath the feet so there was the strange spectacle of men treading as delicately as Agag to save going through, all the while the unloading and repairing was going on.

On the other occasion I had climbed out of a launch into a big canoe with some dry grass in it to be taken half a mile to shore. As soon as we pushed off I noticed there was so heavy a list to port that there was barely an inch of free board and I adjusted my weight to trim the boat. The paddler standing behind me immediately corrected that by putting his weight to the port side. The canoe was too narrow for me to turn round and make signs to him or even to see what he was doing so we went on with our wordless argument, each gaining a point occasionally as to what was an even keel. It was clear from the state of my seat that water was coming in somewhere and my Charon put on a terrific spurt to get us out of deep water. He ran me ashore on a low sandy bank and as I scrambled out I turned and saw that he had a hole as large as his head on the side near his feet but he could keep this above water level by maintaining the list we had started with. His expression showed better than words what he thought of a stupid white man who thought he knew better than the captain. The moral in both cases is, 'Leave it to the Bangweulan, there is very little he does not know about canoe management.'

The next day they continued amongst the ant-hills and again spent the night on one: '. . . a lion had wandered into this world of water and ant-hills, and roared night and morning as if very much disgusted: we could sympathise with him!

'We were lost in stiff grassy prairies, from three to four feet deep in water, for five hours.' Going landward to find their marching party they got into shallow water: '. . . all hands at the large canoe could move her only a few feet. She stopped at every haul with a jerk, as if in a bank of adhesive plaister.'

On such occasions then no doubt, as now, the paddlers would leap out and haul to the shouts of 'Putti! Putti!' by their shanty man. When in deep water again they would jump in with joyful cries of 'Chambezi! Chambezi', which, besides meaning a large river can mean 'deep water again, thank Heaven!'

They did not cross the Munikazi until April 12th, after six days of this kind of travelling, and on that day Livingstone has to write: 'Great loss of blood made me so weak I could hardly walk, but tottered along nearly two hours, and then lay down quite done.' We must infer that they had parted with their hired canoes at the crossing of the Luitikila and were henceforth a land party though walking much of the way through water.

With such a picture in mind it is a revelation to read what is still in his diary—entries on rainfall, on the scenery, on the fish and their habits. We can only quote one sentence, the one which impelled the artist (C. Whymper) to make the fine imaginary engraving printed on p. 296 of the *Last Journals*: 'A blanket is scarcely needed till the early hours of the morning, and here, after the turtle doves and cocks give out their warning calls to the watchful, the fish eagle lifts up his remarkable voice. It is pitched in a high falsetto key, very loud, and seems as if he were calling to someone in the other world. Once heard, his weird unearthly voice can never be forgotten—it sticks to one through life.'

It took them three days to get clear of the Luitikila, borrowing small canoes at the three crossings they had to make, after which he had to be carried part of the way till they reach the Lombatwa river on the 16th where 'a tremendous rain after dark burst all our now rotten tents to shreds. Three hills now appear in the distance.' Every later traveller in this part echoes what Livingstone says of them, 'The Lavusi hills are a relief to the eye in this flat upland.' By the time they reached the Lukulu his state was alarming Susi and Chuma, to whom we are indebted, via Horace Waller, for what happened in the last week. His last long entry in the diary is on April 19th and concludes with: 'No observations now, owing to great weakness; I can scarcely hold my pencil. Tent gone; the men build a good hut for me and the luggage.' Yet the entry ends with three readings of the barometer and the temperature, and he is somehow entering up his plotting sheet.

On the 21st he was too weak to ride on the donkey, and on the 22nd he wrote only 'Carried on *kitanda* over Buga S.W.2¼'. A *kitanda* or *machila* is shown with four bearers in the chapter heading, but for Livingstone's light weight they may have used a single pole and two bearers.

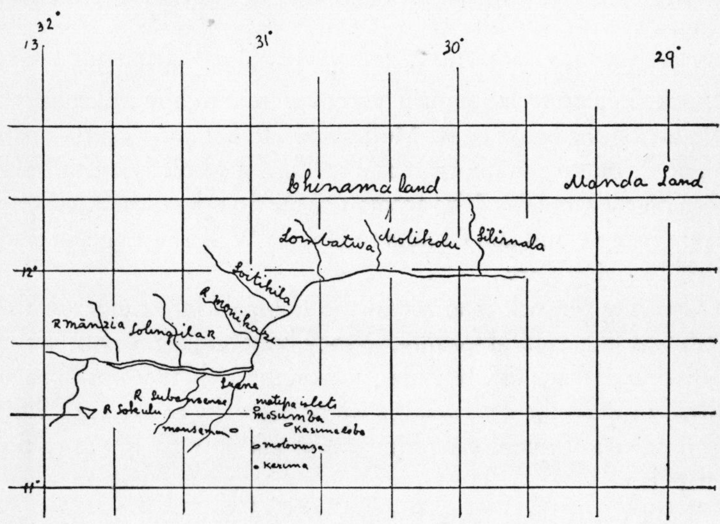

Tracing from part of Livingstone's last map. He reached the Lulimala two days before he died

He was carried thus for the next four days till on the 26th he reached a village on the right bank of the Lulimala belonging to a chief Kalunganjovu (Kalunga the elephant). On these days he was too weak to do more than write the date and the number of hours spent in travelling. On the 26th he added up these hours, a total of eight and a quarter in the five days of kitanda travel and then makes the only mistake I can find in that note-book. He multiplies the hours travelled by four and writes:

'To Kalunga Njovu's
Total $33' = 8\frac{1}{4}$ (where $33'$ means 33 miles).'

The only explanation I can suggest for his giving a rate of four miles an hour is that he was using a figure he dimly remembered. In dry weather on good inter-village paths, travel by kitanda can be at that rate as the men usually go at a jog trot, changing every ten minutes without stopping. But in the present circumstance, with a very sick man, it is not likely to have been more than two and a half miles an hour. A total distance of twenty miles agrees with the modern map between the Lukulu and Lulimala.

The next day, 27th, he makes his last entry in his diary: '27 Knocked up quite and remain = recover: sent to buy milch goats. We are on the banks of R. Molilamo.' His last entry on the map (p. 325), putting in the river and spelling it correctly, must have been on the same day. The account of the doings on these last few days given by Susi and Chuma to Horace Waller in England is in itself a moving story.

Carrying the sick man across the Lulimala in a canoe on the 29th was very painful for him, so they built him a grass hut in the temporary village of Chitambo, and on the 30th he seems to have dozed most of the day, waking up occasionally to speak to Susi. Almost his last question to him was to ask how far it was to the Luapula.

'I think it is three days, Bwana,' replied Susi, and Livingstone sighed saying, 'Oh dear, dear,' as though he wished he could at least reach that river and complete the journey round the swamps. He died some time that night.

To my mind, the most moving incident in the story of the last few days is one which brings vividly before us the desperate hope of this indomitable man that the end of his search was near, a search which had now, for him, almost taken on the guise of a Quest for the Holy Grail.

Just before they reached the Lulimala, they were resting in a village, and Livingstone summoned the elders of the village to speak with him, where he was lying on his kitanda, under a tree. 'They were asked,' told Susi, 'whether they knew of a hill on which four rivers took their rise. The spokesman answered that they had no knowledge of it.'

So disappointment was to remain with him to the very last, that Quest was not for him; our pilgrim had crossed his last river.

His faith, his courage, his enduring and his sincerity under all, have made his name famous.

JOHN BUNYAN

Memorial pillar at the place where David Livingstone died

INDEX

Italic figures refer to illustrations in the text

Index